PERFORMANCE AND KNOWLEDGE

Part of the series Key Concepts in Indigenous Studies, this book focuses on the concepts that recur in any discussion of nature, culture and society among the indigenous. This final volume in the five-volume series deals with the two key concepts of performance and knowledge of the indigenous people from all continents of the world. With contributions from renowned scholars, activists and experts across the globe, it looks at issues and ideas of the indigenous peoples in the context of imagination, creativity, performance, audience, arts, music, dance, oral traditions, aesthetics and beauty in North America, South America, Australia, East Asia and India from cultural, historical and aesthetic points of view.

Bringing together academic insights and experiences from the ground, this unique book, with its wide coverage, will serve as a comprehensive guide for students, teachers and scholars of indigenous studies. It will be essential reading for those in social and cultural anthropology, tribal studies, sociology and social exclusion studies, cultural studies, media studies and performing arts, literary and postcolonial studies, religion and theology, politics, Third World and Global South studies, as well as activists working with indigenous communities.

G. N. Devy is Honorary Professor, Centre for Multidisciplinary Development Research, Dharwad, India, and Chairman, People's Linguistic Survey of India. An award-winning writer and cultural activist, he is known for his 50-volume language survey. He is Founder Director of the Adivasi Academy at Tejgadh in Gujarat, India, and was formerly Professor of English at M.S. University of Baroda. He is the recipient of the Sahitya Akademi Award, Linguapax Prize, Prince Claus Award and Padma Shri. With several books in English, Marathi and Gujarati, he has co-edited (with Geoffrey V. Davis and K. K. Chakravarty) *Narrating Nomadism: Tales of Recovery and Resistance* (2012), *Knowing Differently: The Challenge of the Indigenous* (2013), *Performing Identities: Celebrating Indigeneity in the Arts* (2014) and *The Language Loss of the Indigenous* (2016), published by Routledge.

Geoffrey V. Davis was Professor of Commonwealth and Postcolonial Literatures at the University of Aachen, Germany. He was international chair of the Association for Commonwealth Literature and Language Studies (ACLALS) and chair of the European branch (EACLALS). He co-edited *Cross/Cultures: Readings in the Post/Colonial Literatures and Cultures in English* and the African studies series *Matatu*. His publications include *Staging New Britain: Aspects of Black and South Asian British Theatre Practice* (2006) and *African Literatures, Postcolonial Literatures in English: Sources and Resources* (2013).

Key Concepts in Indigenous Studies

Series Editors: **G. N. Devy,** *Honorary Professor, Centre for Multidisciplinary Development Research, Dharwad, India, and Chairman, People's Linguistic Survey of India* and **Geoffrey V. Davis**, *former Professor of Commonwealth and Postcolonial Literatures, University of Aachen, Germany*

This series of volumes offers the most systematic and foundational literature available to date for use by undergraduate and postgraduate students of indigenous studies. It brings together essays by experts from across the globe on concepts forming the bedrock of this rapidly growing field in five focused volumes: *Environment and Belief Systems* (Vol. 1); *Gender and Rights* (Vol. 2); *Indigeneity and Nation* (Vol. 3); *Orality and Language* (Vol. 4); and *Performance and Knowledge* (Vol. 5). These contain short, informative and easily accessible essays on the perspectives of indigenous communities from all continents of the world. The essays are written specifically for an international audience. They thus allow drawing of transnational and cross-cultural parallels, and form useful material as textbooks as well as texts for general readership. Introducing a new orientation to traditional anthropology with comprehensive and in-depth studies, the volumes foreground knowledge traditions and praxis of indigenous communities.

Environment and Belief Systems
Edited by G. N. Devy and Geoffrey V. Davis

Gender and Rights
Edited by G. N. Devy and Geoffrey V. Davis

Indigeneity and Nation
Edited by G. N. Devy and Geoffrey V. Davis

Orality and Language
Edited by G. N. Devy and Geoffrey V. Davis

Performance and Knowledge
Edited by G. N. Devy and Geoffrey V. Davis

For more information about this series, please visit: www.routledge.com/ Key-Concepts-in-Indigenous-Studies/book-series/KCIS

PERFORMANCE AND KNOWLEDGE

Edited by G. N. Devy and Geoffrey V. Davis

Routledge
Taylor & Francis Group

LONDON AND NEW YORK

First published 2021
by Routledge
2 Park Square, Milton Park, Abingdon, Oxon OX14 4RN

and by Routledge
52 Vanderbilt Avenue, New York, NY 10017

Routledge is an imprint of the Taylor & Francis Group, an informa business

British Library Cataloguing-in-Publication Data
A catalogue record for this book is available from the British Library

Library of Congress Cataloging-in-Publication Data
A catalog record for this book has been requested

ISBN: 978-0-367-25297-7 (hbk)
ISBN: 978-0-367-61576-5 (pbk)
ISBN: 978-1-003-10558-9 (ebk)

Typeset in Bembo
by Apex CoVantage, LLC

CONTENTS

FIGURES

CONTRIBUTORS

Tara Browner (Choctaw) is Professor of Ethnomusicology and American Indian Studies at the University of California, Los Angeles, USA. She is the author of the book *Heartbeat of the People: Music and Dance of the Northern Pow-Wow*, editor of *Music of the First Nations: Tradition and Innovation in Native North American Music*, editor of *Songs from "A New Circle of Voices": The 16th Annual Pow-wow at UCLA* (Music of the United States of America [MUSA]) and co-editor (with Thomas Riis) of *Rethinking American Music* (forthcoming).

Maryrose Casey is Professor of Creative and Performing Arts, College of Humanities, Arts and Social Sciences at Flinders University, Adelaide, Australia. She has published widely on indigenous Australian performance.

Ximena Cordova Oviedo is Assistant Professor in the College of Humanities and Social Sciences at Zayed University, United Arab Emirates. She has a PhD in Latin American studies from Newcastle University. Her research approach is multidisciplinary, borrowing from cultural anthropology, digital ethnography, performance studies, heritage studies and cultural history. Ximena's current interest are the intersections between popular culture, performative practices and identity politics, with a particular focus on 20th-century Latin American history and Andean anthropology.

Kathy Foley is Distinguished Professor of Theatre Arts at the University of California, Santa Cruz, USA. She has also taught at University of Malaya, University of Hawai'i, Yonsei University (Korea) and Chulalongkorn University (Thailand). She is the author of the Southeast Asia section of *Cambridge Guide to Asian Theatre* (1993) and was editor *of Asian Theatre Journal* from 2005–18. She received the 2019 Association for Theatre in Higher Education Award for Sustained Excellence in

Editing. Her articles have appeared in *TDR*, *Modern Drama*, *Asian Theatre Journal*, *Puppetry International* and other publications, nationally and internationally.

Tammy Haili'ōpua Baker is a playwright, director and Associate Professor in Theatre at the University of Hawai'i at Mānoa, USA.

Diana Looser is Assistant Professor of Theater and Performance Studies at Stanford University, California, USA, where she researches Pacific Islands performance.

Hartmut Lutz taught North American literatures and cultures at the University of Greifswald, Germany, until 2011. His doctorate at the University of Tübingen in 1973 was on psychoanalysis and literature (*William Goldings Prosawerk*) (1975), and his habilitation at the University of Osnabrück in 1983 on Indian stereotyping in U.S. and German cultures (*"Indianer" und "Native Americans": Zur sozial- und literaturhistorischen Vermittlung eines Stereotyps*) (1985). He has taught at the universities of Cologne, Osnabrück, Greifswald and Szczecin (Poland), and at native studies programs in North America including UC Davis, Dartmouth College and Saskatchewan Indian Federated College. He has had guest professorships in Denmark, Finland, Iceland, Poland, Romania and Spain. He received Fulbright, ACLS, DAAD and ICCS fellowships, the Harris Chair (Dartmouth College), the Canadian government's 2003 John G. Diefenbaker Award (Ottawa), the 2012/13 Killam Visiting Fellowship at the University of Calgary and a 2013 ICCS Certificate of Merit in recognition of outstanding contributions to the development of Canadian studies.

David O'Donnell is a theatre director and Associate Professor in Theatre at Victoria University, Wellington, Aotearoa/New Zealand. He has published widely on theatre from New Zealand and the Pacific.

PREFACE

The volumes in this series have long been in making. The idea came up in 2011 in a conversation between Prof. Geoffrey Davis and me. The two of us had by then worked on six anthologies related to indigenous studies to which scholars from all continents had contributed. Two of these are published by Orient BlackSwan (*Indigeneity*, 2009 and *Voice and Memory*, 2011) and four by Routledge between 2012 and 2016 (*Narrating Nomadism*, *Knowing Differently*, *Performing Identities* and *The Language Loss of the Indigenous*). However, we felt that we needed to do more, a lot more, in order to firmly establish this newly emerging field. Shashank Sinha and Shoma Choudhury of Routledge showed a keen interest in our proposal. Enthused by the idea of bringing out a set of volumes dealing with some of the definitive themes of the field and assured by the possibility of publication of the volumes, we started our work. Of course, it was not entirely easy going for us. The challenges were many and the scale in which we wanted to cast the volumes was not easy to handle. Despite the difficulties and setbacks expected in such an intellectual venture, we kept up. Most of the editorial work was completed by early 2018. As we were getting ready to send the typescripts, alas, Prof. Geoffrey Davis died in a short internment in an Aachen hospital. His last mail came to me a day before he was to be admitted. The loss was a big blow to me. His friends and colleagues spread over all continents mourned his death deeply. For me, the most civilized way of mourning was to ensure that the volumes to which he had contributed so much care and toil got published. Who was Geoffrey Davis and why was he interested in the indigenous? Perhaps the best way for me to explain this is to repeat here the response I sent to two questions from Prof. Janet Wilson (hereafter JW) of Southampton University.

JW: What were the points of synergy (ideological, intellectual, political activist) that brought you and Geoff together, and when and how did this happen, i.e., what were the particular contexts/motivations? I remember I think Geoff had just retired and was possibly looking for a new project? And might have been inspired through his involvement with ACLALS.

DEVY: I think I met him the first time in 1984 at the EACLALS conference at Sitges, Spain. During the 1980s, I was a "regular" at the EACLALS since India did not have an active Commonwealth Literature culture as yet. But, my memory of that meeting is not very clear. In 1988, Geoff had convened a conference at Aachen, Germany, where Geoff spent most of his academic life. I was invited to it for a plenary. This experience left me impressed by his organizational ability. In between, we had met at other places too – Austria, Hungary, Singapore. But all these meetings were casual; and I do not recall any memorable conversation having taken place between us during these conferences. During the 1990s, Geoff hosted a conference on literature and activism. I left my professorship at Baroda, India, in 1996. Geoff had heard about this move from friends. He asked me to lecture at the conference. I did. It was during this conference I noticed that he was deeply respectful of activism; that his empathy for the dispossessed was genuinely deep. I also noticed that he was extremely wary of using clichéd and fashionable jargon. The impression these qualities made on me was strong. A few years later, he was to attend the ACLALS Triennial in Hyderabad, India. He wrote to me asking if he could visit me after the Hyderabad conference. He knew that I had stopped attending academic conferences and there was no chance of our meeting in Hyderabad. So, I invited him to Baroda, 1500 km north of Hyderabad.

I am not sure if he enjoyed his visit to Baroda. On the day he was to arrive, for reasons difficult for to me know, I altogether forgot about his arrival. I was to meet him at the airport. Baroda in those days was a very small airport and every day only three or four flights arrived there. And overseas visitors were not a common sight. Geoff waited there till almost the last co-traveller had left the meeting area. The last one to leave happened to be an architect named Karan Grover, who is a living legend in the field of architecture. Grover asked Geoff if he was expecting anyone. Geoff mentioned my name. This worked. Karan Grover and I had been friends for decades, and Geoff was made to feel welcome on my behalf, brought to his lodgings and, the forgetting and forgiving over, we met over dinner. The next day, I drove him in my car to the location of the Adivasi Academy (the Tribal University) that I was trying to establish in those years. This location was 90 km east of Baroda. On the way, I talked with passion all about my plans, my dreams. He listened. He spent another day in Baroda meeting Karan and enjoyed the famous Grover wine. I was busy in my work with the tribal academy. The next morning, I drove Geoff to the airport as he was leaving for Bombay and then to Aachen. At the airport, he asked me if I could have him visit the Adivasi Academy again for a longer time, a week or so. I said, "Why do you not stay for a semester?" He was a bit puzzled by my offer, made in such a casual manner. So, I added, "Be a Fellow with us." He took that offer and returned to Baroda the following year, but for a short time. I think it was after two more brief trips that he agreed to spend six months in Baroda.

I must explain that the Adivasi Academy is not like a university. It is a community workstation at best, with really very minimum facilities that makes for most of us what we call "civilization." The "Fellowship" had no set rules. They were made looking at the individual's ability and desire to contribute what one had promised to contribute. . . . The "projects" ranged from writing a book or an article, teaching music or language to children, keeping the library or museum in good order, tending a piece of agricultural land, setting up a community micro-credit group or just documenting any of these activities. When Geoff became a fellow of the Adivasi Academy, there were three others, Brian and Eileen Coates from Limerick, Ireland and Lachman Khubchandani, a linguist from Pune, India. Eileen had accepted to help us with the museum and Lachman was to write a book in linguistics. I was more ambitious with Geoff. I said to him, "If you do not mind, please do nothing, only watch what goes on here and when it pleases you discuss ideas with me." He agreed. The facilities given to the fellows included housing in Baroda and meals when they visited the Academy, 90 km away from Baroda. All my meetings with tribals were transacted in their languages. English words were rarely heard. Only occasionally, some visitors helped Geoff with English interpretations. Geoff, I must say, braved all of this discomfort without a murmur. The impression I had formed about his deep empathy for the dispossessed became firmer. In the fifth month of his stay, I sent a word to him asking if he was available for a serious conversation. He obliged. We met in my Baroda office – the Bhasha Centre – at 2 PM. I asked him if he would join me in imagining an international "non-conference" for looking at the world through the perspective of the indigenous. He said, "I cannot promise, but I will try." Our conversation continued for several hours and, probably, both of us had a reasonably good idea of what all must be avoided in making our idea of conference a completely rooted to the ground. I proposed the name "chotro" (a shared platform); he consented to it with great enthusiasm. Next morning, I found him at Bhasha. He had a "Call for Chotro" ready with him. I made several calls to various offices and individuals in Delhi to finalize the material arrangements for the First Chotro. That afternoon, Geoff sat at the computer and sent out close to 150 mails. Before he left Baroda, we were fully involved in putting together the unusual conference. He made one visit to India before the conference was held in Delhi in January 2008. We met in Delhi. I had to combine some of my other works with the work related to Chotro. One of these involved a visit to the prime minister's office. He was a bit shocked when I told him that after sorting out the conference related arrangements for stay and local transportation, I would be going to the PM's office and he was welcome to join me. Years later, I have heard him narrating this anecdote to friends over a glass of wine. The Delhi Chotro was the first one. We put together several more in subsequent years and worked on the conference volumes, meeting in several countries. Geoff became a frequent visitor to India to Baroda, and also to my home and family. I am not aware if we shared an ideology. In a way, all of us in the field of literature have a varying degree of progressive outlook on life and society. But, what clicked between Geoff and me is something else, and that is his immense patience with me and his ability to cope with surprises and shocks, which could not be avoided considering my involvement in several social causes. John Keats, speaking of William Shakespeare's "genius," had used the term "negative capability" – the ability to live amidst uncertainties. The mutual recognition of this negative capability brought us together for undertaking unconventional kind of work, serious though not strictly academic.

JW: What roles/or positions did Geoff take as collaborator, e.g., in co-organizing Chotro and in working with the adivasis/Bhasha more generally?

DEVY: When we thought of creating the Chotro non-conferences, we had no funding support. We had no sponsors, no funds for international travel. Bhasha Centre was not a full-scale "institution" till then. Besides, "Indigenous Studies" was not any accepted field of academic work. We were not sure if any self-respecting publisher would accept to publish the proceedings. Therefore, in all of these matters, we shared responsibility. But, generally speaking, he dealt with the overseas participants and I handled the Indian issues, material and academic. I accepted to identify publishers, negotiate with them, do the necessary correspondence; Geoff focused on copy editing of the texts. But, this division of work was not sanctimonious. Either of us was free to cross over and even required to do so looking at each other's convenience. Never forget that Geoff had his other major obligations and academic projects, and I had mine. We had no desire to claim credit for the work we were doing. It was born out of our desire to create a legitimate space for the voice of the indigenous.

I hope my response to Janet Wilson will have made it clear why I enjoyed working with Geoffrey Davis on so many intellectual projects. In India's intellectual history, there have been glorious examples of intellectual collaboration between Indian thinkers and scholars and writers and scholars from other countries. W.B. Yeats and Purohit Swamy, Yeats and Tagore, Tolstoy and Gandhi developed their ideas through such collaborations. In our time, with the rising tide of the "Right" political parties and a narrow idea of nationalism gaining a greater currency, such collaborations are difficult to carry through. I am pleased that this series of volumes is seeing the light of the day, bringing my work together with Geoffrey Davis to a successful conclusion.

ACKNOWLEDGEMENTS

The initial idea of this volume and the series to which it belongs came up in 2012. Since then, Prof. Geoffrey Davis, who was to be the co-editor, corresponded with several scholars from the field of Commonwealth literature and from other academic disciplines. These scholars from various disciplines and several continents gave their advice and suggestions for identifying scholars to be involved in the project. They are too numerous to be mentioned individually. I would like to place on record my gratitude to them. The scholars and activists who consented to contribute, and the majority of them who kept their promise, made the putting together of the volumes possible. Their participation in the most tangible way calls for my thanks. Several organizations and institutions offered Prof. Geoffrey Davis and me opportunities of meeting and taking our plans for these volumes forward. They include the Association for Commonwealth Literature and Language Studies, for a conference in Cyprus; Bhasha Research and Publication Centre, Baroda, for various events through these years; the Kiel Voche, organized by Kiel City Council in Germany; the German Academy, for convening a conference at Hamburg; Aide et Action, for convening a meeting in Geneva; and several Indian colleges and universities, for creating spaces on the sidelines of conferences – I thank all of them. I wonder if without these meetings the project would have moved forward at all.

I would like to thank Ingrid, Prof. Davis's wife, for ungrudgingly encouraging him to spend his funds and time on travels to India to work on this project. Surekha, my life partner, has most generously supported the project throughout its years of slow progress by providing ideas, hospitality and courage. I cannot thank them enough.

The publication of these volumes would not have been at all possible had it not been for the abiding friendship and support of Dr. Shashank Shekhar Sinha, Publishing Director, and his inspiring colleague Shoma Choudhury at Routledge. I carry in my heart the comfort drawn from their genuine friendship.

INTRODUCTION

G. N. Devy

The first ever time I visited an adivasi village in Western India, what struck me as its outstanding feature was the exceptionally acute aesthetic sensibility of the families living in it. Going by my idea of wealth and poverty, they were neither rich nor poor. They struck me as being different. The houses in which they lived were all built by them, in most cases collectively, none among them being the "contractor" and none "labourer." They all were makers of the houses. Most of the things and objects adorning the dwellings were made by them. Their houses were not crowded with objects; and practically no object existed purely for "seeing" or "showing." All of the objects had some use, and all of the objects were made "beautifully." As my visits to this village and other villages of the Bhil indigenous community increased in frequency, I noticed that the adivasis do everything with such ease and elegance that they are rarely seen as "doing" anything. I also noticed that it was not easy to distinguish among them "makers" and "users" of things. This was true not just of the tangible things such as houses, objects of use, agricultural implements, clothes and food. It was true of the intangible things such as poems, songs, dances, crafts and arts. Among them, I did not find "poets" and "non-poets," "painters" and "non-painters." All of them were equal singers, equal painters. I did not find among them "critics," as we have in the field of music, theatre, cinema or literature. For them, "to perform" did not mean "to perform for an imaginary viewer or listener." They performed and their hearts responded to their performances. As I moved to live with them, I noticed that "performance" for adivasis is a phenomenon that requires a serious "suspension of the critical faculty" on the part of an outside observer. The complete identification with the performer, the ease with which one soaks in the flow of the narrative or song or dance and the joy that one seeks out of such participation and the joy that one contributes to the community define the "performance" practices of the indigenous. The essays in this volume introduce such practices from various continents – Asia, Australia and America. The reader will find that despite the vast outward differences among them, the aesthetic principle implicit in them brings them together as a cultural singular, the "indigenous performance."

In the chapter presenting the performance scene in the South American continent, Cordova Oviedo's focus is the festive practices that engage with ideas of indigeneity and nationhood in Bolivia and, to a lesser extent, in Mexico. Reviewing the start of the Latin American Republican era, it examines the role of indigeneity as a resource in hegemonic identity-making projects. She studies the Oruro Carnival in Bolivia and how indigenous actors transform these practices into political and ontological quests. In contrast, Tara Brower, through her evocative description of dance and music of the Native Americans, establishes the deep-rooted cultural collaboration evident in their performances. Although European invasion and settler colonialism was devastating for native peoples in the Americas, their music and dance traditions survived, and now old ceremonies and new songs flourish side by side in cultures where continuity, adaptation and innovation have always been vital elements of life. One gets to this simultaneous conflict and collaboration between colonizers and the indigenous on all continents. Baker, Casey, Looser and O'Donnell's joint chapter depicting the indigenous performance practices in Australia, Aotearoa and the Pacific region covers a large range of traditions and innovations within them. They argue that

> performance has occupied a central place in the social and political lives of the peoples indigenous to the Pacific, Australia and Aotearoa. These histories of practice have been forged within heterogeneous geographies, epistemologies and cultural exchanges, yet there are commonalities that bind these activities across Oceania's vast, networked domain. Performers across the region have drawn on performance's multivalent vocabularies to respond strategically to the precariousness wrought by colonial intervention; to seek communion with a spiritual realm that deeply infuses the mundane world; to consolidate, communicate and question cultural norms and customs; and to contribute actively to the construction of existing and emerging communities, both local and international.

Kathy Foley's chapter on Southeast Asia brings in a far more complex sociology than the Canadian and Australian regions. In her region, the definition of the indigenous itself poses a challenge. There are the indigenous "nations" as well as groups that resist assimilation into regional, national or global domains. Hence, she has used three ethnic categories as her canvas. They include the "First Peoples," who inhabited the region prior to the migrations of other ethno-linguistic groups; the "Peripheries," who may be ethnically related to the majority peoples, hold divergent beliefs which are usually animistic and non-normative; and finally some sample groups who use the term indigenous to recuperate culture and resist Western influences. Her chapter brings together descriptions of the performance practices among all these. The case of India is not much different from that of the Southeast

Asia; rather, it is even more complicated. In my chapter, I have attempted to offer an overview of the performance tradition in ancient India, its transformation during the last millennium and its current circulation among the adivasis. In order to demonstrate the continuity and change in that tradition, I have chosen the case of the Garasiya Bhil rendering of an oral epic, which is quite close to the epic *Mahabharata* but is not its copy or a "folk rendering." Another performance practice I have discussed is based on "writing of paintings" as a form of worship offered to the mythical hero of the Rathwa tribal community. The performance of the "Denotified" tribes, a category of people whose human rights have been grossly violated by the colonial government, is described in the chapter. The emergence of their "Budhan" theatre is narrated as an example of how art is used in order to make the world forget the social discriminations of the past. Discrimination, conflict, struggle and marginalization have been components in the lives of indigenous peoples in the recent history of man. One of the important strands of this confrontation is that of knowledge. Hartmut Lutz's chapter offers an extremely perspicuous account of the clash between "knowledges" and how, despite the intrinsic value of indigenous knowledge, the Western world has silenced it. Just as the performance tradition of the indigenous peoples in the world is multifaceted, so is the existential trauma they have to face. That, too, has many sides, as the volumes in this series establish.

Identity, environment, language, gender, belief systems, performance traditions and rights are some of the more central issues relating to the struggles and the survival of the indigenous all over the world. Their local features vary from community to community and from country to country. However, the general narrative is fairly common. Quintessentially, this narrative refers to a colonial experience that hammered a break in the long-standing traditions of the indigenous, and yet they kept close to their traditions and nature while losing control over natural resources, land, rivers and forests in the process and clashing with a radically different framework of justice, ethics and spirituality. For the indigenous, invariably, there are two points in time marking their emergence: one that is traced back to a mythological time enshrined in their collective memory and expressed in their community's "story of origin," and the other that is synchronous with a Columbus or a Vasco da Gama setting foot on the land that was once their dominion. It is true that no established research or theory in archaeology, anthropology, genetics, cultural geography, historical linguistics, agriculture and forestry goes to show that any or all of the indigenous people have been inhabitants of the land where they were when colonialism was inaugurated or that a very small portion of them have been associated with their present habitat since the time the homo sapiens have inhabited the Earth. There were migrations from place to place and from continent to continent during the pre-historic times as well. Yet, despite pre-historic migrations, it is true that indigenous communities have been associated with their habitats for a considerably long time. The European colonial quest, the territorial and cultural invasion associated with it, and the interference of alien political, ecological and theological paradigms brought a threat to the traditions that the indigenous had developed. The absence of desire on their part to accept and internalize the new paradigms made them stand out, be marked as "others," be interpreted as "primitive" and represented as "indigenous." It is common sense that the term "indigenous" as a part of a binary can only have meaning when there are other terms such as "alien," "outsiders," "non-native" and "colonialists." The one without the other would cease to have the meaning that it now has.

Though census exercises in different countries do not use a uniform framework, methodology and orientation, the data available through the carried out by different nations shows that approximately 370 million people in the world's population are indigenous. The communities identified as indigenous on the basis of their location, uniqueness of tradition, social structures and community law number close to 5,000 and are spread over 90 countries. Several different terms are used for describing them in different continents: "Aborigine," "Janjati," "Indigenous," "First Nations," "Natives," "Indian" and "Tribe." In most countries, the identification and listing of such communities is, by no means, complete and has remained, over the last seven decades since the United Nations Organization was set up, an unfinished process. Despite the inadequacy in the world's knowledge about the indigenous, it is clear that their existence, environment, cultural ethos, lifestyles and values have been under a relentless assault by the practices, culture and value of the rest of the world. In recognition of the threat to indigenous cultures and knowledge systems, to their land and environment, languages, livelihood and law, the United Nations came out with a Declaration on the Rights of Indigenous People, accepted by the UN General Assembly in September 2007. The following three Articles of the Declaration address the most fundamental issues involved in the genocidal threat to their survival and their unique cultures:

Article 25

Indigenous peoples have the right to maintain and strengthen their distinctive spiritual relationship with their traditionally owned or otherwise occupied and used lands, territories, waters and coastal seas and other resources and to uphold their responsibilities to future generations in this regard.

Article 26

1   Indigenous peoples have the right to the lands, territories and resources which they have traditionally owned, occupied or otherwise used or acquired.
2   Indigenous peoples have the right to own, use, develop and control the lands, territories and resources that they possess by reason of traditional ownership or other traditional occupation or use, as well as those which they have otherwise acquired.
3   States shall give legal recognition and protection to these lands, territories and resources. Such recognition shall be conducted with due respect to the customs, traditions and land tenure systems of the indigenous peoples concerned.

Article 27

States shall establish and implement, in conjunction with indigenous peoples concerned, a fair, independent, impartial, open and transparent process, giving due recognition to indigenous peoples' laws, traditions, customs and land tenure systems, to recognize and adjudicate the rights of indigenous peoples pertaining to their lands, territories and resources, including those which were traditionally owned or otherwise occupied or used. Indigenous peoples shall have the right to participate in this process.

Given that the population of the indigenous is less than 5% of the world's total population, and also that they are sharply divided in terms of tribe and community within a given country, every indigenous community exists as a minuscule minority within its political nation. To be indigenous is, in our time, to be severely marginalized in economy, politics, institutionalized knowledge and institutionalized religion. The space for the indigenous is rapidly shrinking. The year 2019 has been declared by UNESCO as the Year of the Indigenous Languages. There have been official celebrations and academic conference to "celebrate" the year. However, it is a fact that several thousand of the languages still kept alive by communities are close to extinction. A comprehensive survey of languages that I had conducted of the 780 living languages in India in 2010 showed that nearly 300 languages, all of these spoken by the indigenous peoples, may disappear in the next few decades. In India, the national government passed a law in 2008 requiring the return of tribal community land ownership. However, nearly half of the claims have yet to be settled and the Supreme Court of India has already asked the families whose land title claims not been accepted to evacuate them. This situation is not only in India. It is also so in Thailand, where the tribals in the Chang Mai area have been fighting a bitter battle for land ownership. In Mexico, they are struggling to keep their languages alive; in Australia, despite the best efforts by the government, the status of the Aborigines in professions and educational institutions remains far from what was visualized; in New Zealand, they had been facing social discrimination and continue to do so; and in Africa, their plight still deserves the description "a genocidal neglect." Despite legal provisions aimed at safeguarding the communities and their cultures, they are diminishing and suffering an undeserving obsolescence in a world that is considering when to officially announce that the Anthropocene, the epoch of unprecedented interference with nature fundamentally altering the Earth, has commenced.

On 29 May 2019, I received in my email inbox a press release by ESRC, an international network for economic and social rights networks. It referred to the ongoing struggle of the Ogoni people in Nigeria whose land is slotted to be used for oil drilling. It claims that:

The said oil operation, with military cover, is billed to commence in the coming months, as parties involved have been instructed on their respective roles. Each of the security agencies listed in the plan has been tasked with specific roles and responsibilities, particularly, in tackling voices of dissent in the Ogoni community.

It rued the fact that

> rather than going through the proper and legitimate means and process, the government chooses to ignore the people of Ogoni and prefers to engage and impose an oil prospecting company on them, even with an intent to intimidate, suppress and kill the people more with the use of heavily armed security forces.

The press release concluded by reminding the readers that the Ogoni people have never opposed government activity in the Ogoniland, but have insisted on "the issues of benefits-sharing, community participation and the proper environmental management of the Ogoni ecosystem, including legacy issues arising from the over four decades of reckless oil operations in the land."

For nearly a quarter century now since the internet became a means of communication, I have been receiving such statements in my mailbox from indigenous communities or organizations working on their behalf. They bring a narrative in which the characters change but the plot is predictably the same. It involves a rather helpless indigenous community trying to establish that the natural resource involved is its legacy, and a corporate body supported by the government and aided by the police, military or private security troops are denying the community's right. Normally, the conclusion of this story is in the slow dissemination of the community voice and a gradual success of the state in imposing its will on the community. Rarely do the indigenous succeed in getting their voice heard and respected. From Paraguay to Malaysia and from Canada to Australia – west, east, north, south – the story of the conquest of the natural resources of the indigenous peoples by the "civilized," read exploitative economies and industrial technologies, has been with us as commonplace for the last few decades. An unending environmental degradation of habitats of the indigenous has been the norm, not an exception, implied in the massive movement of capital across countries. Exploitation of natural resources has left the traditional habitats of the indigenous people devastated. This situation is not peculiar to any single country or continent; it is the general condition of the indigenous all over the world. The unjust exploitation of natural resources in indigenous habitats has implications far more profound than either anthropologists or ecologists like to accept. European countries engaged in the hugely exploitative project of colonialism proposed an idea of the "savage" as a descriptive category for the ancient surviving civilizations in distant continents. Initially, the "savage," as in William Shakespeare's *The Tempest*, was a mindless brute, more mindless perhaps than brute. Later, during the 18th century, the "savage" became an object of the colonial curiosity, and because genocide of the ancient surviving peoples was a raging priority in the colonies, a great amount of "literature of curiosity" emerged in European languages. Though Rousseau's "noble savage" was not exactly drawn upon the dispatches about the indigenous sent back home by the colonial administrators and adventurists, the need to weave the indigenous in the grand theory of "society" was beginning to be felt. The three decades after the 1820s were of crucial importance in this direction. On the one hand, the regulations related to land, land measurement, land ownership and forest land were being formulated in Britain, France and Germany with a great gusto during these decades, and on the other, the ideas of citizenship had started taking into account land and forests as inescapable factors. The result of these legal, economic and political shifts within Europe had an irreversible impact on the destinies of the indigenous on all continents. For instance, in India, the entire forest cover in the sub-continent was passed on to the British sovereign as a "non-civil domain." This was precisely where the indigenous communities in India had been living for several thousand years. The transfer of their land at once made them "a little less than the subject citizens." They became isolated from history and reduced to the status of anthropology's laboratory objects. This process has not been, nor it could not have been, exactly identical on all continents, Africa, North and South America, Australia and the Pacific; but the general trajectory of the process on these continents was fairly similar. It began with curiosity, passed through confrontation and ended with a unilateral imposition of sovereignty of the colonial state. When countries in these continents acquired self-rule, in most cases during the first half of the 20th century, the colonially produced "state" had come to be an antagonist for the indigenous "nation." The general theme of this volume is to show, in a non-pedantic way, the complexities in the evolution of the idea of nation among the indigenous peoples of the world.

This five-volume series being brought to the readers is intended to comment on the processes through which the clash of civilizations has played out and is impacting society, culture, belief-systems and languages. Each of the volumes deals with a related set of two key issues crucial to understanding the indigenous and thinking about the processes affecting their culture and life. These are: *Environment and Belief-Systems*, Volume 1; *Gender and Rights*, Volume 2; *Indigeneity and Nation*, Volume 3; *Orality and Language*, Volume 4; and *Performance and Knowledge*, Volume 5. These key concerns were selected for discussion based on my three decades of experience living amidst and working with some of the indigenous communities in western India. A large number of consultations, discussions, workshops and field visits have led me to believe that at this juncture of history, these ten form the "key concepts" that one must understand in order to imagine and understand indigenous peoples. The volumes present in-depth studies in the form of long essays, ranging from 8,000 to 10,000 words, and useful bibliographies. However, these essays are not exactly purely academic studies. Their reference is not so much to the previously accumulated knowledge in the fields of anthropology, linguistics, literature, social sciences, law and art criticism. The essays focus on the lived life more than on any field of knowledge. They relate to the prevailing contexts surrounding the communities discussed, without, however, lacking in academic rigour. Many of the contributors have been activists in addition to being scholars. Besides, they are drawn from all continents, in most cases from the communities themselves, and they bring to these volumes their valuable experience of the indigenous from all of those continents. Thus, the five volumes, focusing on ten key concepts, effectively speak about the indigenous peoples in Australia, New Zealand and the Pacific region; in India and East Asia; in Africa and in the Americas. Each of the volumes has seven or eight intensive essays which open up a range of themes and questions related to the specific key terms discussed. It is hoped that these volumes will form valuable reading for students, researchers and academics interested in knowing what the indigenous communities think about themselves and about the contemporary world.

The publication of this series of volumes brings me a great personal satisfaction. I was trained in literary studies in an era when "excellence" in literature was ascribed to works in the main European languages alone. In my early years as a professor at an Indian university, I started noticing that the rich and unique culture of the indigenous communities was at that time like a continent about to be submerged under the ferocious cultural assault of the urban-industrial values and materials. My unease increased so much that I felt compelled to drop out of academic life and to move to a tiny village where the Rathwa indigenous community lived. That opened a new universe for me. There was so much to experience, see and learn from them, most of all how limited what I had till then imagined as "knowledge." Throughout my years spent with them, it was never my intention to "represent" them to the rest of the world that was on a path of ecological destruction. My task was to let the indigenous express themselves, to create spaces for their voice and to facilitate that expression. I realized that the gap between the indigenous and the universe of formal knowledge, labour and economy was unbridgeable. During the last three decades, all of my intellectual and activist work has remained devoted to bridging this abysmal gap. The publication of this series, Key Concepts in Indigenous Studies, is a small step in that direction. I would like to hope in all humility that it will achieve what it aims to, and will remind the readers that the Earth does not belong to us, we belong to it.

1

INDIGENEITY AND NATIONAL CELEBRATIONS IN LATIN AMERICA

Performative practices and identity politics

Ximena Cordova Oviedo

The "discovery" of America marked the start of the "eclipse" of indigenous American peoples, their systems and structures by European powers. Alongside the annihilation of indigenous people, their histories and previous knowledges have been discarded by "the myth of European superiority over other cultures of the world" (Dussel 2008: 341).

This process started with the Spanish invasion of the continent in 1492, followed by European colonization, later independence from Europe and then nation-building by Eurocentric elites who imposed European literacy, science, Christianity and capitalist industrialism as universal doctrines of progress (Dussel 1992).

Through centuries of survival and struggle against dehumanization, indigenous Americans (alongside other colonized peoples all over the world) have won remarkable victories in recognition of their land rights, their personhood, as well as the right to evolve and to be in the world differently.

More recent widespread indigenous mobilizations coming from Latin America have given indigeneity a new political visibility worldwide. Particularly since the 1990s, to coincide with the commemoration of the 500 years since the arrival of Europeans to the Americas, there has been a Latin American relaunch of indigenous movements.

In Bolivia, Albó (1991) debated the "return of the Indian," as the previous decades had shown that indigenous movements were restructuring their struggle in ways that would find resonance in the changing political and economic global context. The *Declaración de Quito* (Ecuador) in 1991, which was among the first documents to result of an international indigenous gathering (Pratt 2007: 398), served to catalyze a political campaign for the recognition of the rights of indigenous peoples. This was followed by the UN Declaration of 1993 as the Year of Indigenous Rights, and the start of a ten-year period to mark their recognition. Among other important events, indigenous Guatemalan peace activist Rigoberta Menchú won the Nobel Prize in 1992, and two years later, in 1994, the Zapatista movement in Mexico led a political uprising against the government that was covered by media globally.

Since the turn of the millennium, we have witnessed a surge in political participation by indigenous groups with the arrival of an indigenous Aymara to the presidency of Bolivia in 2005, Evo Morales, and the rewriting of the constitutions in Venezuela (in 1999), Ecuador (in 2008) and Bolivia (in 2009) to include indigenous rights, indigenous legislative bodies and the rights of the environment. Some scholars have noted the emergence of indigenous practices, in the Andes in particular, that visibilize the exclusion of indigenous practices from modern ideas of the nation-state, which have accompanied these events (De la Cadena 2010; Blaser 2014). These practices, both political and performative in nature, show encounters between human and natural deities and sacred beings, which are engrained in pre-Hispanic and contemporary indigenous traditions and religions, as acquiring a new relevance in the global political sphere: they expose politics as not universal, but instead a cultural construct (De la Cadena et al. 2017).

The 21 January 2006 presidential inauguration of Evo in the ruins of Tiwanaku, Bolivia's most important remains of pre-Inca civilization, may be seen as an example of this. Here is the report of Evo Morales' "indigenous" inauguration by US-news chain Fox News:

> Bolivian President-elect Evo Morales, dressed in a bright red tunic worn only by the most important pre-Inca priests, promised to do away with vestiges of his country's colonial past Saturday in a spiritual ceremony at an ancient temple on the eve of his inauguration. . . . Morales first walked barefoot up the Akapana pyramid and donned the tunic and a cap decorated with traditional yellow and red Aymara patterns. Then he was blessed by priests and accepted a baton adorned with gold and silver, symbolizing his Indian leadership.
>
> After putting on sandals, he descended from the pyramid to address the crowd in front of the Kalasasaya temple.
>
> *Morales thanked Mother Earth* and God for his political victory and promised to "seek equality and justice," as he closed *the ceremony performed by Indian priests, the cultural inheritors of this pre-Incan city* whose people mysteriously disappeared without written record long before the Spaniards took control of much of South America
>
> *('Bolivian President Evo Morales Takes Part in Inauguration*
> *Festivities' 2006, my emphasis)*

Politicians performing visual antics in front of a supportive crowd is nothing new in presidential inaugurations, neither is the broadcasting of local politics onto a wider global framework, nor an emphasis on indigenous symbolism, or to make a political point or celebrate the achievement by a particular ethnic group. What is new here is the invocation of non-human beings such as the Mother Earth, and the performance of libations to the Earth in such a public and "rational" platform.

De la Cadena (2010: 337) has remarked on the increased presence of political interaction with Andean deities and sacred natural formations in the form of offerings performed during political events in Bolivia, Peru and Ecuador. There were public displays of offerings to the *Pachamama* ("Mother Earth" in the Andes) during the political mobilizations that took place in Bolivia during the Water War (2000) and the Gas Water (2003), which helped to bring down the neoliberal regime in Bolivia (subsequently giving place to the rise of Evo Morales and MAS party to power). De la Cadena (2010) also documented a number of examples in Peru in the form of offerings to *wak'as* (sacred beings or sacred natural formations in the landscape) during political mobilizations. The inclusion of the rights of Pachamama into the constitutions of Ecuador and Bolivia, both countries with indigenous majorities which have undergone major political changes in the last two decades, can also be read as examples of this new way to view the very "logic" of "politics as only pertaining humans" as open to interpretation.

In the case of the Andes, the emergence of nature and "earth-beings" (De la Cadena 2010) as performative subjects in the political global arena articulate indigenous conceptions of the world that do not separate human relations from those with non-humans (De la Cadena 2010; Blaser 2014), whereby humans and not humans "plants, animals, mountains, the rivers, the rain" are seen as related "like a family" (Oxa 2004: 239). De la Cadena sees this current emergence of indigeneity as an energy that could force the reconfiguration of the political, for it proposes that politics exists in a pluriversal frame and not as a single universal concept that rules all. In other words, that the separation of nature and culture that is at the foundation of the very idea of politics is a cultural construct that is being challenged by indigenous groups from the Andes (in this case) in their long struggle against the universal status of Eurocentric modernity as the only way to understand and conduct ourselves in the world (Dussel 1992).

I am interested in applying this new paradigm when looking at the realm of festive and popular practices in Latin America as an alternative to understand ideological debates about culture. For Gramsci, the imaginaries conjured up by folklore and popular culture act as "instrumental values of thought in the development of culture" (1988 [1916]: 195) in generating ideologies which are then used to implement domination. I am also persuaded by Guss (2000: 12), who has spoken of the interconnectedness of cultural performance in Latin America as "sites of social action where identities and relations are continually being reconfigured." I will focus my analysis on contemporary festive practices that engage with ideas of indigeneity in Bolivia and, to a lesser extent, in Mexico. I will start by looking at examples of state-led nation-making projects that used indigenous cultures as a resource for their own hegemonic identity-making agendas. I will then discuss contemporary indigenous strategies to turn these platforms into channels for their own political and ontological quests.

Nation-making and popular culture in the Republican era in Latin America

During the Latin American nation-making processes of the 19th century, after nearly four centuries of Spanish rule, the idea of the "national" was borrowed from incipient European nations post-Enlightenment, with specific mono-linguistic and mono-ethnic characteristics (Thurner 1997). The newly independent countries and their European-descent elites required the establishment of both symbolic and figurative maps of the nation to claim their own idea of civilization and identity as legitimate, and thus counteract indigenous claims to land and ancestry.

The legitimization of the unique identity of new republics called for the establishment of a homogenous national identity that integrated all of members of this "imagined community" (Anderson 1991) into a common project: the integration of the country as a player into the world economy. But first, deep, existing divisions needed to be overcome.

In the Latin American Republican period of the 19th and 20th centuries, the internal limits to the community were marked by positivist racialism, a legacy of the colonial "dual republic system" of the Spanish Empire. *Indians* (indigenous peoples) and Spanish had been clustered separately in early colonial times, as the concept of race determined not only fiscal categories, but also what work, language, location and culture was assigned to each. With time, miscegenation (biological mixing) and processes of acculturation moved the emphasis from race as the mark of distinction onto culture (Rowe and Schelling 1991: 42). In the context of industrialization in the first half of the 20th century, the reconfiguration of boundaries prompted Latin American nations to give a new prominence to ethnicity, history and language, and external markers such as dress, speech and "manners" (Klein 2003: 50).

In Brazil this gave rise to the discourse of *mestizaje* (Freyre 1933), which attempted to transcend old racial boundaries. The racial mix of the region, no longer a sign of impurity, came to be seen in a positive light and as a cultural point of reference (Bakewell 2004: 490), operating in contrast to US-style segregation policies (Wade 2004: 335). Mexico underwent a similar process under the Zapatista government (1910–20). In *The Cosmic Race* (Vasconcelos 1997 [1925]), Mexico's cultural mix was invoked as the basis of a new civilization. In the case of the Andes, with its large indigenous population, the processes of including indigenous populations into national configurations were more tense. This was related to the colonial legacy of protected indigenous territories, which meant that as late as the end of the 19th century, Andean Indians were still holding large portions of land. The hostility of the population against indigenous people, who were perceived to be an impediment to progress and industrialization, delayed the arrival of mestizaje to Bolivia until 1952 (to be revisited later in this chapter).

National celebrations played a key role in this process. Uses of popular culture as a means to forge national identities emerged during the 18th century in Europe with the birth of "folklore" (Burke 1994). This stems from how the folkloric is understood by the upper classes as the "discovery of the popular knowledge," dating back the European Enlightenment (Burke 1994).

In the Americas, uses of the folkloric started to appear in the aftermath of the Mexican Revolution. According to Guss, strategies to "instil faith in the infant state" included making newly important dates coincide with important festivities (such as religious dates on the Christian calendar), and also hosting new commemorations on existing ritual sites (2000: 13). This has been discussed as the tactical management of ethnic identity (Cohen 2000), and relating to "hegemonic processes as a means of shaping and controlling nationhood" (Hellier-Tinoco 2011: 35).

In her ethnographic analysis in Mexico, Hellier-Tinoco (2011) traces and analyzes the dynamics that take place whereby two performed practices by the P'urhépecha peoples, the *Dance of the Old Men* and *Night of the Dead* of Lake Pátzcuaro (Michoacán, Mexico), have been used to perform and construct long-lasting ideas of Mexican nationalism. As I will later show of my own ethnography of Oruro in Bolivia, this author finds strong evidence of the appropriation of selected indigenous practices into the official narratives of Mexico and Mexicanness "with the multiple objectives of incorporating disparate peoples, enabling economic development, fashioning a future, attracting tourists, and creating collective identities" (Hellier-Tinoco 2011: 4).

She documents how certain images of these events – such as the public and private rites of collective mourning for the veneration towards dead relatives of the Day/Night of the Dead, and the masked dancing "old men" wearing colourful ponchos of the Dance of the Old Men – emerged as quintessential icons of Mexico's nationalism and are used in different contexts away from their original lacustrine setting of Janitzio Island in Lake Pátzcuaro (Hellier-Tinoco 2011: 71).

As official markers of the nation, she writes, the Dance of the Old Men dance is performed in government-run buildings by folkloric ballets as entertainment in fully inclusive package tourist resorts in Cancun and Acapulco, by children in school shows, in touristic and cultural publications about Mexicans, and in events attended by Mexicans in the USA and Europe – each and every time conjuring up "authentic and indigenous Mexico" (Hellier-Tinoco 2011: 26).

Another important marker of Mexicanness from the same location is the quintessential Day of the Dead, which conjures up ideas of Mexicanness all over the globe. Since the 1920s, the Day of the Dead is a yearly national celebration that falls on November 1, which was once informally celebrated in Janitzio, away from the public eye. The celebrations in Janitzio by P'urhépecha indigenous people have become a site for more than a hundred thousand visitors who want to witness the communal rituals in honour of the dead, dancing, songs, food and music.

It has featured in several major Hollywood studio films, and certain ideas concerning it are familiar to many people when Mexicanness is invoked: the commemoration of dead relatives with food, gatherings and visits to the cemetery, and the iconic figure of the skeletons dressed as women, called Catrinas. Nowadays, near the date, Mexican restaurants around the globe offer special menus that include skeleton-shaped sugar and bread snacks in surroundings decorated with "typical" altars, orange flowers and fruits. Party suppliers around the world ship Day of the Dead-themed decorations to celebrate Mexican culture in private and public events around the world. Apparently, Mexico City recently started an annual parade after an invented depiction of a massive parade during the Day of the Dead for a James Bond movie.[1]

These displays of Mexicanness are promoted as a source of authentic culture, yet very few of us abroad are aware of the P'urhépecha (among other groups) from which these traditions emerge, or how these traditions have developed over time.

Celebrations such as the Dead/Night of the Dead in Mexico are the product of cultural "hybridity" at many levels. Existing pre-Hispanic traditions have had to adapt for survival through the centuries, avoiding strategies of domination such as the colonial Extirpation of Idolatries applied in the Spanish Americas in the 17th century to brutally and publically eliminate traces of indigenous beliefs and practices that were deemed a threat to the political power of Spanish institutions.

To counteract this and improve their chances of survival, existing religious practices had to undergo a process of transformation and negotiation which resulted in both Catholicism and local religiosity adapting to one another and acquiring a different set of characteristics.[2] In Mexico, like in Peru and Bolivia, the festive has been one of the main outlets for these conflictive juxtapositions and transmissions, as an expression of both the tensions and encounters between indigenous and European epistemological frameworks.

The ritual celebration of All Saints in the Christian calendar, with performative practices that honour the link between the dead and the living, is practiced throughout the Americas as a whole. Yet the Day/Night of the Dead have become iconic constructs of Mexicanness. The incorporation of these previously local traditions into global displays of Mexican culture was launched when a group of intellectuals, artists and politicians came from the capital to visit the region in the 1920s to observe and register P'urhépecha practices, which had stubbornly survived the decimation of indigenous populations by the Spanish better than other indigenous groups (Hellier-Tinoco 2011: 69; Zárate Hernández 1993).

Hellier-Tinoco (2011: 6) argues that with the projection of this celebration as national icon, "a particular set of meanings was molded, circulated" with the aim to be later reproduced in nationalist and sometimes commercial contexts that brought the different subjects of the nation together under a blanket of embedded rootedness and homogeneity. These associations, based on particular places, histories and corporal activities, rely on ideas of "authenticity" and "indigeneity" at their core, and have accompanied the Mexican nation-building project into the 21st century and the development of a foundational agenda "in opposition to purportedly inauthentic foreign entities, both internal and external, which were usually perceived as European and from the United States" Hellier-Tinoco (2011: 46).

One of the consequences was the designation of the people of Lake Pátzcuaro and their practices as "folkloric" (Hellier-Tinoco 2011: 5), with their ethnicity reconstructed (as per MacCannel 1984, 1992) for touristic and commercial ends.

These political concerns, which have emerged from the historical developments of Latin American nations – the role of indigeneity in the making of national identity, the rural/urban dichotomy, the visibility of selected indigenous practices in popular imaginaries, and the rights and duties of indigenous people towards the nation and the rest of the population –also find profound resonance in the festive in Bolivia.

I have found important points of historical/cultural/political convergence in the festive that mirror the development of Bolivian nation-making. This will be the context for my interpretation of certain contemporary indigenous performative practices in Bolivia as a catalyzer of ontological and political transformations.

Performative practices as interaction

Performance has been discussed in the social sciences to reflect on two worlds: the world of symbolic and aesthetic activities (theatre, music performance, protest), when people are set apart from their everyday lives (Bauman 1986, quoted by Schieffelin 1998: 195); and the world of "the everyday" – our daily practices.

Schechner (2002) differentiates the two worlds as "is-performance" and "as-performance." In the first case, people participate by people either performing or watching, and ideas of virtuosity and expressive competence become relevant (Bauman 1986, quoted by Schieffelin 1998: 195), whereas "as-performance" reflects the daily dynamics of interactions between individuals and the others (Goffman 1959; Schieffelin 1998). This area of performance is associated with theories of practice (de Certeau 1988; Bourdieu 2000) and the idea that human expressivity is affected when human beings come into contact with one another, establishing the meaningfulness of culture and society, and their social identity through their voice, gestures and appearance.

Festivals, such as Janitzio's Night of the Dead singing, dancing and praying, are clearly performance in the "is-performance" sense, as a spectacle that is bracketed apart from everyday life and judged on the virtuosity of the display. The 150,000 tourists that visit Janitzio every year are most certainly largely attracted by the displays of choreographed dancing and P'urhépecha music and art that take over the public spaces, as much as the witnessing of the ritual aspects.

However, I propose to concentrate on the "as-performance" aspect of the festive because of the rich meaning that can be extracted from festive practices beyond the realm of spectacle. Howard-Malverde (1997a) identified the interconnectedness of text-context in cultural practice in the Andes, which is of use here to identify how the contextual aspect of the Oruro Carnival, in terms of ritual, social and economic organization, can have an effect on transformations and continuations of the performed event in question.

In looking at the Andes, previous scholars have exposed the idea of Andean rituals and celebrations generating new meanings and processes.[3] I propose to focus on dance because of its acknowledged significance as a medium of information transmission (Gilbert 2006) and, as I will show, the agency invested in it by Andean indigenous groups to expand their political and ontological agendas (Cordova 2012).

Mendoza (2000) has explored the significance of popular parade dancing in Peru, practised extensively on special dates on the ritual calendar in the Andes. Beyond the visual, the commemorative or the entertaining, she has found that dance in Peru helps dancers in the redefinition of the identities that emerge from everyday links to occupation, ethnicity, class, age and gender in interacting with each other.

Viewed in this way, dancing in the Andes emerges as a site with identity-making properties; as a way to comment on important sociocultural values "such as decency, elegance, genuineness, modernity, and folklore" (Mendoza 2000: 41) for those taking part, as well as on the dichotomies that dancers have to confront in their daily lives with regard to their own subjectivity: rich/poor, White/indigenous, rural/urban, etc.

Carnival in Oruro (Bolivia)

Carnival is a moving date on the Christian calendar, celebrated around February or March, just before Lent. In Oruro, celebrations include a four-day public holiday, a street party with food and drink stalls, private and public rituals, and a dance parade made up of around 20,000 dancers – including locals and visitors.

Oruro is a quiet city for half of the year. It gets transformed in a momentous crescendo of activity from November onwards that explodes in the Carnival. Once the festivity arrives, it consumes the whole city.

Catholicism plays an important part, as the parade is performed under the supervision of the church, and in honour of the Madonna of the Mineshaft (also celebrated by Aymaras in Southern Peru in the Festivity of Candelmas on February 2). Its timing in the regional agricultural calendar coincides with the end of the rainy period, considered since pre-Hispanic times in the Andes to be linked to fertility and abundance (Stobart 2006; Véliz Lopez 2002), so both the Catholic and the Andean have a place in this celebration.[4]

The pageant is officially Bolivia's most prominent cultural expression, attended by the country's authorities and mediatized all over the world as a source of Bolivian national pride. The festivity is organized jointly by the church, with their Catholic agenda; the cultural authorities that work to help coordinate the event at local government level; and the organizing committee, representing the dance troupes.

For the last few decades, and particularly since its 2001 entry in the UNESCO list of Masterpieces of Intangible Heritage of Humanity, the state and the organizers present the parade as a source of cultural capital and national pride for its ability to bring the nation together. It is mediatized all over the world as a symbol of the nation coming together to display their best, often through one of its most emblematic dance: the Devil dance, which is also the oldest on record.

The Devil dance, one of 18 types of Carnival dances, has become the most iconic symbol of the Carnival as a whole. The significance of the figure of the dancing devil in Oruro is clear as soon as a visitor approaches the city. There is a huge sculpture of a devil dancing just after the military post that marks the entry to the city, and images of Devil dance figures all over the city. The logo of the local football club, the region's well-loved San José, shows a devil, as do advertisements of many other Oruro service providers, and there are Devil dancers in all of the media produced by Bolivia's national tourism department. In short, the devil and Carnival are seen as iconic of Oruro, just like Day of the Dead and the Dance of the Old Men, as shown by Hellier-Tinoco (2011), have come to represent Mexicanness.

There is also a widespread view that "everyone" takes part in Carnival. According to the highest Catholic priest in the city at the Church of the Mineshaft:

> Here in Oruro Bolivian cultural traits from all places converge . . . here are all the expressions. The Fatherland is united in the forty-eight dance troupes.
> *(A fray at the Church of the Mineshaft, in interview)*[5]

However, I found that participation, even if wide-ranging, is subject to determinant factors outside the festive: Oruro, as with all cities in the region, is home to a fragmented society, and hierarchies of place of origin, gender, ethnicity and socio-economic status help to determine if and how an individual may take part, and what transmission processes they will take part in.

Oruro: location and memory

Oruro is a small city located inside the department of Oruro, about 230 km from La Paz (site of government). The surrounding landscape is mostly arid and cold, stretching over the treeless plateau of the country's central highlands.

The Carnival's urban location has wide socio-cultural significance, for an analysis of its urban backdrop can also be informative of particular contexts that are relevant to the past and present of Oruro as a whole.

Oruro has a definite urban feel to it, as it was, along with silver-rich Potosí, the first modern city of Bolivia during the height of mining in the 17th century; but the countryside does not feel far away either. Nowadays, trade is Oruro's main activity, attracting people from all over the country. Men in suits and men in indigenous ponchos share the pavements and the small buses. Women dressed in *polleras* (the skirt worn by some urban women of indigenous descent) and in "European-style" dress both act as sellers and customers in the markets and shops, and women in traditionally woven indigenous dress are also seen about, carrying their children or goods in traditional back carriers. It is obviously more urban than rural, but the presence of nearby rural communities is significant and noticeable. Many of the provinces around Oruro city are rural, and many still operate under Andean forms of organization.[6]

Out of the total of the population in 2001, 38.9% lived in moderate poverty and 27.3% in extreme poverty, which is 6% more than the national average, most of them in the rural area (INE 2009: 20).

Local historians suggest that the location of Oruro had been occupied by several civilizations previous to the Conquest (Murillo Vacarreza 1999; Condarco 1999; Revollo 2003). The last group to inhabit the area had been the Urus of Paria, an ancient lacustrine group settled around the area near the lakes Titicaca, Poopó and Coipasa (Wachtel 1984).

Like Carnival, mining is at the core of the city's identity, and has shaped many of the practices that make up the body of "Carnival traditions" that most troupes follow.

Mining was first carried out informally by some of the earlier European settlers that came to the area in search of gold and silver (Wachtel 1984; Pauwels 2006). Inside the mines, the Aymara Indians were the majority, working as *mitayos* (Klein 2003: 55). The *mita* system, borrowed from existing Inca practices to designate "turns" or shifts for working in the many activities that the expansion of the Inca state required (Harris 1995), was adapted to sponsor mining under Spanish authorities with very disadvantageous conditions for indigenous workers (Klein 2003: 39).

By the second half of the 17th century, disease, repressive abuse, war and migration had significantly weakened the indigenous population (Wachtel 1984: 213). Many of the existing Inca economic, political, cultural and religious institutions had been brought down, and only elements of it were used to prop up the colonial regime.

Oruro's rapid growth as a result of the prosperity of the mines prompted its urban expansion, with new buildings and institutions, hospitals, churches and convents constantly being raised. By 1680, Oruro had a population of 80,000 (De Mesa and Gisbert 2001: 178–9), including thousands of indigenous people employed in the mines, and others serving the needs of the mine, selling food items and offering their services to mine owners and their employees. It is significant that the first Carnival dancers, at the start of the 20th century, were grouped on the basis of trades that delivered goods to the mines during the colony, as meat, candle and coca leaf traders all formed Carnival troupes.

Mining defined the city from its foundation as a Spanish colonial mining settlement in 1606 to the 1980s, when state mines were closed down. The city's original layout had two urban settlements, or "republics," one for the "Spanish" and one for the "Indians." Even today, the Ranchería – as the site of the old Republic of Indians and today's location of most of the workshops of costume-makers and other Carnival artisans – holds a particular sense of community, with own cultural traits that are different from the rest of Oruro. Interviewees from the Ranchería will often mention that they were "born and bred" there.

In 1904, a group of butchers started a Devil dance troupe in the Ranchería known as the *Auténtica*, and it is the oldest Carnival dance troupe on record. Other troupes were formed by those who held stalls in markets: the butchers danced the Devil dance, the match sellers danced the Inca dance, the coca leaf sellers danced the Moreno dance, and so on. For the first decades, due to a municipal ordinance in place until the end of the Chaco War which banned Indians from the main plaza (originally in the Spanish quarter of the city), the dance parade was an indigenous affair in the city outskirts; whereas the elites celebrated "Carnival" in dance halls, dressed up and away from the public eye.

There was a major cultural reframing during the 1940s and 1950s in Bolivia, which coincides with the time when the Carnival was undergoing its most significant transformations. The 1940s marked the end of the marginal period of the "indigenous carnival" in Oruro, with the first performance of the Devil dance for national authorities in 1944, followed by the introduction of members from the upper classes in the parade. Oruro's elite had recently immersed themselves in Carnival dancing, moved by an ideological push to incorporate indigenous peoples into the mass of national citizens, previously described as "indigenismo," and the adoption of "mestizaje" as the main cultural project to accompany the nation-making projects from the 1950s onwards, which had also taken place also in Peru, Mexico and other countries with large indigenous populations. However, as we shall see, the Euro-centric bias of the national populism of the 1940s and 1950s (Zavaleta Mercado 1987) had a profound effect on the processes of reconfiguration of the festivity during this period.

In the Andes in the 1940s, and as part of the 1952 Nationalist Revolution in Bolivia, the discourse of mestizaje acknowledged the presence of indigenous elements in the making of the nation, "as an ingredient which gives a certain particularity to national identity, through the appropriation of certain symbols and cultural features," but resting all along on the premise that the indigenous contributions are not part of "worthy" culture (Oliart 2002: 9; see also Barragan 2006; Morales 2010 for Bolivia).

In the subsequent years of the 1960s and 70s, as the nation struggled to endorse mestizaje as a unifying identity during an era of great political instability and military intervention, the Oruro Carnival also became more heavily loaded within nationalist discourse. In 1970, then president General Ovando (1969–70), who came to power through a *coup d'état*, named Oruro as Folkloric Capital of Bolivia by national decree, raising the profile of the Carnival parade to a national level. Specialist institutions were created to safeguard the "interests" of the dancing troupes, which have since then endorsed the standardization of many elements of the event, i.e., costumes and dance steps, as the appropriation of the celebration by the elites became officialized and reached new dimensions. During this period, as regulations were drafted to manage the event in a more structured way, Catholic affiliation became an official requirement for participation. In the 1970s and 80s, masses of the urban middle classes joined in the parade and created dances in imitation of indigenous cultures, directed at the consumers of folklore. Seated tickets for watching the parade also started to be sold.

Thus, from its humble beginnings, over the course of the second half of the 20th century dancing in the Oruro Carnival had become a modern source of social status and a spectacle to behold: the costumes were now extravagant and reassuringly expensive, starting to prevent poorer people from taking part.

Two main strands of interpretation are constantly projected in official discourses about Carnival in Oruro (Araoz 2003; Lara Barrientos 2007): the parade as an expression of Christian-Catholic devotion, and as a carrier for the transmission of national traditions through folklore. This view is corroborated in the documentation produced as part of the bid to win UNESCO's recognition (ACFO 2000), prepared by a selected group of cultural authorities, which I analyzed in a previous work (Cordova 2012). In it, I found that through the use of local myths to create authoritative interpretations of the symbolic capital of the festive in Oruro, and the Christianization of Andean symbols as a source of symbolic capital, Carnival is presented as univocal: representing the coming together of all memories and cultures into the mestizo and Catholic identity of Bolivians as a whole (Cordova 2012).

To gain meaning beyond these established discourses, I looked at the multivocality of Carnival (Bakhtin 1984), as well as how Carnival parade dancing produces discourses through daily practices (Harvey 1997; Mendoza 2000; Femenias 2005), by focusing on the Devil dance troupes – the stars of the parade.

Devil dancing

Carnival troupes are divided into subgroups, each with their own costume and choreographic displays, headed by a lead dancer.

Joining a troupe can be very expensive, costing at times hundreds of US dollars in fees and costumes. The more prestigious troupes, given their standing and media coverage, attract a large numbers of participants and sponsorships. A few struggle to survive in this competitive arena due to low numbers and get threatened with closure by the organizing committee.

According to Haraway, there is a personal body and a social body, and the emphasis is on location (1991: 10). I found that choosing a dance troupe becomes a way to indicate where a dancer's social mobility is taking place, as the personal body gains meaning from attaching itself to the social body of particular troupes in Oruro, and any values associated to them: their high standards in performance, their sense of innovation or their international recognition.

The Butchers troupe, for instance, as the first troupe on record, is the holder some of Carnival's oldest traditions. It continues to mainly be made up of families in the meat trade in market stalls around the city. Newer troupes have more of a socio-economic mix.

During the political and cultural changes of the 1940s, the Butchers' troupe split in 1944, prompting the creation of new Devil dance troupes. The Fraternidad, founded by Oruro's elite, emerged from the split as a new Devil dance troupe and went onto become Oruro's most renowned Devil dance institution.

I interviewed the son of a dancer from the Butchers' troupe who had helped to found the Fraternidad as their first choreographer – a very prominent role for the history of any troupe and, given the high standing of the Fraternidad, the history of Carnival as a whole. He recalled how his father, a butcher, had tried to join the Fraternidad:

> My father was one of the . . . founders of the [elite troupe], but . . . as a result of racial and social discrimination [there], which had middle class people, [my father] was erased from their Foundation Certificate. He isn't even mentioned as the first [choreographer]. . . . My father was [a founder], but he is not mentioned in the records.
>
> *(Carnival dancer and researcher, in interview)*

Indeed, many of the members of the Butchers' troupe speak indigenous Andean languages, such as Quechua or Aymara, and many women wear indigenous skirts – both markers of indigenous descent. The emergence of the Fraternidad in the Carnival scene, made up of bank managers, business people and people with high social capital who self-identified as "mestizo," is usually described in terms of being an improvement for the festivity, as having brought in positive changes and a sense of evolution to an otherwise marginal celebration, such as the inclusion of women and the standardization of the costume and steps:

> A less conservative, more updated version. . . . The trademark of the Fraternidad is a sense of innovation, improvement, and the evolution [of Carnival].
>
> *(Carnival dancer, in interview)*

Indeed, the need to innovate the spectacle dimension of the parade needs to be understood within the dialogue between Carnival in Oruro and the mediazation of other large street festivals and commercial spectacles around the world. New global standards are set with each new transmission of the Rio Olympics and the Olympic Games opening shows – on aesthetic and logistic levels.

However, the common knowledge that the institution has brought innovations to the dance translates, in some contexts, into a sense of ownership, despite the popular nature of the event. According to the son of one of their founders: "everything related to the devil dance in the Oruro Carnival is the work of the Fraternidad" (Carnival dancer, in interview).

In the book *La Diablada de Oruro: sus máscaras y caretas* (1998), used as a reference book for those researching the Devil dance in Oruro, Jorge Enrique Vargas Luza describes and explains the meanings of the symbols of the Diablada, in terms of mask, costume and choreography. He says,

> we standardised the costumes and instituted a rehearsal costume, we diagrammed the steps and movements, and designer [choreographic] figures according to the message of the sacramental plat [that inspired the dance].
>
> *(Vargas Luza 1998: 28)*

The author states that in coding these dances through writing, all of those elements became the "legal patrimony" of the Fraternidad (Vargas Luza 1998: 28). This commentary becomes pertinent when we link it to accounts of how writing as a method of coding knowledge is connected to how "other" epistemologies have been excluded from historical narratives in the Andes (Howard et al. 2002).

Despite being the first troupe in the history of the parade, the Butchers' troupe is among the least visible, as they dance in the early hours of the parade (when people are still asleep from partying the night before), and their participation is not usually covered by the media or sponsorship deals. Their communal and preparatory ritual practices directed at Andean deities, borrowed from traditional mining rites and among the oldest practices related to the parade in Oruro, are also not mediatized, as only the rituality that is related to Christianity and the Temple of the Mineshaft is broadcast.

As founders of the most prestigious national celebration, butchers remain a subaltern group, and their practices, performed year after year and rooted in Aymara culture and religiosity, are not visible to most. The folkloric dimension of the Oruro Carnival parade leaves all traces of being indigenous firmly in the past, like Janitzio's "folkloric" P'urhépecha traditions in Mexico, performed in museum-like displays of the nation, without a hint of any of the debates that concern contemporary indigeneity.

In the face of Oruro's entry to UNESCO's List of Masterpieces of Intangible Heritage of Humanity, there is the issue of who represents an "authorized" voice in the dynamics of the heritage content of the parade. In seminars with Oruro's cultural authorities, it was often expressed that performers have to understand that when they make, in the words of representatives of Comité de Etnografía y Folklore, "distortions" to the dance, or "unfounded innovations" (with an emphasis on the need for "scientific" research), "they are damaging the [UNESCO] masterpiece" (CEF 2007). The concept of transgression is often in the air when discussing the changeability of culture and what types of evolution are considered "legitimate."

More often than not, these distinctions operate within larger power discourses that work to keep the status quo in the hands of the powerful. I'll bring your attention to the aesthetics of female Carnival costumes to illustrate this point (Figure 1.1).

Polleras (urban indigenous skirts) are major signifiers of the historic resistance of urban and countryside indigenous women to modernize and adopt mestizo European ways. Carnival polleras, however, serve another purpose. They are short and worn with high-heeled boots that elongate the body. The waist is reshaped by a

FIGURE 1.1   Oruro Carnival women dancers

Source: All photographs in this chapter are by the author. © Ximena Cordova Oviedo

hidden corset inside the blouse, giving dancers a flat stomach, and a long and thin waist. These costumes reshape the female body to project an "improved" embodied identity that matches current global ideas of beauty and femininity, whilst its configuration around the traditional attire of the urban indigenous woman of the highlands keep it within the framework of "authenticity."

Thus, certain "traditions" are preserved, even commodified to acquire meaning outside of their original context, like the shortening of the pollera that no longer serves to cover from the Andean cold, and is now used for new projections of different femininity and modernity. Other types of memories, like the banning of the first Carnival troupes from the city's centre until the 1940s due to racial segregation, less useful for national discursive projections or touristic branding, are edited out of official narratives.

It is interesting to see that the official discourse of "safeguarding the masterpiece" does not extend to the continuing shortening of the pollera, which has not caused any claims of unfounded innovation among the (mostly male) gatekeepers of the parade.

The lack of visibility of some key Carnival actors in representations of national heritage in Oruro reflects, in my view, the unceasing racialization of culture, whereby contemporary indigenous actors are "eclipsed"[7] from hegemonic transmissions of national memory, whilst at the same time (as seen in Mexico's Dance of the Dead and the Dance of the Old Men), "folkloric" indigeneity is used as a source of legitimacy to accompany nationalist projects that depend on a claim to territory legitimized by communal memory.

However, despite elite-led management strategies to appropriate or even "eclipse" indigeneity in favour of the projection of a homogenous mestizo identity, festive performance, thanks to its dialogical nature, creates new meanings and relations, as performers strive to negotiate their participation, interests and needs through different discursive and structural forms. The Butchers' troupe does contest their invisibility, although I have not had a chance to discuss how here. One of the ways is that they continue to dance and perform according to what they call "the ways of our grandparents," year in year out, regardless of the powers that be. The P'urhépecha, in Mexico since 1983, have started to celebrate the P'urhépecha New Year, *Kurhikaueri K'uinchekua*, on 2 February (which commemorates the Lady of Candlemas in the Christian calendar), honouring Mesoamerican deities and inserting elements symbolic of P'urhépecha ethnicity, such as the P'urhépecha flag, the calendar stone and the icon of fire. This more explicitly indigenous performance, which engages sacred forces and deities in the public display, is an attempt to expand the cultural display of P'urhépecha peoples to "a new sphere of public discourse and spectacle," according to Roth-Seneff (2014).

I found that Oruro, too, has produced a new type of indigenous performance that turns festive practices into sites to challenge invisibility and bring opportunities to attain wider social and political recognition. I will briefly discuss the Anata Andina parade, an explicitly indigenous parade that enters the city of Oruro during Carnival time.

The anata (meaning "play" in Aymara language) is one of the yearly Aymara rainy season celebrations centred on the Pachamama (Véliz Lopez 2002: 72). People celebrate by decorating their houses, and ritual activity in the countryside is also directed to the natural deities and sacred beings in charge of the fertility of the land, animal and humans. At the end, there is a celebration with music and drinking for the rites of the dispatch of rain until the following year.

The Anata Andina parade in Oruro started in 1993, framed by the surge in social and indigenous movements around Latin America previously discussed (Abercrombie 2003). This parade of dancing troupes is made up of indigenous people from rural areas around Oruro, and is accompanied by live music performers playing local handmade instruments. At the end, a jury assesses their performances and the winners emerge, receiving agricultural goods as prizes. It follows the same route as the Carnival parade, and is performed a week before. It is clearly a performance in dialogue with the Carnival parade, so it is necessary to establish some comparisons.

Interestingly, one of the main points of contrasts between the two parades is the different approaches to religiosity in the public space. Carnival parade dancers mostly save any religious expressions for when they arrive inside the church, perhaps because the dancing itself is often described as a religious pilgrimage. The Anata dancers, on the other hand, perform a number of indigenous rural rituals in honour of Andean natural deities before, during and at the end of the parade (Figure 1.2).

These types of rites are common for important dates on the agricultural calendar, as indigenous groups who survive as rural agriculturalists continue to observe

FIGURE 1.2 Coca offerings during Anata Andina parade

Source: © Ximena Cordova Oviedo

practices linked to the fertility of the land that have survived, albeit changed, from pre-Hispanic times. What is of contrast here, as already discussed at the start of the chapter, is that these rural practices, ritual drinking, communal chewing of coca leaves, burning of sacred items as offerings to Andean deities and animal sacrifice (Figure 1.3) are not usually performed in urban public spaces.

I accompanied the Anata organizers, many of whom were members of the local and politically powerful Oruro Peasant Union (the FSUTCO, Federación Sindical Única de Trabajadores del Campo de Oruro in Spanish), to perform preparatory rites before the parade. We went to a number of Oruro sacred sites, moving at leisure from one location to another, led by a local Andean shaman (*yatiri*) who had us make offerings to request that the natural deities would cooperate with each of our lives and worlds and reflect on our "Andean rituality," as he called it.

The next day, however, during the Anata parade that crossed the urban environment of Oruro, I observed many troupes perform similar rituals. This time, perhaps under the gaze of the cameras and the urban Orureños, some of the rites seemed more resonant, as llama blood and beer trickled into the ground whilst performers danced and played music requesting for well-being and prosperity. This did not fail to shock some in the audience, who were perhaps more accustomed to folkloric displays of indigeneity, and not the "real thing" as such.

During interviews, one of the Anata founders said that the Anata Andina was launched to "show the nation what goes on in the countryside with the Indians." He also described the Anata in terms of a struggle with the Catholic Church.

FIGURE 1.3   Llama sacrifice during Anata Andina

Source: © Ximena Cordova Oviedo

> The Catholic Church didn't want the Anata Andina parade to take place. . . . Because . . . we remembered with force the five hundred years of resistance, the Spanish invasion. . . . There was a powerful confrontation with the Church, [by] the Aymaras and the Quechuas. We advanced with force since 1993, we made our own priests. We researched and we have our own Aymara priests now. That's how we had our first Anata on 1993. Thanks to the impetus of those who lived in exile abroad, we were able to identify our identity and see that we had been confused by the Spanish evangelising invasions.
>
> *(Anata founder, in interview)*

Here, there is a potent anti-mestizaje and anti-Catholic standpoint that directly challenges the official discourse that Carnival in Oruro represents all the peoples of the nation in their coming together as Catholic mestizos. It serves, in my view, to inscribe Carnival practices in Oruro as evidence of indigenous agency to engage as political subjects in the construction of national discourse of Bolivia and Bolivianness.

There is also another dimension at play with the public inclusion of rituality towards Andean deities in the public sphere that challenges the fact that since the arrival of Hernan Cortez in Mexico in 1521 and Francisco Pizarro in Peru in 1535, indigenous peoples' claims to be at one with nature and natural forces have existed outside of what Blaser calls "reasonable politics" (2014). That is, that the presence of natural deities and non-human beings in politics "disavows the separation between 'Nature' and 'Humanity,' on which the political theory our world abides by was historically funded" (De la Cadena 2010: 342).

Yet, I also observed that many of the participants made the Christian sign of the cross when performing some of the rituals in the parade, and others changed into jeans and a T-shirt when the parade was finished. Unlike the museum-like heritage management of indigeneity as pristine and in the past of the Oruro Carnival, Anata participants were free to mix and match religions and fashion styles, and to adopt and adapt from many identities available to Bolivians as a whole.

This, and the public performance of rituals towards nature normally reserved to the sphere of the community, emerge as political statements in the discussion the role of indigenous peoples in official national memory discourses. This was not lost on the elites, and cultural and religious authorities who refer to these rural parades as "people from the countryside" who are not well mannered with the tourists – they get drunk, they urinate everywhere and they act up – they spoil the city for the "real Orureños." The Anata parade day is the only day in the year when the Church of the Mineshaft closes.[8]

Whereas the Carnival parade is celebrated as an amalgam the nation, these rural parades that invade the city are referred to as "autochthonous" – marking the difference in terms of their national value and also the quality of the delivery. I noted that something was perhaps not explicit in this distancing: that the "otherness" of the Anata is not merely inherent by their being so "backward" as to be repulsive (for that can go away when Indians finally surrender to modernity, as the discourse of mestizaje is constantly trying to do). The Anata's subversiveness is also in its summoning of non-humans (Mother Earth, mountains, the dead) into this particular stage, which under the gaze of the world and media starts to bring to life more political and ontological questions. How do you explain the unsettling of the "universality" of the separation between nature and humans in the context of folkloric performance?

In 2008, one of the founders of the Oruro Anata helped change the rules of the game. He said it promoted the identity of first nations in Bolivia, and ultimately, the structural changes of the country which led to an Aymara Indian (Figure 1.4) becoming the nation's president (in interview).

The visibility of Aymaras in Bolivia and the powerful emergence of an Aymara, Evo Morales, as a global political leader confirm new understandings of indigeneity whereby it is no longer assumed to relate to something intrinsically backward, but has to be looked at amidst the moving goalposts of political, cultural, national, territorial and epistemological boundaries (De la Cadena and Starn 2007: 3). The project to "eclipse" or folklorize indigeneity becomes (to an extent) redundant when both the president of the nation and other indigenous promoted to the role of authorities reflect the changing configurations of indigenous identity and are engaged in the restructuring of how political meaning is produced.

In fixing national heritage through institutional management of Bolivian folklore, hegemonic versions of national identity are projected nationally and globally – mestizaje, Catholicism, homogeneity, the "folkloric" Indian – and become validated

FIGURE 1.4   Supporters of Evo Morales, president of Bolivia 2006–19 and first indigenous president in the Americas

Source: © Ximena Cordova Oviedo

in festivals at home and cultural events abroad. In Bolivia, both the Butchers' troupe and the Anata Andina groups contest the notion that national heritage (inherited values, selected traditions and beliefs promoted as the embodiment of the nation) can be homogenously represented by the performative actions and symbols of an increasingly exclusive group. In Mexico, the P'urhépecha have ditched their folkloric indigeneity for an explicit one during the P'urhépecha New Year celebrations, *Kurhikaueri K'uinchekua*, whilst continuing to take part in the tourism economy that they have become dependent on.

More than a nostalgic revisit of the past, these performances offer the possibility of envisioning a future in accordance to a more authentic framework for the generation of political and religious meaning, and to expose an alternative sense of self that is self-consciously indigenous, proud and creative.

Abbreviations

ACFO   Asociación de Conjuntos Folklóricos de Oruro. Body run by authorities of each of the dancing troupes, in charge of coordinating the management of the Oruro Carnival Parade.

CEF   Comité de Etnografía y Folklore

FACLD   Fraternidad Artística y Cultural La Diablada

FSUTCO   Federación Sindical Única de Trabajadores del Campo de Oruro

GTADO   Gran Tradicional y Auténtica Diablada Oruro

MAS   Movimiento Al Socialismo. Bolivian's ruling party under the leadership of Evo Morales.

UNESCO   The United Nations Educational, Scientific and Cultural Organization

Notes

1 According to *The Guardian* newspaper, www.theguardian.com/world/2016/oct/29/day-of-the-dead-parade-james-bond-mexico-city (accessed June 17, 2017)
2 On this topic, see Celestino 1988; McCormack 1991; Estenssoro 1992; Nash 1993 for the Andes. For Mexico, see Nesvig 2006.
3 See the works of Sallnow 1987; Estenssoro 1992; Howard-Malverde 1997a, 1997b; Cánepa 1998; Mendoza 2000; Stobart 2006; Lara Barrientos 2007; Tassi 2012, among others.
4 Villarroel 1908; Zaconeta 1925; Beltrán Heredia 1962; Fortún 1961; Boero Rojo 1993a, 1993b, 1993c; Condarco 1999, 2002, 2003, 2005, 2007; Revollo 1999, 2003; Murillo Vacarreza 1999; Nava 2003, 2004; Cazorla 2003; Véliz 2003; Cazorla and Cazorla 2005; Llanque 2005; Gisbert 2007; among others have discussed this topic in relation to Oruro.
5 This figure is from 2008; the current number of dance troupes in 2017 is 52.
6 The central structure for organization in rural communities are *ayllus* (pre-Hispanic social and political units of community organization). These are led by indigenous authority figures that act in parallel to those provided by the state. See the work of Platt (1982) for a more detailed discussion of the Ayllu.
7 I called this process the "eclipse of the Indian" in honour of Dussel's interpretation of the Conquest and the inauguration of modernity as leading "universal" epistemology as the "Eclipse of the Other" (Dussel 1992).
8 At least this was the case up to 2008, when I did my fieldwork.

References

Abercrombie, Thomas. 2003. 'Mothers and Mistresses of the Urban Bolivian Public Sphere: Postcolonial Predicament and National Imaginary in Oruro's Carnival,' in Andrés Guerrero and Mark Thurner (Eds.), *After Spanish Rule*, pp. 176–222. Durham: Duke University Press.

Albó, Xavier. 1991. 'El retorno del indio,' *Revista Andina*, 9(2): 299–345.

Anderson, Benedict. 1991. *Imagined Communities: Reflections of the Origin and Spread of Nationalism*. London: Verso.

Araoz Sanjines, Gonzalo. 2003. 'Heavenly and Grotesque Imageries (Re)Created in the Carnival of Oruro, Bolivia,' PhD dissertation, St Andrew's University.

Asociación de Conjuntos Folklore Oruro (ACFO). 2000. *Formulario para la candidatura UNESCO*. Oruro, http://docs.google.com/viewer?a=v&q=cache:VrPsa49hZlgJ:www.carnavaldeoruroacfo.com/documentos/FORMULARIO%2520DE%2520CANDIDATURA.pdf+acfo+formulario+para+la+candidatura&hl=en&gl=uk&pid=bl&srcid=ADGEEShZ-FJp3j0DnorJPLefIi2Ma-V0yy4AUiVPlL_dsdOnK_IB-HSt6PwQWJ0WqEMC1jxUq_MGOv6FVT2E8im8NiUEvmY6I7Y8wu7qboaiKrLnnbWKjf91DUJbVGW2MfvDaqPP69w-&sig=AHIEtbTuibp3–2F9iETAQnqpXZ6hkSpXlA (accessed 2 September 2010).

Bakewell, Peter. 2004. *A History of Latin America: c. 1450 to the Present*. Malden and Oxford: Blackwell.

Bakhtin, Mikhail. 1984 [1965]. *Rabelais and His World*. Bloomington: Indiana University Press.

Barragan, Rossana. 2006. 'Más allá de lo mestizo, más allá de lo aymara: organización y representaciones de clase y etnicidad en La Paz,' *América Latina Hoy*, 43: 107–130.

Bauman, Richard. 1986. *Story, Performance, Event*. Cambridge: Cambridge University Press.

Beltrán Heredia, Augusto. 1962. *El Carnaval de Oruro y Proceso Ideológico e Historia de los Grupos Folklóricos*. Oruro: Edición del Comité Departamental de Folklore.

Blaser, Mario. 2014. 'Is Another Cosmopolitics Possible?,' *Cultural Anthropology*, 31(4): 545–570.

Boero Rojo, Hugo. 1993a. 'Panorama del folklore,' in *Bolivia mágica, Tomo II*, pp. 247–257. La Paz: Editorial Vertiente.

Boero Rojo, Hugo. 1993b. 'La fiesta andina,' in *Bolivia mágica, Tomo I*, pp. 175–256. La Paz: Editorial Vertiente.

Boero Rojo, Hugo. 1993c. 'Oruro,' in *Bolivia mágica, Tomo I*, pp. 247–255. La Paz: Editorial Vertiente.

'Bolivian President Evo Morales Takes Part in Inauguration Festivities.' 2006. *Fox News*, 21 January, www.foxnews.com/story/2006/01/21/bolivian-president-evo-morales-takes-part-in-inauguration-festivities.html (accessed 14 May 2017).

Bourdieu, Pierre. 2000. *Capital Cultural, escuela y espacio social (3ra edicion)*. Mexico: Siglo veintiuno editores.

Burke, Peter. 1994 [1978]. *Popular Culture in Early Modern Europe* (2nd edition). Cambridge: Cambridge University Press.

Cánepa Koch, Gisela. 1998. *Máscara: Transformación e identidad en los Andes*. Lima: Fondo Editorial de la Pontificia Universidad Católica del Perú.

Cazorla, Fabrizio and Maurice Cazorla. 2005. 'La Fraternidad en su historia,' in C. Condarco (Ed.), *El Carnaval de Oruro IV (Aproximaciones)*, pp. 105–121. Oruro: Latinas.

Cazorla, Maurice. 2003. 'Presencia histórica de la Virgen del Socavón,' in C. Condarco (Ed.), *El Carnaval de Oruro III (Aproximaciones)*, pp. 72–85. Oruro: Latinas.

Celestino, Olinda. 1988. 'Transformaciones religiosas en los Andes peruanos, 2 Evangelizaciones,' *Gazeta de antropología*, 14, www.ugr.es/~pwlac/G14_05Olinda_Celestino.html (accessed 4 October 2007).

Cohen, Anthony. 2000. 'Introduction: Discriminating Relations: Identity, Boundary and Authenticity,' in A. Cohen (Ed.), *Signifying Identities: Anthropological Perspectives on Boundaries and Contested Values*, pp. 1–13. London: Routledge.

Comité de Etnografía y Folklore. 2007. 'Presentation' at the *Seminario "Puesta en valor de la danza de la Diablada",* 4 December, Casa Municipal de la Cultura, Oruro.

Condarco Santillán, Carlos. 1999. *La serranía sagrada de los Urus.* Oruro: Latinas.

Condarco Santillán, Carlos. 2002. 'La Virgen María y los diablos danzantes,' in C. Condarco (Ed.), *El Carnaval de Oruro I (Aproximaciones)*, pp. 19–32. Oruro: Latinas.

Condarco Santillán, Carlos. 2003. 'La "Pakarina" del "Tío",' in C. Condarco (Ed.), *El Carnaval de Oruro II (Aproximaciones)*, pp. 143–152. Oruro: Latinas.

Condarco Santillán, Carlos. 2005. 'Tres leyendas marianas en el contexto del Carnaval de Oruro,' in C. Condarco (Ed.), *El Carnaval de Oruro IV (Aproximaciones)*, pp. 139–162. Oruro: Latinas.

Condarco Santillán, Carlos. 2007. *"Uru-Uru": Espacio y Tiempo Sagrados.* Oruro: Latinas.

Cordova, Ximena. 2012. 'Carnival in Oruro (Bolivia): The Festive and the "Eclipse" of the Indian in the Transmission of National Memory,' Unpublished Ph.D. dissertation, Newcastle University.

De Certeau, Michel. 1988. *The Practice of Everyday Life.* Berkeley: University of California Press.

De la Cadena, Marisol. 2010. 'Indigenous Cosmopolitics in the Andes: Conceptual Reflections beyond "Politics",' *Cultural Anthropology*, 25(2): 334–370.

De la Cadena, Marisol and Orin Starn. 2007. 'Introduction,' in M. De la Cadena and O. Starn (Eds.), *Indigenous Experience Today*, pp. 1–30. Oxford: Berg.

De la Cadena, Marisol et al. 2017. 'La ontología política no es realista,' Paper presented at the Latin American Studies Association Annual Congress, 30 April, Pontificia Universidad Catolica, Lima.

De Mesa, José and Teresa Gisbert. 2001. 'Libro III: El Virreinato. La Audiencia de Charcas en el Siglo XVII,' in de Mesa et al. (Eds.), *Historia de Bolivia. Cuarta Edición corregida, actualizada y aumentada*, pp. 172–234. La Paz: Editorial Gisbert.

Dussel, Enrique. 1992. *El encubrimiento del Otro: Hacia el orígen del mito de la Modernidad.* La Paz: Plural Editores.

Dussel, Enrique. 2008. 'Philosophy of Liberation, the Postmodern Debate, and Latin American Studies,' in Mabel Moraña et al. (Eds.), *Coloniality at Large: Latin America and the Postcolonial Debate*, pp. 335–349. London: Duke University Press.

Estenssoro, Juan Carlos. 1992. 'Los bailes del los indios y el proyecto colonial,' *Revista Andina*, 10(2): 353–456.

Femenias, Blenda. 2005. *Gender and the Boundaries of Dress in Contemporary Peru.* Austin: University of Texas Press.

Fortún, Julia Elena. 1961. *La danza de los diablos.* La Paz: Ministerio de Educación y Bellas Artes, Oficialía Mayor de Cultura Nacional.

Freyre, Gilberto. 1987 [1933]. *The Masters and the Slaves/Casa-Grande and Senzala.* Berkeley: University of California Press.

Gilbert, Helen. 2006 [1995]. 'Dance, Movement and Resistance Politics,' in Ashcroft et al. (Eds.), *The Post-Colonial Studies Reader*, pp. 302–305. London: Routledge.

Gisbert, Teresa. 2007. *La Fiesta en el Tiempo.* La Paz: Unión Latina.

Goffman, Erving. 1990 [1959]. *The Presentation of Self in Everyday Life.* London: Penguin Books.

Gramsci, Antonio. 1988. 'Ethico-Political-History and Hegemony,' in David Forgacs (Ed.), *An Antonio Gramsci Reader: Selected Writings 1916–1935*, p. 195. New York: Schocken Books.

Guss, David. 2000. *The Festive State: Race, Ethnicity, and Nationalism as Cultural Performance*. Berkeley: University of California Press.

Haraway, Donna. 1991. 'A Cyborg Manifesto: Science, Technology, and Socialist-Feminism in the Late Twentieth Century,' in *Simians, Cyborgs and Women: The Reinvention of Nature*, pp. 149–181. New York: Routledge.

Harris, Olivia. 1995. 'Ethnic Identity and Market Relations: Indians and Mestizos in the Andes,' in Olivia Harris and Brooke Larson (Eds.), *Ethnicity, Markets, and Migration in the Andes: At the Crossroads of History and Anthropology*, pp. 351–390. London: Duke University Press.

Harvey, Penelope. 1997. 'Peruvian Independence Day: Ritual, Memory, and the Erasure of Narrative,' in Rosaleen Howard-Malverde (Ed.), *Creating Context in Andean Cultures*, pp. 21–44. Oxford: Oxford University Press.

Hellier-Tinoco, Ruth. 2011. *Embodying Mexico: Tourism, Nationalism and Performance*. Oxford: Oxford University Press.

Howard-Malverde, Rosaleen. 1997a. 'Introduction,' in Rosaleen Howard-Malverde (Ed.), *Creating Context in Andean Cultures*, pp. 3–20. Oxford: Oxford University Press.

Howard-Malverde, Rosaleen (Ed.). 1997b. *Creating Context in Andean Cultures*. Oxford: Oxford University Press.

Howard, Rosaleen et al. 2002. 'Introduction,' in Rosaleen Howard and Henry Stobart (Eds.), *Knowledge and Learning in the Andes*, pp. 1–16. Liverpool: Liverpool University Press.

Instituto Nacional de Estadística de Bolivia (INE). 2009. '10 de febrero del 2009: Estadísticas e indicadores sociodemográficos del departamento de Oruro,' www.ine.gov.bo/publicaciones/Boletines.aspx?Codigo=08 (accessed 27 January 2010).

Klein, Herbert. 2003. *A Concise History of Bolivia*. Cambridge: Cambridge University Press.

Lara Barrientos, Marcelo. 2007. *Carnaval de Oruro: Visiones oficiales y alternativas*. Oruro: Latinas.

Llanque, Jorge. 2005. 'Ritos, Leyendas y Símbolos de Oruro; la base contextual del Carnaval de Oruro,' in C. Condarco (Ed.), *El Carnaval de Oruro IV (Aproximaciones)*, pp. 163–176. Oruro: Latinas.

MacCannel, Dean. 1984. 'Reconstructed ethnicity, tourism, and cultural identity in third world communities,' *Annals of Tourism Research*, 11(3): 375–391.

MacCannel, Dean. 1992. *Empty Meeting Grounds. The Tourist Papers*. London and New York: Routledge.

MacCormack, Sabine. 1991. *Religion in the Andes: Vision and Imagination in Early Colonial Peru*. Princeton, NJ: Princeton University Press.

Mendoza, Zoila. 2000. *Shaping Society Through Dance: Mestizo Ritual Performance in the Peruvian Andes*. Chicago: University of Chicago Press.

'Mexico City's James Bond-inspired Day of the Dead Parade Gets Mixed Reviews.' 2006. *The Guardian*, 30 October, www.theguardian.com/world/2016/oct/29/day-of-the-dead-parade-james-bond-mexico-city (accessed 17 June 2017).

Morales, Waltraud. 2010. *A Brief History of Bolivia*. New York: Infobase Publishing.

Murillo Vacarreza. 1999. 'Intento para una historia de la Virgen del Socavón de Oruro,' in J. Murillo Vacarreza and A. Revollo Fernández (Eds.), *La Virgen del Socavón y su Carnaval*, pp. 7–38. Oruro: Cedipas.

Nash, June. 1993. *We Eat the Mines and the Mines Eat Us*. New York: Columbia University Press.

Nava, Ascanio. 2003. 'El Carnaval de Oruro y la danza del caporal,' in C. Condarco (Ed.), *El Carnaval de Oruro III (Aproximaciones)*, pp. 35–52. Oruro: Latinas.

Nava, Ascanio. 2004. *Referencias sobre el Carnaval de Oruro*. Oruro: Latinas.

Nesvig, M.A. 2006. *Local religion in colonial Mexico*. Mexico: UNM Press.

Oliart, Patricia. 2002. 'Los desafíos para los procesos de identidad y la cultura de los pueblos indígenas de América Latina: Síntesis de los talleres sobre identidad y cultura en Lima, Antigua y Manaos,' in Carrasco et al. (Eds.), *Doce Experiencias de Desarrollo Indígena en América Latina*, Fondo para el Desarrollo de los Pueblos Indígenas de América Latina y el Caribe. Series Documentos, No. 21.

Oxa, Justo. 2004. 'Vigencia de la Cultura Andina en la Escuela,' in Carmen Maria Pinilla (Ed.), *Arguedas y el Peru de Hoy*, pp. 235–242. Lima: SUR.

Pauwels, Gilberto. 2006. *Oruro 1607: El Informe de Felipe de Godoy*. Oruro: CEPA.

Platt, Tristan. 1982. *Estado boliviano y ayllu andino: tierra y tributo en el Norte de Potosí*. Lima: Instituto de Estudios Peruanos.

Pratt, Mary Louise. 2007. 'Afterword: Indigeneity Today,' in M. De la Cadena and O. Starn (Eds.), *Indigenous Experience Today*, pp. 397–404. Oxford: Berg.

Revollo Fernández, Antonio. 1999. 'Ensayos sobre el Carnaval de Oruro,' in J. Murillo Vacarreza and A. Revollo Fernández (Eds.), *La Vírgen del Socavón y su Carnaval*, pp. 67–125. Oruro: Cedipas.

Revollo Fernández, Antonio. 2003. *Apuntes del "Carnaval Sagrado" de Oruro*. Oruro: Latinas.

Roth-Seneff. 2014. 'Spectacle and Discourse of Decommoditisation in the Construction of Subaltern Public Spheres: the P'urhépecha New Year and P'urhéecherio,' in Helen Gilbert and Charlotte Gleghorn (Eds.), *Recasting Commodity and Spectacle in the Indigenous Americas*, pp. 167–183. London: ILAS.

Rowe, William and Vivian Schelling. 1991. *Memory and Modernity: Popular Culture in Latin America*. London and New York: Verso.

Sallnow, Michael. 1987. *Pilgrims of the Andes: Regional Cults in Cusco*. Washington: Smithsonian Institution Press.

Schechner, Richard. 2002. *Performance Studies: An Introduction*. London: Routledge.

Schieffelin, Edward. 1998. 'Problematizing Performance,' in Felicia Hughes-Freeland (Ed.), *Ritual, Performance, Media*, pp. 194–207. London: Routledge.

Stobart, Henry. 2006. *Music and the Poetics of Production in the Bolivian Andes*. Aldershot: Ashgate.

Tassi, Nico. 2012. '"Dancing the Image": Materiality and Spirituality in Andean Religious "Images,"' *Journal of the Royal Anthropological Institute*, 18: 285–310.

Thurner, Mark. 1997. *From Two Republics to One Divided: Contradictions in Postcolonial Nationmaking in Andean Peru*. Durham and London: Duke University Press.

Vargas Luza, Jorge Enrique. 1998. *La Diablada de Oruro: sus máscaras y caretas*. La Paz: Plural.

Vasconcelos, Jose. 1997 [1925]. *The Cosmic Race: A Bilingual Edition*, Translated by D.T. Jaén. Baltimore: Johns Hopkins University Press.

Véliz Lopez, Vladimir. 2002. 'Anata Andina,' in C. Condarco (Ed.), *El Carnaval de Oruro I (Aproximaciones)*, pp. 67–84. Oruro: Latinas.

Véliz Lopez, Vladimir. 2003. 'La estructura de la danza de la diablada a partir de un mito de origen,' in C. Condarco (Ed.), *El Carnaval de Oruro III (Aproximaciones)*, pp. 98–121. Oruro: Latinas.

Villarroel, Emeterio. 1908. 'Novena de la Virgen del Socavón,' reproduced in J. Murillo Vacarreza and A. Revollo Fernández (Eds.), (1999) *La Vírgen del Socavón y su Carnaval*, pp. 40–48. Oruro: Cedipas.

Wachtel, Nathan. 1984. '7: The Indian and the Spanish Conquest,' in *Cambridge History of Latin America. Vol 1. Colonial Latin America*, pp. 207–248. Cambridge: Cambridge University Press.

Wade, Peter. 2004. 'Images of Latin American Mestizaje and the Politics of Comparison,' *Bulletin of Latin American Research*, 23(1): 355–366.

Zaconeta, José Victor. 1925. 'La Vírgen del Socavón y la Corte Infernal,' in *Odas y Poemas*, pp. 259–276. Oruro: Imprenta La Favorita.

Zárate Hernández, José Eduardo. 1993. 'Procesos políticos en la cuenca lacustre de Pátzcuaro,' in Sergio Zendejas Romero (Ed.), *Estudios Michoacanos IV*, pp. 205–232. Zamora, Michoacán: El Colegio de Michoacán.

Zavaleta Mercado, René. 1987. *El Poder Dual: Problemas de la Teoría del Estado en América Latina*. Cochabamba: Los amigos del libro.

2

PERFORMANCE IN NATIVE NORTH AMERICA

Music and dance

Tara Browner

The creation and performance of music and dance have played an essential part in the lives of North America's indigenous peoples since their settlement of the continent. Although European invasion and settler colonialism was devastating for native peoples in the Americas, their music and dance traditions survived, and now old ceremonies and new songs flourish side by side in cultures where continuity, adaptation and innovation have always been vital elements of life. Contemporary American Indians participate in age-old religious rituals, dance in intertribal celebrations, sing native-language hymns in church and listen to the latest in Indian country, rock and hip-hop music. Indigenous American performance is a broad category, and includes "classical" (art) music by native composers (such as symphonies and ballets), Christian hymns and popular music, as well as professional dance theatres and age-old ritual drama (contemporary native theatre is more connected to oral literature traditions). In this chapter, the primary focus is upon the two most widespread musical performance genres: traditional musics associated with specific tribes, and intertribal musics, which can be performed by native people regardless of their tribal affiliation. In traditional and many contemporary performance contexts, music and dance are not separate elements, but instead interlocking components in a larger performative setting that often includes gesture and utterance intended for tribal compatriots and not outsiders, and as such is not intended for a non-tribal audience.

Although many large-scale generalizations about Native American music and dance are possible, Indian peoples of the past and present have distinctive tribal repertories of songs and dances, enhanced and expanded by occasional sharing with neighbouring tribes. Because their spiritual and religious beliefs grew from the life experiences and needs of those who practiced them, Native American ceremonies reflected (and continue to reflect) a remarkable diversity, mirrored in the accompanying music and dance. Intertribal music (sometimes known as "Pan-Indian" music) such as pow-wow and flute music styles are derived from the sharing of tribal-specific traditions with other groups, and often through the process of one community "purchasing" the right to perform a specific style of music and dance. This practice expanded throughout the 20th century, resulting in the contemporary intertribal pow-wow, a kind of organized music and dance event that can be found within a few hours' drive of any geographic locale in the continental United States.

Part I: tribal specific traditional performance

Culture area theory and traditional styles

Before the arrival of Europeans, the indigenous peoples of the Americas did not think of themselves as a single racial or ethnic group. Native North Americans (north of present day Mexico) spoke more than 200 languages, and had ways of life adapted to their environment, whether it was in the Arctic Circle or the desert Southwest. Even when Europeans began to arrive on the shores of eastern North America, the native tribes and confederacies in many cases simply saw them as a different tribal group – perhaps one that could be traded with or serve as allies – and it was not until the late 1700s that a sense of "Indian" ethnic identity began to develop. Although contemporary native people identify themselves as a larger group in a variety of ways including "Indians," "Natives," "First Nations," "Inuit" and "Aboriginal," traditional music associated with specific tribes has in most ways stayed unchanged for centuries, making it difficult to discuss North America as a single unified musical region, and necessitating the continent be divided into multiple cultural/geographic areas in order to study the music, for example as the Northeast, Southwest, Pacific Northwest and Great Plains. These regions are known as "culture areas," and music from one area is often compared and contrasted with music from another as part of learning to understand how music works in a given context (Figure 2.1).

One reason we know that many forms of traditional Indian music have remained relatively unchanged is that beginning in the 1880s, ethnologists began fanning out across North America, making recordings and documenting musical performance and dance traditions. In fact, the earliest "ethnomusicological" dissertation – Theodore Baker's *Über die Musik der nordamerikanischen Wilden* (*On the Music of the North American Savages*) – was completed for the University of Leipzig in 1881, and the earliest known ethnographic music recording was done on an Edison cylinder machine in 1890 by Jesse Walker Fewkes in the Passamaquoddy of Maine. Probably the most famous of these early musical ethnologists was Frances Densmore (1867–1957), who spent more than 40 years crisscrossing the continent with her wax cylinder recording machine in tow, interviewing and recording elderly singers and storytellers (in one case she recorded an Ojibwe [Chippewa] singer born in 1819). Densmore's recordings are now an invaluable resource for researchers and tribal members alike, and the Federal Cylinder Project at the US Library of Congress is

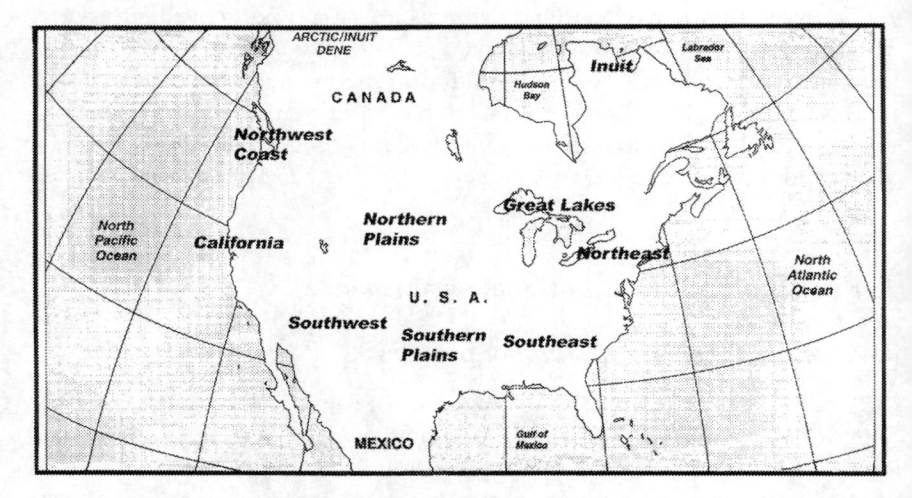

FIGURE 2.1   Geographic locations of culture areas commonly recognized by scholars of native North American music

Source: This image and all photographs in this chapter are by the author.

now repatriating copies to tribal groups. Other important musical ethnologists of this era include Alice Cunningham Fletcher (1838–1923) and her research partner and adopted Omaha son, Francis LaFlesche (1857–1932).

It is essential to understand that in traditional native cultures, there is no over-arching concept of "music." Instead, there are a variety of "song" types, classified by their function in culture and/or their connectedness with other cultural aspects, most notably dance. For example, songs can be categorized as "flute" songs, "war dance" songs, "social dance" songs or "curing" songs, but are *not* known as "music for flute" or "music for social dancing." Vocal song types in native North America include ceremonial/ritual songs (religious, curing, etc.), social and war dances, animal songs, work songs, songs to proclaim social status, lullabies and many other genres. Rarely "composed" in the Western sense, songs in their entirety often come to life through a dream or vision, with the singer serving as a musical conduit and caretaker. Contemporary traditionalists use the term "made" (or occasionally "caught") to describe songs acquired through personal creation, which are then learned and preserved by individuals via oral tradition, or through the recorded mediums such as compact discs or digital media. With the exception of ethno-musicological transcriptions, native music has bypassed the stage of printed nota-tion, moving directly from oral tradition to dissemination by modern recording technology.

Musical and vocal styles are as varied as song types. Most song texts are made up at least in part of *vocables*: disconnected syllables specific to a culture area that are often remnants of archaic languages. Song texts including narratives or even scattered terms in an Indian language are called "word songs," and often refer to historical events in a somewhat cryptic fashion. The origins of dances within Indian communities are similar to the origins of songs: dreams or visions, imitations of animal movements, and the exchange of dance styles and regalia with neighbouring tribes, usually done in a formal ceremony of transmission. Some dances are "owned," and as individual or communal property, should not to be used without their owner's permission. Most dance forms have a specific body of songs that accompany them, and these are traded in conjunction with the dance from group to group through a process known as *diffusion*. As time passes, the new group layers their own footwork and regalia onto the inceptive dance and creates new songs in their own stylistic language. Gradually, tribal distinctions develop between formerly similar types. Through this process, continuity and change occur side by side, with older forms retained while new ones evolve.

Almost all Native American songs have a steady pulse, usually referred to as its "beat," because they are performed in conjunction with group dances. Native songs, even the most basic ones, will have a formal structure (or song form) of some kind, which also fits them into specific categories of songs known to the dancers. Form is a very important attribute of music, because knowing the form allows the dancers to prepare for what is coming, and use dance footwork and gestures that are appropriate to the specific song they are dancing to. Often the form is in a series of phrases, similar to phrases in a sentence, with a stereotyped rhythmic vocal pattern at the end functioning as a cadence, much like the period at the end of a sentence. Finally, the vast majority of American Indian songs are monophonic, meaning that all singers sing the same melody at the same time (women and men usually an octave apart) but some traditions value heterophonic music, resulting in a looser style of singing. A few native song types, especially in the Northwest Coastal areas (Washington State, British Columbia and Alaska) and in the Southeast (Cherokee/Creek) use harmony in parallel intervals, and hocket (interlocking short phrases) occurs in California and the Southeast (only among the Choctaw).

Musical instruments

Due to the diversity of native cultures in North America, it is impossible to present a generic "Indian" worldview. Native North American peoples, however, do hold many shared concepts about music and dance. For example, common to most Indian societies is the belief that musical instruments are living beings brought to life when created, and worthy of care and respect. The most widespread instruments used in both tribal-specific and intertribal music are drums, rattles and flutes, although flutes almost never accompany dances north of Mexico (with the exception of the Central California Maidu/Concow people). However, male dancers do at times blow whistles while performing, for a variety of reasons as will be described later.

Flutes and whistles are the only common melodic instruments, and flutes were traditionally played across North America except in the Pacific Northwest (where whistles predominated) and Inuit areas. In pre-contact cultures, flutes were almost exclusively a solo instrument (played by a single individual), and not played for dance music, except in the mountains of California, where the Maidu people performed a kind of dance to the music of multiple flutes and a large log drum known as a "foot drum." In contrast to flutes, whistles are specifically associated with dancing, and usually played by the dancers while in motion. In the pre-European settlement Southeast, pan-pipes were used, but disappeared before 1700. Only two known stringed instruments exist in North America, one being the stuck musical bow (played lying flat) in California, and the other the Apache fiddle, a one-stringed, bowed fiddle made from a hollow Cholla cactus, and possibly an indigenous variation on the Spanish violin.

Drums vary in size from small hand-held types to large barrel-shaped instruments (common to the Pueblo peoples), and the large multi-player drums known as "big drums." Drums are always played with a single stick, and there are no exceptions to this practice north of Mexico. In many parts of the Great Plains and Woodland regions, "Drum Houses" are built for drums to inhabit, and when played, the instruments are honoured with tobacco, eagle feathers and other gifts, as drums are considered to be living beings (Vennum 1982). Concepts surrounding the nature of drum sounds are complex as well. They can be as simple as a basic beat for dancing, or anchored in the belief that sounds produced by a drum transcend the boundaries of time and the physical universe, mediating between the spiritual realm and our own. In the Great Lakes region, the *Midewiwin* religion of the *Anishnaabeg* "Three Fires" confederacy (made up of the Ojibwe, Ottawa and Potawatomi nations) teaches that the world was made from sound that slowly congealed into a solid object (the physical Earth). One of their ceremonies employs a copper-sheathed shaker played by a woman in conjunction with a gourd shaker played by a man, opening a door into the past and bringing the sound heard in the great void before the Earth was created to the present.

Rattles and clappers of different kinds also play very important music roles, especially in women's musical performance (clappers are used only in California). While cultural outsiders tend to perceive musical expression in native communities as being dominated by men, it is better understood as a kind of gendered sound spectrum, where men dominate on lower pitched instruments, flutes and whistles that are "played," while women's sounds are brighter, higher, more sustained and are *danced* into the web of sound. Women's danced instruments include metallic cones and shells sewn onto dresses (Apache, Pueblo, Great Lakes regions), layers of loose necklaces made of shells that rhythmically clatter as women bob up and down, and in the Southeast, turtle-shell shackles. These are worn strapped to the lower legs by Cherokee and Creek women when dancing the "Stomp Dance" during ceremonials in Oklahoma and Choctaw women during social dances, and provide a strident musical accompaniment to the singing, which is traditionally only done by men (except for the Choctaw, where women sing but do not lead the singing).

Traditional music and dance by culture area

The Inuit people, while resident in North America and Greenland, are not considered to be part of the large native "First Nations" grouping, and their ties to peoples in Siberia are widely recognized. Nevertheless, they have been present in the Americas for thousands of years, and have separated into a number of cultural groups that are categorized under the cultural-linguistic term Eskimo. This includes the Inuit proper, the Yupik, Inupiat, Alutiiq and, more loosely, the seafaring Aleut (Unangan). Inuit culture-area performances are dominated by game songs and drum dances – a style where a large single-headed drum with a handle is played by striking on the rim and whirling, so the instrument serves as a resonator (Conlon 2009). A large variety of game songs are regularly sung, but perhaps the most well-known style is Inuit throat-singing – a hocketed improvisation that involves a kind of rhythmic heavy breathing in and out, with melodic components based on words and animal calls. Although normally done between two women, contemporary artist Tanya Tagaq has developed solo throat-singing as the basis of an original avant-garde vocal concert performances, and composes using throat-singing as a central element of her pieces.

The other primary Arctic/Sub-Arctic cultural group is the Dene (or Northern Athabaskans). They live in interior areas in small family bands and, in pre-contact times, subsisted through hunting, trapping and gathering. Dene society is egalitarian in nature, both in social rankings and gender roles. Their primary instrument is the hand drum, which is unique in that it possesses a number of snares stretched over the hide that create a buzzing sound when struck. The Dene drum is more than an instrument in that it is a visual metaphor representing unity of self, others, and the spiritual world and land. The reasons behind this belief are that drums come from the trees and animal hides the Earth provides. The major Dene dance with drums is known simply as the Drum Dance, and there are also various animal dances performed without drums, including most importantly, the Tea Dance, which is said to attract migrating herds of caribou. Major song repertories are love songs and love of land songs (Lafferty and Keillor 2009).

The culture area known as the Pacific Northwest covers coastal areas from southern Alaska to the northern Oregon coast. Rather than politically organized "nations," these were/are large coastal villages affiliated by language and family ties. Commonalities in lifeways include dependence on the sea and salmon, intensive use of cedar wood for construction and, at the time of early European contact, extremely hierarchical societies with stratified ranks of nobles, commoners and slaves. In a general sense, the northern-most groups are matrilineal (Tlingit, Haida, Tsimshian); the central Canadian coastal groups are mixed matrilineal and patrilineal (Kwakiutl, Bella Coola); and the southernmost groups in the Vancouver and Washington State areas are patrilineal (Salish, Nootka/Makah). Musical performance in this area is characterized by large-group choral singing, sometimes in harmony and sometimes monophonic. Most songs are sung in the lower male vocal range, with limited melodic range and an open, relaxed throat. Songs often begin with slow tempos followed by bursts of fast-tempo singing and loud drumming on either hand-held drums or large log drums (literally split logs) played with club-like sticks.

The Northwest Coast is renowned for masked dances that function as community ritual dramas. The best-known of these is the Kwakiutl (Kwakwaka'wakw) *Hamatsa* coming of age ceremony for young men, where they leave the community as boys and roam the wilderness for one to three months. During that time, the boys go "wild" and are possessed by the spirit of the Cannibal Bird of the North: *Baxwbakwalanuxwsiwe*. After a certain period of time, the wild boys return to village and are "tamed" in the *Hamatsa* Ceremony, which features the bird as a masked dancer squawking and screeching through the use of whistles powered by air bladders under the dancer's arms, and loudly snapping its beak (often four-plus feet long) at onlookers through a hinge system. The boy initiates leave the ceremony as men, and are then reintegrated back into the community. The Makah have a similar ceremony called *Klukwali* using a wolf instead of a cannibal bird.

Another cultural practice common to the Northwest Coast peoples is the *Potlatch*, a large community event that reified the status of chiefs and noble families, who gained status by giving away wealth. In these cultures, wealth is made up of not only material objects, but also intellectual property such as songs, as well as right to perform them (Goodman 1992). Every event during a potlatch highlighted the host's status by demonstrating his wealth or expounding on his inherited privileges. Ownership of such privileges determined status. Potlatches serve as a means to redistribute wealth in the community and a kind of social glue, but historically were completely misunderstood by the Canadian authorities, and potlatching was outlawed in 1884 and did not resume until the 1950s. Potlatch seizures, where the authorities would appear at a potlatch, confiscate the goods to be given away and arrest the participants, were not uncommon, and some natives were sentenced to jail for the crime of giving away their property. Even today, objects confiscated at these seizures – including musical instruments – have not been returned to their rightful owners and instead sit in museum collections.

The state now known as California was in many ways geographically isolated from the rest of the continent, and forms its own unique culture area. Selected tribes of the north include Yurok, Hupa, Tolowa, Maidu, Nisenan and Concow; of the central area Pomo and Yokuts; and of the south, Chumash, Tongva, Cahuilla, Serrano and Kumayaay. Anthropologists estimate that up to 500 distinct small tribes of 500–900 people each lived in California at the time of early European contact, with a population of roughly one million. In the year 1900, approximately 25,000 Indians remained. This population decline started with Spanish missionization beginning in 1769 (which brought with it new forms of music that the friars taught to the native people), and hit its peak from 1848–80, when the California Gold Rush and its aftermath resulted in the wholesale slaughter of Indians, and a type of legalized slavery where children deemed orphans could be enslaved – often by the very men who orphaned them. By 1900, the Indian tribes who survived with musical and dance practices at least somewhat intact tended to be those either

associated with missions (in Southern California), or those who lived in more isolated areas that were less coveted by white settlers.

Native peoples in California traditionally lived in small village settings, and
those in desert and mountain areas often had traditional summer lands and separate
lands for winter residence, with unique food sources in each. The abundant land
provided a good living without the need for agriculture, especially through the
widespread processing of acorns for a staple bread and mush (oak trees are nearly
everywhere). This meant that with the exception of the desert peoples, life was
good, with a great deal of leisure time, leading to the development of complex
music and dance cultures. Native California has a unique and vibrant collection of
musical instruments, ranging from clappers and musical bows to flutes, rattles and
tuned square drums (Gendar and Siva 1988). And unlike the common terraced
(from high to low) melodic contour common to so many native songs, California
songs feature a "rise" in the melody, which is a type of melodic plateau. In the far
northwest corner of the state, songs are sung in an improvised close harmony with
a microtonal interval between a major second and minor third, and also in a hock-
eting style with parts divided between male and female singers.

Song types include animal songs, acorn songs (asking the trees for abundance), a
lively culture of gambling songs and, in the southern areas of the state, bird songs,
which are a celebration of the tribal oral tradition that humans followed birds to
where they live today. The song cycles, which can last all night, feature a half circle
of men singing and keeping time with gourd rattles (women will occasionally sing
along but do not play), and a group of women in the front facing the men who do
a kind of hopping dance, with their hands clasped together and held out in front
of them. The lyrics are metaphorical teachings about life, and the songs themselves
are often polymetric and end with a rhythmic cadence pattern of "ah-ha ha-ha."
This song repertory is widespread in the south, and can be found from Santa Barbara down to the Mexican border (south of San Diego), and east to the Mojave
people of the Colorado River basin. Bird singing (known as "singing bird") nearly
died out, but was kept alive by a small group of elderly singers, of whom the best
known was probably the Cahuilla Elder Alvino Siva, and is today enjoying increasing popularity among Southern California Indians, who see it as a unique symbol
of their culture and survival.

Southwestern culture area peoples live in a harsh, desert environment, crossed
by mountain ranges, mesas and great rivers. In a place of such extremes, a variety
of lifeways can be found, from farming in the many pueblos to sheep ranching on
the Navajo reservation. Historically, the Pueblo people have inhabited the region
for thousands of years (anthropologists refer to ancestral Pueblo peoples as the Ana-
sazi), while the Navajo (*Diné*) and Apache (*Tiné*) arrived from the north only about
a thousand years ago during a time of drastic climatic change. At one time the
Navajo and Apache were a single culture, but post-1690 the Apache ancestors of
the contemporary Navajo gave shelter to Pueblo Indian refugees fleeing from the
Spanish, and the Apache host families learned farming, weaving and other aspects
of culture such as ceremonies from their guests. The resulting cultural shift was

great enough that a new syncretic culture, the Navajo (Diné), gradually developed, although the Navajo and Apache languages are still somewhat mutually intelligible.

Traditional Apache singing employs a wide melodic range and a vocal quality known as *naldehé*, meaning to hold the voice up in the throat (Aplin 2009). Songs are strophic, with an AB form of alternating sections. Section "A" is the chorus, with the text most often made up of vocables sung to a wide-ranging melody, while section "B" contains the verse in Apache words sung to just one or two repeating notes. Navajo singing styles and musical forms are very similar to Apache ones, with two major differences: women do not sing in Navajo ceremonial contexts (but can in Apache) and, in order to have the female deities represented, Navajo men will sing in falsetto (light, high-pitched) voices for the purpose of impersonating women (Frisbie 1989). The gender roles in musical performance are a holdover from Pueblo styles, where women's voices are not heard in public ceremonial contexts. Pueblo songs are dramatically different from those of the Navajo and Apache, and are carefully composed and rehearsed before ceremonies, and then sung in a low natural voice with a limited range and heavy drum-beat. Rehearsing the songs together with the dances allows for a more complex metrical base to be created, and Pueblo songs often have sections of polymeter shifting back and forth between duple and triple groupings. Pueblo women do participate extensively in ceremonial dancing.

One of the most interesting aspects of Navajo musical culture is how song types have broken off from ceremonies and become the basis for separate secular musical events in the social and even competitive realms. One of these song types are the *Yei-bi-chai* chants from the "Nightway" ceremony. The *Yei* are the grandmothers and grandfathers of the Navajo gods, and originally, the chants were sung by masked dancers in ceremonies that occurred only in fall or winter, as part of a healing ritual. Masked Yei dancers perform in teams, and each team is expected to perform 12 times during the ceremony. Although women may dance, they do not sing, and men sing the female deity parts. In recent years, Yei team dancing (and singing) has turned into a competitive event completely separate from the Nightway, and Yei competitions can be found on the reservation in tourist venues in the fall and winter months.

In addition to the tribal groups already mentioned, the Southwest includes the Pima and Papago (Tohono O'odham and Tohono Akimel) and the Yaqui/Yoeme, the latter of whom migrated north from Mexico into Arizona in the early part of the 20th century, fleeing an enslavement campaign by the Diaz government. The Yaqui are famous for their Deer Dance, a ritual performance that portrays the struggle between good (the sacred deer) and evil (either hunters or coyotes). In the performance itself, the musical accompaniment to the deer is almost always indigenous instruments such as the rasp, water drum and reed flute, whereas the hunters (or coyotes) are often accompanied by European instruments (violin and harp). The vocal songs (*maso bwikam*) are densely poetic and metaphorical, and sung by a single individual during the drama, which always begins with the deer living in freedom and beauty, but in the end being slain by the hunters and/or coyotes.

The Great Plains culture area stretches from central Canada down through northern Texas, and into the Rocky Mountain/Great Basin regions. These were the "Horse Cultures" who lived a nomadic existence following the buffalo herds, or in the case of a few groups (Pawnee, Caddo, Mandan) stayed part of the year in earth lodge villages and practised horticulture. In the North, the Lakota, Dakota, Cheyenne, Crow and Blackfeet peoples were large and powerful confederacies, and in the south could be found the Kiowa and Comanche. All of these groups had common musical forms and shared ceremonialism, much of it centred on ritualized warfare and buffalo hunting. From the 1820s through the 1890s, a loose grouping of songs and ritual practices known as the Omaha Dance passed from tribe to tribe and developed into the foundations of contemporary pow-wow song and dance styles, but Plains peoples still preserve their tribe-specific songs and dances as well, which are based upon voice, drum (both large and hand held) and solo flute playing.

The Lakota (also known as the Sioux) have one of the best-documented musical cultures of the Plains tribes, and in their tradition the core repertory of their ceremonial song practices was a gift from the spiritual figure known as the White Buffalo Calf Woman (*Pte Ska Win*). The male vocal style is distinctive, with a tight-throated quality and tendency towards singing in the high part of the range (melodies start high and descend in a contour known as a terraced melody, and then cycle up again in a repetitive pattern). In religious contexts, the singing often has a "crying" quality, as the singer is a supplicant to *Tunkashila*, and in order to get Grandfather Creator's attention must make himself "pitiable." Up through the 1950s, in group performance settings, a heterophonic musical texture was the norm; however, Western styles have increasingly influenced social and war dance performance, and in those genres monophony is common, although heterophony is still found in older ceremonial contexts such as the Sun Dance (*Wiwanke Wacipi*). Women's performance practice is known as *wicaglata*, and they sing an octave higher than the male singers in a piercing voice without vibrato. In some situations, women will sit at the drum and sing alongside the men, in which case they sing the men's part rather than the women's. Dances were at one time fairly free form, with the requirement of keeping feet in sync with a double or triple drum-beat, but with the advent of pow-wow competitions, dance styles and regalia are more systematized.

Southern Plains music and dance shares many features with Northern Plains styles – most specifically musical form – but vocal production is quite different, with the male voice in a lower more natural range (women sing one octave high than men). Both Kiowa and Comanche tribes had their own versions of the Sun Dance, but both groups dropped the ceremony in the late 1870s/early 1880s when they converted in great numbers to Christianity (this was less common in the North) (Bridwell-Briner 2016). The Sun Dance did not completely disappear, however, but was instead incorporated into the revitalized Gourd Dance (*Tiah-Piah*), which was the rebirth of a Kiowa Warrior Society in the late 1950s (the Comanche version of the Gourd Clan is known as the Little Ponies). The "new"

Gourd Dance includes an opening section where the men symbolically emerge from their lodges, arranged around the periphery of the dance circle. Music is provided by a drum group located in the centre of the circle, and male dancers carry rattles made of gourds which they play at specific times during the songs. Songs are in sets of seven, and increase incrementally in tempo and volume, creating an intensification that builds excitement as the dance moves forward. Other extant warrior societies are the Kiowa Black Leggings (for Veterans) and the War Mother's Society, which honours the female family members of veterans. War Mother's includes dances where women dress in the regalia of male family members and parade around in celebration of victories with faux scalps on lances in imitation of the 1800s practice where the real object was used.

The Southeast is part of an interconnected area known as "Eastern Woodlands" that includes the Northeastern and Great Lakes regions. Although the larger territory was crisscrossed by trade routes, music and dance performance styles are quite distinct in each area. Major tribal groups in the Southeast include Choctaw, Chickasaw, Creek, Seminole (all Muskogean) and Cherokee, the latter of whom are more closely related the Iroquois of the North, having moved south about 4,000 years ago and having adopted elements of Southeastern musical performance over the centuries. The Cherokee retained the Iroquoian tradition of masked dances (most notably in the Booger Dance), and added the Muskogean Stomp Dance with its call and response structure, as well as the Green Corn Ceremony (Busk) common to the Southern tribes (Heth 1992).

The primary Muskogean peoples are all descended from the earlier Mississippian cultures of the Southeast – various groups of which survived the depredations of the Hernando DeSoto's incursions (1540–42) and reformed afterwards as large confederacies. Their performance traditions also survived from this earlier time period, and those that are extant today are remnants from a second period of disruption, that of settlers from Western Europe and later the United States. Approximately three-quarters of the indigenous inhabitants of this area were "removed" between 1830–40, and were forced to cede their lands and migrate to Indian Territory (now the state of Oklahoma). Loss of musical culture varied from community to community, with one small Creek remnant tribal town – Pine Arbor – managing to retain the majority of their older ritual performance traditions in isolation (Koons 2016). Most of the Southeastern tribes were only able to retain the Green Corn Ceremony and its requisite stomp dance as a connection with the maintenance of each town's Sacred Fire, which was carefully transported from older territories in the American South to new villages in Oklahoma. In performance, the dance is fairly basic and resembles the coiling of a snake, with women playing turtle shell leg shackles, and men singing in a call and response form. The Choctaw no longer practice Green Corn, and instead the old dances have been recontextualized into small family group dances (Lindsay-Levine 1993) performed at social gatherings. In the Choctaw performance tradition, family groups march out one at a time in a square formation to the playing of a 1700s-era military drum, modelled on one captured from the French in the 1720s. Each family dance group has its own singers (and unusual among Southeastern tribes, this can include women), and presents dances from the surviving corpus of 28. No new songs or dances are being made, and these dance groups are a recontextualization of the older songs and dances from a town-based large ritual format to a small group activity showcasing Choctaw identity to other Choctaws and local tribes (in Oklahoma). Choctaw and Chickasaw music and dance repertories are identical.

In the contemporary Great Lakes region, Algonquian peoples predominate, including the Chippewa/Ojibwe, Ottawa, Potawatomi (together, the Three Fires *Anishnaabeg* Confederacy) and Menominee. This area experienced constant warfare and depopulation during the "Beaver Wars" of the 1600s, and the Anishnaabeg were essentially those who survived and repopulated the area. Historic Anishnaabeg peoples lived in small extended family units known as "bands" during much of the year, and traditionally came together in the fall to harvest wild rice and maple sugar, and for harvest festivals celebrating nature's bounty. They participated in a common religion, the *Midewiwin* (Heartway) lodge, and had mutually intelligible languages. The Menominee are somewhat separate, having lived in Wisconsin for approximately 4,000 years, yet they share the same cultural and religious underpinnings. Large numbers of contemporary Great Lakes Indians are involved in the Midewiwin, which serves as an engine to preserve traditional culture.

The foundation of tribal musical performance in this region is the Midewiwin lodge, and the ceremonial songs brought to life in that context. Songs are "caught" in dreams and visions and shared with others, and at one time rituals were preserved through a kind of picture writing on birch bark scrolls. The instruments used are gourd and copper shakers and water drums, and both men and women participate. Older songs can be distinguished by their five-beat phrase patterns that arose from the Algonquian base five-number system. Outside of the lodge, the "big drum" (a large drum with a greater diameter than depth) predominates, and it is almost always played by men, having been gifted to the community by a mythic figure known as Tailfeather Woman in the 1880s, with the idea that if men played the drum, they would no longer be violent with one another (Vennum 1982). The big drum and much of the music and dance style that goes with it have an origin from the Great Plains that dovetails with the spread of pow-wow styles, and was layered onto Anishnaabeg culture through the Dream Dance ceremony (external to the region) in the 1890s–1940s.

The Northeast, including New York State and the Canadian province of Ontario, are the traditional home to members of the Six Nations of the Iroquois Confederacy, also known as the *Haudenosaunee*. This confederacy, made up of the Onondaga, Seneca, Cayuga, Oneida, Mohawk and Tuscarora nations, was the dominant regional power in New York State and Northern Pennsylvania before the American Revolution. Other groups still in place are the Mi'kmaq, Maliseet, Passamaquoddy, Abenaki and Penobscot, who together make up the Wabinaki Confederacy and are culturally and linguistically Algonquian. The Iroquoian peoples were far more organized, with a clear governmental structure, and dominated the region from 1600 through the end of the American Revolution, when many were driven from New York State into Canada for having sided with the British. Their overarching confederacy organization, established by Hiawatha and The Peacemaker in the 1400s, withstood the diaspora, and is directly reflected in traditional singing and dancing practices.

Because Iroquoian people live in geographically far-flung communities, they have created a means for tribal members to gather twice a year in what are known as "Sings," a series of music contests that rotate around the various reserves and reservations. These Sings feature performances in a musical genre known as *Eskanyeh Ganiseh*, or "Women's Social Dance Songs." Part of the larger Iroquoian musical category called "Earth Songs," Eskanyeh, are only danced by women, but can be sung by both women and men at Sings. Song texts can be old or newly made, and include words in English and/or Seneca, plus vocables. Seneca is the only native language used, because it is considered the most pleasing language to the ear of the various Iroquoian languages. Interestingly enough, Eskanyeh song texts can include bits and pieces of popular songs (especially country music songs), adapted into the Eskanyeh stylistic matrix.

Iroquoian social dance music uses repetitive verse forms, with cadence patterns made up of vocables completing each larger phrase unit. Eskanyeh is usually performed in sets of seven songs, with each song being repeated twice. The singers sit in two rows facing each other, and the lead singer plays a small water drum while the others play cow-horn rattles. Singing Societies are benevolent organizations, and the members donate whatever profits they make from singing to charity. While some groups are all-female, all-male groups predominate, but in either case, single gender is the rule. Singing Societies come together twice as year for competitions called "Sings," where they perform their new songs and old favourites for an appreciative audience of dancers. The dance itself a group freeform style of dancing, where an individual follows a leader but still has a degree of freedom to improvise. The other popular Iroquois contemporary dance style is known as Smoke Dancing, and is performed by both men and women to upbeat, fast-tempo songs sung by a single singer playing a water drum. This style is a more recent development – since the 1950s – and has been introduced to Iroquoian pow-wows as a competitive dance.

Part II: contemporary intertribal performance styles

Song and dance traditions have been shared at multi-tribal meetings since time immemorial. These gatherings tended to occur at important annual ceremonials, from harvest celebrations to healing ceremonies. Especially among nomadic societies – who typically split into small family bands during the winter – seasonal get-togethers were social occasions to visit with family and friends, for possible courtship, for trading and the ubiquitous practice of gambling. These interactions served as the cultural precursors for modern intertribalism, which can mean everything from one-on-one cultural exchange to large celebrations involving hundreds of singers and dancers from many different tribal backgrounds. In this next section, two different styles of intertribal performance will be described: one that involves the creation and spread of a small-form intertribal musical style (flute), and the other the development of a larger multi-faceted music and dance performance (pow-wow).

Flute performance: traditional to contemporary

In pre-contact North America, flutes (Figure 2.2) were associated with a number of different performance practices, including courtship on the Great Plains and curing rituals in the Northeast. Within woodlands areas, crisscrossed by pathways through dense forests, travellers playing the flute as a signal of peaceful intentions when approaching an unfamiliar town was not uncommon. Flute melodies were most often derived from vocal songs, and played on the flute in alternation with the sung version.

Playing the flute in Lakota (Northern Plains) society was a culturally acceptable way for a man to court a woman in an attempt to "make" her fall in love with him. The Lakota way of courtship was complex. A man not only had to win the heart of a woman, he also had to convince her parents that he was capable of supporting her. So before a young man could even consider looking at a woman, he had to showcase his desirability by earning war honours; killing buffalo or other large, dangerous animals; or stealing horses as a gift for his potential wife's parents. When a young man felt he was finally ready for marriage, he would go *winole* (to seek a woman). His first stop was at the home of the local "Elk Dreamer" – a spiritual figure who claimed special "medicine" or powers over women. The Elk Dreamer would give the young man a flute called a *Siyotanka* – a flute with the open end carved and painted like the head of a waterfowl – and a love medicine song, with the power to enchant the selected young lady. These love songs, called *Wioste Olowan*, had both melodic and vocal/textual components. Customary Lakota performance practice was for the man to sit outside of his intended's lodge in the early evening, first playing the song on the flute and then singing the same melody with a text about love. If the song was powerful enough, the young women would fall in love with him. If not, the spurned suitor reconfigured the text into a kind of teasing song, sung from a woman's point of view.

During the post-reservation era from the 1890s though the late 1960s, flute performance traditions (including the art of making flutes) nearly died out, and were kept alive by only a few elders such as Richard Fool Bull (Lakota) and Belo Cozad (Kiowa). Beginning in the early 1970s, Comanche flute player Doc Tate Nevaquaya single-handedly revived the native flute-playing tradition, creating new songs inspired by programmatic influences such as the weather and beauty of the seasons, the Oklahoma landscape and personal relationships with others. Since that time, Native American flutes have gained popularity with both Indian and non-Indian musicians. Influential players and teachers today include Kevin Locke (Lakota), the late Edward Wapp (Comanche/Sac and Fox), Arnold Richardson (Tuscarora), R. Carlos Nakai (Navajo/Ute) and Mary Youngblood (Lakota).

FIGURE 2.2 Undecorated flute in the style common to the Eastern Woodlands and Great Plains regions

Pow-wows: traditional and contemporary

The contemporary intertribal pow-wow has become a major force for music and dance innovation among today's Indian populations, especially those with far-flung tribal memberships. Pow-wows provide a gathering place for Indian people to celebrate their culture through music and dance, and fertile ground for change, as members of diverse tribal groups interact and share music, dance styles and dance regalia. Consequently, a new Pan-Indian culture, with regional music and dance layered upon a Plains Indian framework, is shaping an overarching "Indian" identity for native and non-native alike (Browner 2002). Pow-wows can be grouped into two broad divisions of "competition" and "traditional" events, with competition pow-wows offering prize money in various categories.

Historically, gatherings similar to pow-wows existed in many native communities long before the advent of European settlement. For example, the Lakota *wacipi* (dance) was a time when scattered bands of tribal members converged in one location for religious ceremonies, homecoming celebrations honouring successful war parties, celebrations of new or reaffirmed alliances, and events sponsored by various warrior societies or extended family groups. These dances were often the only time that young people from different bands could meet, and young men took great care to look their finest for the female spectators. One major difference between old-time events and modern pow-wows is that the latter are intertribal and inclusive, meaning that they are open to all who wish to attend, whereas pre-contact events only allowed tribal members and those from friendly neighbouring tribes on the dance grounds.

Within the larger pow-wow circuit there are two basic types of events: "Northern" and "Southern." The Northern style, originating from the northern Great Plains and the Great Lakes regions, now takes place throughout the northern tier of American states and Canada. Tribal styles of music and dance that are considered Northern include the Lakota, Dakota, Blackfeet and Ojibwe. Southern-style pow-wows have their genesis in the Central and Western areas of Oklahoma and the cultures of the Southern Plains tribes, including the Kiowa, Comanche, Pawnee and Ponca peoples. For the most part, the dividing line between Southern and Northern events is geographic and, in many ways, Northern and Southern pow-wow formats are similar, differing only in the Southern dance categories of Men's Southern Straight and Women's Southern Cloth, and the Northern styles of Men's and Women's Traditional dance. Other categories, such as Women's Jingle Dress and Men's Grass dances, began in specific tribal communities but have spread throughout the pow-wow circuit, and are no longer associated with particular geographic areas. Additional common dance categories are Men's and Women's Fancy Dances (Figure 2.3), with origins in the Wild West shows that toured from the late 1800s through the start of World War I. The Fancy Dance was an entertainment style encouraged by "Buffalo Bill" Cody, who told dancers to "fancy up" their routines.

The musical ancestors to today's pow-wow repertory are the songs – and especially the song-forms – of the Omaha and Ponca Nation's *Heluska* War Dances. The Omaha inhabit a mid-Plains region in Iowa and Nebraska (at one time, the Oklahoma Ponca also lived farther to the north when the two tribes were a single entity), and their musical style and dance regalia greatly influenced surrounding peoples. Generally speaking, pow-wow singing, as with events, is categorized by its practitioners as being one of two styles: Northern or Southern (Figure 2.4). The Northern style area included drum groups from the Central and Northern Plains,

FIGURE 2.3 Women's fancy dancer

Canada and the Great Lakes regions, while Southern singing is synonymous with Oklahoma. Singers typically learn their songs from other tribal members, or occasionally, in the case of urban drums, pow-wow musicians currently refer to songs with indigenous language texts as "traditional" or "word" songs, and vocable-only songs as "straight" songs.

The established formal structure of pow-wow music has remained unchanged for almost half a century. This form, most often termed "incomplete repetition" by scholars, has distinct Northern and Southern variations. In Oklahoma, when the

FIGURE 2.4 Porcupine singers

Omaha *Heluska* Warrior Society was taken up by the Comanche and Kiowa, they referred to its music and dances as "O-ho-ma," most likely a mispronunciation of Omaha. Although the Warrior Society was spread from tribe to tribe by the Kiowa and Comanche in the post-reservation era, the geographic distance between tribal groups in Oklahoma (the state with the largest native population) was much less than in the North, allowing fewer deviations from the original *Heluska* style. Also, the Oklahoma Ponca share the same language and music with their Northern cousins the Omaha, and have been influential in maintaining *Heluska* songs in the South.

Pow-wow songs are in a *repetitive strophic* (verse) form, which serve as flexible yet codified framework for new song creation. Plains pow-wow music uses an AA'_ BC_ BC_ form, with each phrase grouping ending with a formulaic cadential pattern of genre-specific vocables. This "Omaha" form (named after its originators) traditionally repeats four times, with three drum accents called "hard beats" between the two BC phrase groupings in the Southern Plains style, and four to five "honour beats" within the interior of a BC phrase grouping in the Northern. In general, Southern singing has a slower tempo (with the exception of Fancy Dance songs), more flowing vocal lines and softer dynamic levels, while Northern musicians tend towards a faster tempo and more active rhythmic structures. Northern songs also sound louder to the listener, but this is probably because the higher notes in the melodies and tighter vocal production style of the singers combine for greater sound projection.

Songs come in a variety of categories defined by whether or not the song has a steady two-beat or three-beat underlying pattern, and its function within the larger dance event. Songs organized in steady two-beat patterns are derived from the old *Heluska* war songs, and are used for general intertribal dancing and competition. Three-beat pattern songs – with the actual drum beats on one and three – are social dance songs for "round-dance" or "two-step" categories. Songs with a series of single accented drum beats are for "Crow-Hop" (Northern) or "Horse-Stealing" (Southern) dances.

Pow-wow dance styles in urban areas and outside of the Plains regions tend towards the generic, with personal interpretations of the various dance style/regalia categories (Traditional, Fancy, Grass and Jingle). The term "recontextualization" best describes how in pow-wow settings, older pre-contact forms of music and dance such as war dances can survive and flourish in the same cultural venues as contemporary "fancy" styles. And, in recent years, Southern pow-wows have become hosts to sessions of Kiowa Gourd Dancing, with a strong conservative influence on musical tradition. Although the process of recontextualization may seem threatening to those outside of the pow-wow community, native people know that their elders will ensure that older forms of songs and dances are preserved for the younger generations within the pow-wow setting, invigorating the pow-wow arena with infusions of older tribal traditions.

References

Aplin, T. Christopher. 2009. ' "This Is Our Dance": The Fire Dance of the Fort Sill Chiricauhua Warm Springs Apache,' in Tara Browner (Ed.), *Music of the First Nations: Tradition and Innovation in Native North America*, pp. 92–112. Urbana: University of Illinois Press.

Bridwell-Briner, Kathryn Eileen. 2016. 'Nmn Hubiyan: Comanche Hymns as Art, Identity, and Resistance,' Unpublished M.A. thesis, Florida Atlantic University.

Browner, Tara. 2002. *Heartbeat of the People: Music and Dance of the Northern Pow-wow*. Urbana: University of Illinois Press.

Conlon, Paula. 2009. 'Inglulik Inuit Drum-Dance Songs,' in Tara Browner (Ed.), *Music of the First Nations: Tradition and Innovation in Native North America*, pp. 7–20. Urbana: University of Illinois Press.

Frisbie, Charlotte J. 1989. 'Gender and Navajo Music: Unanswered Questions,' in Richard Keeling (Ed.), *Women in North American Indian Music: Six Essays*, pp. 23–38. Urbana: Society for Ethnomusicology.

Gendar, Jaime and Ernie Siva. 1988. 'Special Report on Musical Instruments,' *News From Native California*, 2(4): 25–36.

Goodman, Linda. 1992. 'Aspects of Spiritual and Political Power in Chief's Songs of the Makah Indians,' *The World of Music*, 34(4): 23–42.

Heth, Charlotte (Ed.). 1992. *Native American Dance: Ceremonies and Social Traditions*. Washington, DC: Smithsonian Institution Press.

Koons, Ryan. 2016. 'Dancing Breath: Ceremonial Performance Practice, Environment, and Personhood in a Muskogee Creek Community,' Unpublished Ph.D. dissertation, University of California, Los Angeles.

Lafferty, Lucy and Elaine Keillor. 2009. 'Musical Expression on the Dene: Dogrib Love and Land Songs,' in Tara Browner (Ed.), *Music of the First Nations: Tradition and Innovation in Native North America*, pp. 21–33. Urbana: University of Illinois Press.

Lindsay-Levine, Victoria. 1993. 'Musical Revitalization Among the Choctaw,' *American Music*, 11(4): 391–411.

Vennum, Jr., Thomas. 1982. *The Ojibwa Dance Drum: Its History and Construction*. Washington, DC: Smithsonian Folklife Studies, No. 2.

3

INDIGENOUS PERFORMING ARTS IN SOUTHEAST ASIA

Kathy Foley

One must recognize that Southeast Asia, with its 655 million people, includes a plethora of ethno-linguistic groups continually forged into new configurations over millenniums. What is more, former colonies with independence after World War II inherited borders defined by colonial footprints rather than earlier ethno-linguistic formations, creating disparate minority-majority relations in places that had previously not thought of themselves as a united nation. This creates a situation where people use the term "indigenous" to cover an array of behaviours in performing arts: from the arts of literal "First Peoples" (sometimes darker skinned and both linguistically and ethnically diverse from majority groups); to groups living in more remote areas whose bloodlines may or may not relate to majority group, but whose culture/religion contrasts (for example, "hill tribe" Tai verses "Central Thai"); to regional cultural-religious groups, who find themselves juxtaposed against the national majority group (Balinese, Sundanese or Batak as opposed the amalgamated national majority of Javanese and/or modern urban Indonesians). We also see efforts by modern urbanites assimilated as national subjects, but seeking revivals of indigenous local cultures/values to resist global forces of consumerism, environmental degradation and/or religious fundamentalisms.

This chapter will first introduce "Patterns of performance" found across the region. Next, it will talk about groups by region that resist assimilation into regional, national or global domains, distinguishing three major variations: literal "First Peoples" who are often negrito/mixed blood groups who inhabited the region prior to the migrations of Austronesian, Tai and other ethno-linguistic groups, and who have continued to avoid full assimilation; secondly, in "Peripheries," I will discuss sample groups who may be ethnically related to the majority peoples, but due to their adherence to older and divergent beliefs, usually related to animism, may be considered as non-normative; and finally, in "Revivals," I will discuss sample groups who use the term indigenous to recuperate culture and resist influences coming from the West, Middle East and the majorities of their nation-state.

The first two groups tend to live outside major cities and are politically disadvantaged *vis-a-vis* the centre. They live deeper in the forest (for example, Semai of Malaysia or Dani of West Papua), higher on the mountains (for example, Hmong and the Lahu of mainland Southeast Asia, Baduy of Java and Igorot of Luzon, Philippines) or they reside on "outer islands" (Iban of Borneo/Kalimantan). The revival group is often spearheaded by assimilated urbanites who may or may not share ethnicity as they collaborate with indigenous groups to seek roots that may focus on spirituality, environmentalism or an intangible culture heritage marker of local identity. For example, the revitalization of rice harvest rituals by a village in West Java by Sundanese revivalists is in part a rejection of Westernization, fundamentalist Islam and Indonesia's Java-centric politics (Baier 2017: 66). For the last group, the indigenous imaginary is filtered through contemporary needs and can range from documenting ancestral arts to mounting intangible cultural heritage campaigns to creating modernizations reminiscent of the "invented tradition" paradigm of Hobsbawm and Rangers (1983).

Patterns of performance

Southeast Asia is not a unitary linguistic/culture area, so generalizations will always have exceptions. Nonetheless, patterns emerge and they will be here discussed in two categories: images and functions.

Images

Images that are important in indigenous thinking of the area include "representations of the whole" (in which I will discuss the importance of the tree image and the clown/shaman/narrator) and animal icons (where tiger, bird, snake/dragon and water buffalo rise to the fore). Such conceptualizations, very evident in Indo-Malay groups, may come from early and widespread ways of thinking about humans in relation to nature.

Often, it is thought in local cosmologies that an underlying unity of the cosmos gives rise to dualism (male/female; left/right; living person/dead ancestor; sky/sea; rice fields/forest, etc.). Dualism may in turn yield ideas of the four directions and centre ("five directions" equalling, again, a whole); or, in places like Bali, this may further morph into the nine directions (four directions, their quadrants and centre). These thoughts on wholeness lead towards images that correlate the universe to physical entities that metonymically stand for everything. Especially for the islands of Southeast Asia, the unitary image might be the great tree/banyan or looming mountain/volcano, whose human metamorphosis is often a solo exemplary performer who often combines spirit/multi-character manifestations, shamanic healing, storytelling and clowning.

The tree/mountain image is perhaps most graphically displayed in the Indonesian *kayon* (tree)/*gunungan* (mountain) and corresponding Malay *pohon beringan* (banyan tree) puppet that is the beginning, ending and serves many other functions in *wayang*, the shadow, rod or scroll puppet genres, but may also appears in human dramas of the Indonesian and Malaysian area. While this figure is impacted by Hindu-Buddhist thinking, it appears indigenous, as it rises in groups that have not experienced deep Indic influences (among the Ngaju of Kalimantan where it may be associated with head-hunting/status ceremonies, or the skull tree of ship cloths of Lombok, where a tree [with heads] is mounted on a boat which represents journeying between this and the ancestral world). As an image, the tree appears in theatre and a central pole/tree/stone structure around which dance/performance may happen. Perhaps it comes from the fact that many villages are established on slopes of mountains and that trees are natural sites of shade and protection where performances and ceremonies take place. The mountain/tree can be thought of as a kind of theatrical axis mundi that connects different levels of the cosmos. We find widespread versions of the tree/mountain figure in puppetry, and it may be linked to an older history of performers using masks, puppets and character types to heal and promote fertility and good luck. Perhaps an older pattern of the performer as a shaman/healer who links life and death is behind this performance image.

Other related performance objects or performers may have some of the same aura of a whole – for example, the significance of the largest and slowest moving gong in a gong chime ensemble or drum in a drum ensemble (other parts can be thought of as splitting off and out from the central time keeper). Early lithophones (rock instruments) have been found, though we do not exactly understand how they were played. In contemporary music, the most seldom sounded and deepest toned sounder – whether bamboo resonator, drum or gong – may be thought of as the central tone/note and is often associated with the "ancestor." Wood rice-pounding blocks were also widely used, with the pounding stick creating the deep musical sound; perhaps this sound models the gong, which is linked to ancestral presence/spirit/dead. The rice goddess/ancestor Dewi Sri in Malay and Indonesian areas is often thought of as the female who dies to give us life. In island areas, the bones of the dead were sometimes kept by or inside the large gongs. Headhunting, which was rather widespread in some outer islands prior to colonization, was often linked to dancing while playing gongs and, even today, symbols of the skull (often now represented by a coconut) remain linked to the use of gongs and dancing among the Iban of Borneo/Kalimantan or Igorot of the Philippines.

The clown in many traditional theatres is likewise a figure of this wholeness and, in puppet and mask theatre especially, we get the story that the clown is a high god of the universe (Pak Dogel in Malay *wayang*, Semar in Javanese *wayang*, Teu in Vietnamese water puppetry). The clown may have shaman-like powers (for example, clown figures like Pa Jantuk in Sundanese *topeng banyet*, a courtesan dance of the Jakarta area) and performances could bring rain. The character of Java's chief clown Semar, for example, is half male and half female, and his mythos says that he was the first principle that came out of the cosmic egg initiating the beginning of our world. His face is white to represent day and his body black to represent night. He is said to have a huge belly because he swallowed the cosmic mountain. The emergence of transgender groups as associated with spiritual powers, as with the now vanishing *bissu* of Sulewesi (Lamb 2015), or the spirit mediums of Burma who are often female, but also transgender men, may have some relation to this sexually ambiguous clown who combines spiritual potency, fertility and curing functions. While she/he is at the bottom of the social scale, she/he is also the top. The black-bodied clown is seen on Java as the *danyang* (guardian spirit) and first inhabitant of the island, and this figure could embody the dim cultural memory of negrito "First Peoples" who preceded the Austronesians as inhabitants. In any case, the combination of shamanic healing and comic entertainment by a single person who uses voices/characters as a storyteller or curer may be the reason for preferring healer-entertainers who embody multiple persona in this region. The solo puppeteer/mask dancer/storyteller is ritually important throughout the region and, even in the contemporary world, continues to be respected as with the *dalang* (puppet master) of the Indo-Malay area. The interpenetration of the cosmic and mundane, clowning and epic ancestral narrative is a hallmark of Southeast Asian theatres and may come from cultural roots that in the early days delivered shamanic ritual, healing and entertainment in one performance package.

Solo performers as ritual or narrative specialists lead towards a system of character types/conventions – demons may have a deep, guttural voice; refined divinities may use a more medium register, and so on. This one performer with many voices may derive from shaman-related trance genres, which are/were done for both healing and community amusement. While with urbanization and modernization trance forms have become less pervasive, we still find traces – healing done via entertaining séances in forms like *main peteri* ("playing the princess") in Kelantan (Malaysia) or the Hmong shaman's healing rites. The need for stylized differentiation of beneficent ancestral and fierce demonic voices may rise from using one performer/shaman who had to make clear what spirit was manifesting in a ritual.

While the performer was often a solo healer, there is a tendency for such forms to have a second artist who is often playing an instrument and commenting or questioning the trance performer. His (since this is most often a male, while the trancer can be female) music helps bring on the trance, he controls the flow of the performance and returns the entranced performer to consciousness, as needed. This relation of dancer/medium/character and musician (often a percussionist)/commentator/controller is found in a variety of performance forms.

Animals have importance, but not all animals are equal. The monkey, tiger, dragon-snake, bird, water buffalo and sometimes horse have become significant performance tropes in different genres across Southeast Asia. The best-known monkey in performing arts is Hanuman, the monkey general from the Indian *Ramayana*, who appears in classical genres of the region – but his popularity may derive from older precedents. In the Indo-Malay martial arts dance (*penca silat*) we find "monkey" forms that feature leaps and loose wrists and relate to "trance" versions of dance-fighting accompanied by a drum and gong. Among the Sundanese of West Java, the *pantun* (storytelling to a plucked zither [*kecapi*]) tells the *Lutung Kasarung* (Castaway Monkey) story: the son of the high goddess Sunan Ambu who, due to his incestuous dreams about his mother, is banished from heaven and lives in monkey form until the kind-hearted Purbasari (youngest daughter of a king) helps him return to his handsome shape. Freud would approve. The monkey found in many genres is normally a stand-in for a human being who is driven by appetites, but, by making the right choices, can achieve noble potential.

Today, there are very few tigers in Southeast Asia, but this animal continues to loom large in the Southeast Asian mythos. In Sunda (West Java), the song "Kidung" is said to summon tigers and is used in exorcisms during puppet shows. Performers doing the martial arts dance *penca silat* also perform a "tiger" (*macan*) form that is associated with trance. In séances of the Semang in Malaysia, the ritual specialist in trance acts as a tiger, the ancestral spirit. Tigers are dangerous – representing the wild, the forest, the dead, the spirit world – but also protective ancestral symbols of fertility and strength. Historically, ritual fights took place in palaces in Java that pitted the tiger against the water buffalo (the wild/raw vs. the tame/cooked). While the importance of the tiger fades on the outer islands of Southeast Asia, in mainland Southeast Asia, Sumatra and Java this figure still tends to be linked to the ancestors and leads to performance icons (young boys riding on tiger/lion figures carried by martial dancers in circumcisions in West Java, tiger and leonine *barong* [body masks] paraded in Bali, etc.). Dances exist where young people (usually adolescent males) go into a trance and become wild animals – sometimes the tiger/lion, but often a horse, monkey, *naga* or dragon-snake. These performances are exciting and have similarities to mosh pits of the 1980s rock bands and other frenzied dance events in the contemporary West. The tiger is beyond full human control, but with proper attention will contribute to human well-being. Youthful performers rolling on the ground and snarling impressively in a *penca silat* or *kuda kepang* (horse trance dance) allow performers and audiences to let off steam and promote social integration of what can otherwise be overwhelming energy.

The bird is also associated with beneficence – especially the hornbill in Island Southeast Asia (Sumatra, Kalimantan), the bird of paradise (West Papua), peacocks and the Indic Garuda (eagle). In island societies, the bird is often associated with beneficent ancestral aspects, beauty, freedom and the soul flying free. The bird figure has a link to the top of the body and bird feathers appear on dance headdresses of island areas, while Garuda visages appear on the rear of classical Javanese dance headdresses. Birds seem to soar when Iban male dancers wear hornbill feather headdresses doing their *ngajat* ("jumping in place") dance, with their arms gracefully extended and holding a sword and shield as they pivot and, dancing in place, rotate around their centre. They give the illusion of flight as they execute dances historically done in rituals associated with head hunting/war games for Gawai Burong (Bird Festival), but now these dances are displayed at regional festivals or tourist venues.

The dragon/snake (*naga*) or sometimes a lizard is another important entity. The *naga* is associated with the earth and/or sea, fertility, and water or river, yet is a more dangerous or ambivalent figure than the bird. When one reaches the outer islands of the archipelago, the dragon-snake may be a crocodile or another lizard-like creature. The *naga* is generally associated with death, rebirth (as the snake sheds its skin) and rain – the hill tribes of Thailand have festivals/parades to honour the *naga* king who brings rain.

The final animal that recurs is the water buffalo representing strength. In Vietnam, water buffalo were sacrificed in Kho community rituals where people danced to percussion in Lom Dong (until animal rights activism resulted in a ban in 2016). Among the animist Toraja of Sulawesi, water buffalo are ritually killed during funeral rites. Palaces on Java used them in ritual animal combat with tigers.

Other animal figures have significance, of course. Pigs have faded as significant animals in Islamicized regions, but in the animistic highland groups of the mainland, non-Muslim and Melanesian areas (Bali, Biak, West Papua) in Indonesia, or Christian areas of the Philippines, they are important in stories and playlets, and are sacrificed during dance rites/festivals involving group music, dancing and feasting.

Functions

Occasions for performance repeat across the region. Among indigenous groups, music and dance are largely participatory rather than professionalized, with the notable exceptions of the shaman and the storyteller (the latter may be blind and still have some shaman-like connection, as with the story-singer of the Baduy of West Java). Performance is associated with important life-cycle events and functions: courting/marriage ceremonies/rice harvests, coming of age/initiations/martial events, death ceremonies/ancestral remembrances, and healing and divination. There may be linkages between the old traditions of shamans using stringed instruments making contact with ancestors/spirits and the storyteller forms with tales of ancestral times, where narrators accompany themselves on a plucked or bowed string instrument, as with the multi-stringed *kecapi* (zither) of the Baduy in West Java and the *kucapi* of Kalimantan.

Courting song-dance is widespread. On mainland Southeast Asia and the Indonesian archipelago, especially where rice cultivation is important, there are many song-poetry forms that involve either a representative couple or two groups of singers (male vs. female) taking turns by gender in semi-improvised sung debates that often include sexual innuendo and comic banter. These forms are sung with lyrics that are sometimes improvised by the talented soloists with choruses by gender group. Traditionally, these forms might be done during rice cultivation (planting, harvesting, pounding). They might also include simple, improvised group (or solo) dances with males doing more energetic moves with martial stances and stamping, and woman often dancing in a group circle (with contained steps and circling wrists). Today, couples dances with traditional-style movements are seen frequently. Forms like Khmer *ayay*, Lao *pa-nyah*, the Hmong *kwv txhiaj* chanting songs, *pantun* of the Indo-Malay world and *quan ho* in Vietnam are examples of these playful performances. These song-debates are sometimes around the traditional practice of gatherings at the village rice-pounding block, where the large wooden pounding poles (often used by women) created the interlocking beats. Improvised sung poetry, which sometimes alternates with a set chorus sung by the larger group, is normal. Such forms may be the basis of more professionalized genres like the Indo-Malay *ronggeng*, which features courtesan-singer dancers (females or transvestite/transgender males). A number of regional dance-music and theatre forms derive therefrom. Communal solidarity as well as individual romantic love matches may develop in such game-like performances. Woman may do rice-pounding percussion (though the pounding block is now gone) as they sing and dance. Males sing, clown and play more complex musical instruments (drums, gongs, xylophones and plucked or bowed instruments, as these additional instruments take over from the pounding block). Lullabies are another genre that may use the same poetic structures as game-singing.

Male coming-of-age ceremonies/initiations/martial or war celebrations involved performing arts. Dances, songs and stories were involved with these initiation rituals as youths (mostly males) prepared themselves under elders' directions. Such dance and music was usually participational, including both those undergoing the rites (usually male adolescents) as well as many others in the community. In times past in outer islands of Southeast Asia, ritual warfare (head-hunting) was sometimes practiced until the early 20th century. Today, celebrations that remember such practices symbolically continue. In parts of Indonesia, Borneo and the Philippines, headhunting was often associated with post-harvest ancestral rites. Referring to contemporary Sulawesi, Kenneth George notes that today, remnants of such practices have been given a clear narrative structure and a symbolic coconut replaces the "head": lively improvisational banter of male and female groups (related to courting songs previously discussed) has been developed into written texts in upland Sulawesi and has become part of heritage festivals (George 1996).

Funerals and commemorations of the dead were linked to music almost everywhere (be it stylized wailing, soft flutes or cacophonous songs of grief). Ceremonies to commemorate the dead might be held annually and include the whole village (as with the Mah Meri Aboriginal people of Malaysia or the Kamoro of West Papua) or, alternatively, be events that honour a specific person. In many areas, the rites traditionally promoted movement of the spirit of the deceased from a potentially haunting ghost to a beneficent ancestor.

Almost all groups have some kind of storytelling tradition, and a number call for musical accompaniment. This may be a stringed instrument as with the Vietnamese *xam xoan*, the Sundanese zither (*kecapi*) or the northern Malay brass bowl used by the *penglipur lara* (storyteller). Stories are normally local mythologies and legends, and some may have a healing function or strengthen connections to powerful ancestors, as with the *tukang pantun* story singers of the Baduy in West Java who begin each story with a mantra, which is felt to have beneficent impacts. In some ethnic groups these story specialists were blind males who had developed special expertise in knowing the tales, lore, poetic meters, appropriate improvisational modes and musical accompaniment through oral-aural study with the teacher. More recently,

YouTube has become the teacher, and intangible cultural heritage concerns and local nostalgia – rather than ritual blessings – have become the reasons for reviving languishing arts.

Healing was another time for song and role-playing. When an individual is/was ill or some kind of collective need emerges/d, a specialist is/was often required. In many areas, this shaman-like figure was a societal specialization. Sometimes they came from being born into a family of ritual specialists, but in other instances this work was due to personal interest or a "calling." Some specialists may experience a classic shamanic process (Eliade 1972) – sickness, apprenticeship with a specialist to heal him-/herself and then practising alone. Males, in a number of traditions, were seen as superior to women as healers. But women, especially older women, could take the role too. Music, song, dancing and taking on the roles of various spirits (both comic and fierce ones) while in trance/diagnostics might occur until a bargain was struck with the spirit world to alleviate the problem.

In the contemporary period, a literal belief in healing through performance has weakened as formal schooling, modern media and urban life prevail. Elders die without a student to inherit their expertise. However, younger members of the groups have sometimes chosen to rework traditional genres in new ways as part of group identity, tourist endeavours, politico-social efforts or intangible cultural heritage projects.

First Peoples

The terminology of "First Peoples" is new to Southeast Asia, but could be applied to the darker-skinned people of the mainland and islands of Southeast Asia, as well as the Melanesians of Biak and West Papua. These performance traditions have, in general, only been modestly studied.

The very small population of negritos in the mainland areas had a culture that was traditionally spatially removed from the major population group. However, they have become more permanently settled in the last century, and today, cities and resource extraction encroach on their sites. Sometimes such groups, at present, are engaged in performing acts with traditional blowpipes and neo-traditional costumes made of leaves and other natural materials in tourist enclaves, as with the formerly nomadic Maniq in Phuket in the south of Thailand. Another group includes people formerly termed Sakai ("Slave") in the Indo-Malay world – the group is now differentiated into Semang (a negrito group) and the lighter-skinned Senoi, which includes (among others) the Temiar of Malaysia, who speak a Mon-Khmer language. The Temiar have been rather extensively documented given their "dream songs," which attracted the attention of western psychology in the 20th century. Small groups of negritos are also found in Sumatra and Riau. In the Philippines 15,000 negritos from different ethno-linguistic heritages are scattered over a number of islands; the Aeta (Agta) are one example of these Filipino groups. Though the Melanesians are often discussed in terms of Pacific Island performance (see, for example, Chenoweth et al. [1998]), their incorporation and interactions over centuries with Southeast Asian majorities must be recognized, and examples from Biak and West Papua are noted later.

Instruments used by such indigenous groups may vary, but are usually easily made of forest materials. For example, for the Temiar, bamboo stamping tubes, a tube zither, jaw harp and the nose flute are found, with gongs added. Dances were a communal activity with costumes of leaves, feathers and other natural materials.

Temiar use dream inspirations in song composition. Temiar mediums are, Roseman (1991, 1998) notes, singers of the landscape – translating the rainforest into performance materials, as local spirits inspire shaman/healers to compose songs which are connected with dreams and presented in ritual night-long performances in which the main singer (often male) leads and a female chorus responds with bamboo pounding percussion and song. Participants engage in a graceful, swaying trance dance which can climax in intense quivering, leaps and head twirling (patterns also seen in Malay trance dance healing of *main peteri*). Entranced participants then collapse and are revived. Fire swallowing or touching flames is involved. The composer receives the curing songs complete with melody, movement, text, rhythm of the bamboo tubes and costumes from the spirit world. Tiger ancestors, trees, rivers and other natural phenomena are celebrated. The songs keep up with the changing political-social environment – healer Abilim Lum of Bawik, Kelantan, Malaysia did a song taught to him by the nationalist spirit of the state of Kelantan for healing demonstrations organized by Roseman (Benjamin 2014: 333). Another genre of the Temiar includes singing of both males and females in gender-grouped choruses at the end of the mourning ceremony. Nose flutes are played as part of traditional courting.

The Aeta are a negrito group of traditional hunter-gatherers in Luzon (Philippines), and while today many have converted to Christianity, they were traditionally animists. The instruments they used in the 20th century included the gong, bamboo flute, bamboo violin, bamboo two-stringed zither, jaw harp and guitar. Community dance was traditionally done before and after pig hunts. Women also danced before fishing, both as an apology to and a charm for catching fish. Men danced before harvesting honey. These occasions reflected the then hunter-forager life of the group. The spirit séance was an Aeta healing ceremony to drive away evil spirits: the patient would be covered with a red cloth and the shaman (*balyan*), along with the patient's relatives, would threaten the spirits (*aitu*) who were thought to cause disease/psychic disorder, offering them gifts to leave the ill person. After the red cloth was pulled away, the whole community joined in a shuffling walk dance with skipping or shaking (Vilarus and Obusan n.d.). Christianization has led to changes, but events are held for education or tourist groups, and at the annual Aeta Festival in Mabalacat that celebrates indigenous heritage (see "Caragan Festival of Mabalacat City: Aeta Fiesta 2017"). Such fiestas combine traditional dances, demonstrations of bows-and-arrows and blow pipes, beauty pageants, and traditional and neo-traditional/pop-inflected music and dance. Choreographed street parades by large groups of students in synchronized movement patterns with elaborate, matching costumes are performed in displays that are part Aeta revival and part

Western colour guard. Traditional elements – crouching monkey hops by male dancers and swaying movements by female groups with up-swinging arms – are included. Loud percussion is featured in the ensemble music that mixes traditional and Western instruments. Aeta and non-Aeta performers participate, with most sporting blackface (see 'Caragan 2015 – Tribung Camachiles'). Such festivals – including the non-indigenous public imitating Aboriginal peoples and remembering moments of their confluence with Austronesian settlers – combine themes of indigeneity, settler culture and Christianization, and are celebrated with non-stop dancing, as with the Ati-Atihan Festival of Kalibo, Aklan, Panay Island (Peterson 2016: 129–51).

Elaborate feasts with dance and music, sometimes involving trance behaviours, were part of traditional culture in the Melanesian areas of Indonesia, including Biak and West Papua (see Chenoweth et al. 1998: 597–600). Important activities included male initiations where secret songs were shared, sometimes accompanied by paired flutes. Lyrics obscured full understanding – spirits understand what eludes human comprehension. Celebrations after or in preparation for warfare were common, as were laments for the dead. Healers sometimes sang medicinal songs (as with the Yali). Groups sang and danced to celebrate the erection of a new men's house (Asmat) or the making of a canoe (Kamoro). Hunting, courting (among the Yali, with alternating male and female choruses) and magic – these were all times for song, dance and ritual. Song/music-composing was often a specialization (and might require spirit inspiration or training). Dance, by contrast, was a community activity – one learned by following. Gongs, drums (especially the hourglass *tifa* drum), bamboo flutes and jaw harps are common instruments. From the early 20th century, many changes in community life occurred as Christian and Islamic missionizations, which disallowed traditional rites, brought conversion and formal schooling became standard. However, there have been various revival movements (see Rutherford 2002: 188–226).

For example, in Biak-Numfor the *wor* was an important dance-music-poetry gathering that celebrated life-cycle events (introduction of a child, nose piercing, initiations into adolescents, dowry and wedding celebrations). In the 20th century, the *wor* was associated with the story of Manarmakeri (Scabby Old Man) who captures the Morning Star and learns the secret of Koreri (Cargo). Angganeta Menufandu (1905–4?) was a gifted *wor* singer-poet who revived this myth of Manarmakeri in a "cargo cult" group, and she gathered a large following from Biak and nearby islands in the years leading up to World War II. She combined the indigenous myth of wealth from across the seas (Manarmakeri and Morning Star) with Christian imagery and a vision of a coming utopia. Followers would be possessed by spirits of snakes or rocks, and Angganeta would exorcise them. However, she was imprisoned and killed by the Japanese during the World War II occupation of the Dutch East Indies.

More recently, *wor* revivals became associated with regional political self-determination. Arnold Ap (1946–84) was from Numfor, educated on Biak and was jailed in 1969 for protesting the union of West Papua with Indonesia. In 1974, he became the curator of the museum at Cendrawasih University in Jayapura, the capital of the then Irian Jaya Province. He collected folk songs and initiated a radio show (*Rainbow of Irian Jaya Culture*), which featured aspects of Papuan song, myth and story. Local music was reworked by his popular music group, Mambesak, which also included artist/folklorist Sam Kapissa (1947–2001). These researcher-artists led a resurgence of *wor* which was ideologically linked with the Free Papua Movement (OPM) of the 1970s. Ap was arrested for supporting Papuan independence from Indonesia and shot while in prison in 1984.

Danilyn Rutherford (2002: 211–16), while doing research in the 1990s, helped yet another revival of *wor* as the Raewena Troupe gained recognition. Kaleb, Yesaya and Agustus Burwa (raised in a family of pro-independence OPM separatists) recorded music and presented the *wor* tradition in Jakarta at a national festival. The group performed for a Smithsonian Folklife recording and sparked another *wor* revival. Soon after, school children were taking up this rather chaotic group dance/singing, but were performing it in a disciplined colour-guard manner in parades and festival events.

Both *wor* and *aker* (fishing dance) have been acknowledged as part of the local intangible cultural heritage of West Papua. Also popular in Biak is *yospan* dance, and its movement is said to be inspired by the fighting of Dutch vs. Indonesian airplanes prior to the vote for incorporation of the area in Indonesia in the 1960s. *Yospan* song-dance uses Western-style ukuleles, guitars and double basses along with traditional drums.

Groups like the Asmat (Pouwer 2010; Smidt 1996) and Kamoro (Pouwer 2010; Jacobs 2003) in West Papua have organized significant revivals in local festivals of music, dance and carving, as old missionary resistances to historical rites of initiation and ritual warfare have been replaced by general support of cultural revivals. Head hunting in these events becomes symbolically represented, and festivalization and touristification of traditional culture becomes part of the annual events sponsored by the tourist department. Masks and sculptural images, formerly used in local ceremonies, have become coveted artefacts for international "tribal arts" markets. Today, locals, collectors and tourists gather to sing, dance and auction artefacts at annual events: heritage and commerce join in modern life.

Peripheries

Other groups (living upland and on outer island) in both mainland and archipelagic Southeast Asia see themselves and their performances as far from centres of power by location and lifestyles (see Miller and Williams 1998: 527–913). Some groups are ethnically different: two of the many mainland examples of ethnically and linguistically diverse peoples are the Hmong (Vietnam, Laos and Thailand) and Lahu (Thailand and Vietnam). Other groups have ethnic roots related to the majority, but retain older practices that contrast with the majorities. The Mah Meri and Temuan of Malaysia are such groups, and they correspond to many archipelagic groups, for example, the Baduy in West Java and "Dayaks" (represented by the Iban, "Sea Dayaks") of Kalimantan/Borneo, who share bloodlines with the national majorities. The Igorots in the highlands of Luzon are another example of an upland group. Hundreds of such groups with distinct local rituals, stories, dances and music exist, but, as global forces (social media/internet, conversion, national culture and standard education) prevail, weakening of tradition grows, even as concepts of intangible cultural heritage, ethno-political solidarity, sustainability and eco-consciousness rise to counterbalance.

Many of these groups practiced swidden (slash and burn) agriculture rather than wet rice cultivation. Other groups, like the Bajau/Orang Laut, lived on boats travelling between Malaysia, Indonesia and the Philippines as itinerants who followed marine resources. Many such groups held longer to older, animist-shamanic religious practices, even if most groups are now settled and participating in national cultures. Only a few regional examples will be given. Hmong and Lahu will represent upland or "hill tribe" examples in the northern mainland. Mah Meri and Temuan (Mainland Malaysia), Baduy (Java), Iban (Borneo/Kalimantan) and Igorot (Luzon) from the upland Philippines will be other examples.

Hmong

Hmong of upland Vietnam, Burma and Thailand are traditionally animists, whose ritual specialist use a gong (played by an assistant), sistrum (iron clacker) and rattle as a shaman sings to cure illnesses during *ua neeb* ("honouring spirits"). Texts tell of a flying horseman who defeats offending spirits and lyrics may even relate to Central Asian shamanic concepts. Ritual texts are chanted for funerals and weddings.

The funeral rites are accompanied by a free reed mouth organ (*qeej*) and drum. The lamenter sings as the spouse mourns; then comes the procession to the gravesite. The circles and spirals of the *qeej* player's dance create complexity as his musical tones emulate the tones of the spoken language. Performances are said to entertain the dead spirit and keep it from wandering until the soul is sent to heaven. Other Hmong musical instruments include the jaw harp, flute, rice-pounding block and (in Vietnam) lutes, oboes, etc.

Secular music includes *kwv txhiaj* – songs which often focus on love. This genre is featured in courtship games during the New Year festival month when unmarried boys and girls traditionally tossed courtship balls back and forth, singing verses to *qeej* music. The poetry relies on repetitions of each verse, where the first iteration is the riddle and the second substitutes words that deliver the message. The tonal nature of language complicates this game/singing: those who can perform accurately and creatively are respected.

Narrated legends were also popular (called *khau xia* in Vietnam). In Thailand, the storyteller-performers may alternate between singing the verses and playing the mouth organ as the tale is delivered. Since the Southeast Asian War, with the diaspora of Hmong, popular music, hip-hop and rap have become intermixed with more traditional styles. Western guitars and electric mouth organs can mesh. Traditional ceremonies are sometimes abandoned for Christian hymns or contemporary pop culture (see discussions by Ruriko Uchida and Amy Catlin in Miller and Williams 1998: 550–59).

Lahu

The Lahu (Burma, Laos, Thailand and Vietnam) practice slash and burn agriculture. Though conversion has caused some groups to embrace Christianity (and learn American Baptist church hymns), shamanism is the traditional practice and it includes music in curing rituals. Traditional instruments include free reed mouth organs (especially the *naw*), the jaw harp, lute, gong and goblet drum.

The New Year is a time of music, fun and group dance, as the spirits return to visit an altar, with male and female figures of paper representing dead souls. The village headman and ritual specialist offer prayers and rice cakes at this altar, the symbolic New Year's tree, and ancestral shines. Male groups dance, stamping their feet in unison, as swaying women form a semi-circle line moving around the men to the tunes of the *naw* mouth organ. Groups of boys and girls sing love songs back and forth all night during New Year celebrations and on other occasions throughout the year. *Naw* (song) and dance traditionally accompanied work, such as planting, harvesting and pounding rice. At weddings, the bride, groom and guests all sing to each other, delivering good advice for happy living. Funerals are also occasions for song. Harvest festivals are elaborate communal song and dance celebrations (see discussion by Miller in Miller and Williams 1998: 538–40).

Malaysia's Mah Meri and Temuan

One Malaysian example of a group ethnically related to the majority, but socio-culturally different, is the Mah Meri (People of Forest) Orang Asli (Indigenous People) of Carey Island, Selangor, Malaysia, whose *tarian jo'oh* (mask dance) or *sewang* (trance ritual) represent spirits of the tiger, iguana and other significant animals. For Hari Moyang ("Ancestors' Day"), for example, the village would gather at a spirit house filled with flowers, incense and food to pay homage. Burnt offerings would alert the spirits, and then the maskers would appear with the dancers in pandanus leaf costumes, moving to music of a bamboo pounder, drum and violin. The Mah Meri mask-carving heritage has now been recognized as intangible culture heritage by UNESCO. Traditional dance showed everyday activities including hunting and fishing. Curing was also a time for traditional singing and dance performance, as the *bomoh* (shaman) helped those suffering from emotional, physical or psychological problems caused by spirits. Such patterns are related, as mentioned previously, to *main peteri* ("playing the princess") in Malay-Kelantanese curing rituals.

Today, traditional practices are reproduced in touristic representations at a Carey Island cultural village, and most of the masks are for sale. Claire Chan (2015) argues the Orang Asli are right to present embellished performances of their ancestral heritage and realize they must alter things for the tourists' gaze, savvy of what attracts. Noted performers and carvers, such as Kemi bin Khamis, find the outside recognition by UNESCO crucial to local heritage preservation. Carvers use image research by earlier anthropologists (Werner 1973) as a guide for their present carving patterns, showing the interpenetration of earlier ethnographic research and current cultural regeneration. A 2017 attempt to displace the Mah Meri group for commercial developments was being strongly resisted and arts were part of the protests (Mayberry 2017).

Another notable Malaysian example of cultural revival among Orang Asli is the work of the Temuan music group Akar Umbi (Tap Root), which is a collaboration between two Malays – Atares and Rafique Rashid – and Mak Minah Anggong, a Temuan ceremonial singer. Mak Minah's chanting is preserved in *Song of the Dragon*, a CD giving honour to the *naga* (snake/dragon spirit of the river). Mak Minah rose to prominence in an Akar Umbi 1994 benefit concert for Bosnia that was broadcast on Malaysian national TV, and the group later appeared during the 2nd Rainforest World Music Festival (1999). This annual festival at the Sarawak Cultural Village in Kuching combines the themes of environmentalism, tourism and world music. Akar Umbi fused sacred *sewang* trance chant music in the Temuan language to bamboo tubes struck on a long block of wood and contemporary pop music (see D'Cruz 2000; Tan 2005). Now performing with Malay-, Chinese- and Indian-Malaysian players on guitars, keyboard and drum set, Akar Umbi has helped launch Malaysian eco-pop. Songs include "River Makao" ("Sungai Makao"), which protested logging and land degradation from resource extraction. Indigeneity, ecology and sustainability intertwine in this Malaysian intra-cultural project.

Baduy

The Baduy are swidden cultivators in Java who have attempted to maintain local traditions and rejected both the 16th-century Islamization and subsequent modernizations. They are Sundanese speakers who attempt to preserve traditional religion (Sunda Wiwitan [Original Sundanese Religion]) and have blocked outsiders' entrance to their isolated villages and ancestral sites since at least the first European documentation of the group in the colonial period (1822). For the ethnic Sundanese of West Java, this group is now seen as the keepers of ethnic heritage. Though entry into core sites (with only an estimated 5,000 "Inner" Baduy inhabitants) is blocked to outsiders, ethnomusicologists like Wim van Zanten (1995) give some insight into their performing arts. *Angklung* (shaken bamboo instruments) are played in rites for Dewi Pohaci, the rice goddess, as part of the harvest festival. People sing *sisinderan* riddle poetry in *pantun* (8-8-8-8) rhymed meters. The *anklung* along with bamboo rice carriers (which sound as the bundles of stalks are carried/danced to the village) make musical sounds for this processional performance. Storytellers (*tukang pantun*) playing a *kecapi* (zither) share stories of gods who become monkeys (*Lutung Kasarung*) and other old stories. These nightlong stories are performed for coming of age ceremonies (circumcision, tooth filing). Other instruments for the most removed group include the rice bounding block, jaw harp, xylophone, flute and a large bowed lute.

Iban

As an example from Borneo/Kalimantan in both Malaysian and Indonesian areas is Iban performance (see Matusky in Miller and Williams 1998: 823–38). Iban traditionally lived in long houses on rivers. Major performance was associated with shamanic curers (*manang*) who use chants (*timang*) delivered with gong and drum music, while storytellers (*lemambang*) shared *ensera* (narratives) of epic heroes. Examples of narratives are stories of Keling and Laja making a hornbill statue while courting, and Keling obtaining the tree of life from overseas. Other instruments include the lute (*sape*), flute and jaw harp (the latter formerly used in courting).

Dance (*ngajat*) was associated with major festivals (*gawai*), which included harvest celebrations, funerals, headhunting events (historically) and marriages or weaving celebrations. Currently, 1 June in Malaysian Borneo is celebrated as a collective *gawai* combining rites that in the past might have been celebrated at different times in a large heritage festival. While animism was the traditional religion, conversion to Christianity and other world religions, along with universal education and national integration, have brought modifications. Headhunting, which was important in song and dance as part of the Gawai Burung (Bird Festival), has, of course, been long abandoned, and this ritual dancing/ceremony that once marked men's upward shift in social status has become symbolically reworked, with coconuts replacing heads. However, old symbols such as the *ranyai* (tree of life) or the hornbill (representing dead/ancestral power controlled by great men) persist. The striking hornbill-feather headdresses of men, who dance holding a sword and shield as they circle on the spot and then leap and advance, impress. Hornbill-feather fans held by the female dancers wave gently as they sway, dressed in beaded sarongs: they curve their wrists and hold graceful plies, and the dance evokes bird imagery. Comic male dances represent monkeys, drunken men and frogs. Martial dances (*kuntau, penca silat*) are other frequent displays.

Today, daily performances at the Sawawak Cultural Centre show such dances, especially during the Rainforest World Music Festival in Malaysia. Similar presentations can be seen in Kalimantan regional festivals in Indonesia. Dance and music of the Iban and other groups are, in these instances, done in stage presentations. Additional tourist enterprises include short programs of dance and music during organized tours to longhouses of Iban (and other groups). Heritage efforts funded by local governments produce new dance dramas: *Raja Langit* (King of the Heavens, December 2016) is a Sarawak production of 35 actor-dancers and 14 musicians to tell the old tale of a god who descends to earth and was intended to perpetuate Iban heritage among contemporary youth (Pilo 2016). School and university performances feature Iban and other indigenous groups' arts as part of cultural night performances and national holidays, and include dancers in traditional garb.

Igorot

Igorot is a general term to refer to a number of tribal groups of the Cordillera range of Luzon (the Philippines), a few of which (Bontoc, Kalinga, Ifuago) are mentioned here (see Maceda in Miller and Williams 1998: 913–28). Their flat gongs (*gangsa*) punctuate performances at rice harvest ceremonies, weddings, martial dances (formerly linked to head-hunting rituals) and funerals. The nose flute, jaw harp and various bamboo instruments (including zithers) are common. During Bontoc courting, girls would sing responsorial songs to draw their suitors out of the darkness. In the men's dwelling, compound choral and solo songs were sung. For weddings, the older men would sing group songs during sacrifices of water buffalo and other animals. Among the Bontoc, groups of men and women at a traditional funeral would honour the dead person's corpse (which was normally tied in a chair) to show respect and lament. Group responsorial choruses came at the end of the verses. Among the Kalinga, gongs might play as an older woman feinted off her male partner who playfully pursued, earning the audience's laughter. At weddings of the Kalinga, the bride's side and groom's party became two choruses that sing advice in turn. Shamanic practitioners (*balyan*, often older women) sang chants for healing and other rituals. Groups of Ifuago women sang epic songs (*huhud*) for harvests and funerals (a form declared as UNESCO Intangible Cultural Heritage in 2008, and currently in revival).

Mountain-area dance and music have represented the Philippines internationally from at least the St. Louis World Fair (1904), which included negrito and Igorot representation. Research on folk music-dance of indigenous groups in the early 20th century by folklorists like Francisca Reyes-Aquino led to the use of hill tribe and Muslim dances by Bayanihan (founded 1958), the national dance company, on its many international tours. Such re-choreographed versions of local dances were, and are, often then taught back to members in these ethnic enclaves by the city choreographers and then performed in school and fiesta venues. Such standard dances have become part of the transnational Filipino diaspora. However, large-scale community participatory dances resist such balleticization and remain an important factor in community life. Groups are part of events like the Baguio City Grand Cordillera Festival each November, where locals share, reinvent and celebrate with music and dance. Parades, staged performances and general dancing proliferate as traditional and contemporary music and dance elements fuse in group celebrations of local culture (see Peterson 2010).

Revivals

This discussion of indigenous practices in Southeast Asia only gives a few examples of revivals. Every country or region has its indigenous other, and that indigenous other may have its own other. In the contemporary period especially we see urban, educated groups rediscovering heritage and reinventing or reinvigorating roots in response to national and/or global forces that seek to assimilate. In Java, well sheltered during the coronavirus/COVID-19 outbreak, *dalang* (puppeteer) Purbo Asmoro started a solo *ruwatan* (making safe) performance on 25 March 2020 which he streamed via YouTube as a response to – and hopefully to help bring about the end of – the global pandemic. The Bali Ajeg (Strong Bali) movement in response to the Islamic fundamentalist bombing in 2002 was another example of curing via performance, where a whole island gathered forces to reaffirm its differences (Hindu–Buddhist–animist) and passionately engaged in performances of mask dances like *Topeng Sida Karya* or *Calonarang* (named after the eponymous witch) to ritually cleanse the island of the political and spiritual pollution as tourism tanked and livelihoods languished (see Kodi et al. 2005). Within Bali itself the performances of the indigenous group residing in Karangasem and the mountain area, known as the Bali Aga (Original Balinese), are seen as more pristine in traditions than the Hindu–Buddhist Balinese (Dibia and Ballinger 2004: 56). And all Hindu–Buddhist Balinese stand in contrast to the Muslims and Christians of the rest of Indonesia.

Sundanese urbanites in West Java visit Desa Naga (Naga Village), where traditional rice-pounding music will still greet eclipses and *anglung* shakers play for rice harvest. Other city dwellers go to Seren Tahun (traditional New Year), an annual ceremony to honour the ancestors in Cigugur near Cirebon, West Java. Contemporary choreographers like Irawati Durban create neo-rice harvest festival dances for the proscenium stage to reconnect urban Sundanese with traditional culture and ideas. Modern dance forms based on traditional rice-pounding songs and dances create modern music crazes like *jaipongan* (Manuel and Baier 1986). Sundanese ethnomusicologist Endo Suanda makes *kecapi* and other instruments out of bamboo to revive traditional, natural and sustainable music traditions in a land that has for centuries been overrun with Javanese bronze gongs. In resistance to Islamic fundamentalist strains that seek to impose conservative anti-music/dance interpretations, local groups start to espouse Sunda Wiwitan or original Sundanese religious practices, dress in the traditional styles of the Baduy villages and recuperate heritage practices (Baier 2017: 66).

Modern ethnomusicologists and pop artists collaborate to create events like the Sarawak Rainforest World Music Festival, discussed earlier. Contemporary choreographers like Filipina Agnes Locsin create "neo-traditional" work, such as her 1987 *Igorot*. Indonesian modern dancer Sardono Kusumo worked with the Iban in Kalimantan and created new choreographies in the early 2000s involving Iban and national audiences in rainforest preservation and eco-dance initiatives. Thus, the music and dance of indigenous people becomes an icon for modern artists of diverse ethnicities exploring ideas of sustainability and community. Artists aim at re-endowing secular life with visions of natural balance, ancestral voices and local self-determination in the face of secular capitalism, imported religions (both Islam and Christian) and national financial imperatives that seek resource extraction and higher GNP. Provincial government bureaus put together files to declare vanishing arts as intangible cultural heritage for local offices, national councils and UNESCO heritage recognitions. Universities archive audio–visual materials and publish reports. NGOs and foundations sponsor projects where indigenous groups and major artists mount new works in national festivals to highlight the loss of land, heritage and political self-determination. Heritage projects are created to pass endangered traditions of story, dance and music from elders to the next generations. Rituals are revived and roots re-examined to carry the arts of the past with new meaning into the future.

References

Baier, Randal. 2017. 'Sound from within and Sound from without: Maintaining Indigenous Media Soundscapes in Ciptagelar, West Java, Indonesia (Abstract),' p. 66, https://ictmusic.org/sites/default/files/documents/study%20groups/publications/PASEA%20Proceedings04_upload.pdf (accessed 30 November 2017).

Benjamin, Geoffrey. 2014. *Temiar Religion, 1964–2012: Enchantment, Disenchantment and Re-enchantment in Malaysia's Uplands*. Singapore: National University of Singapore Press.

'Caragan Festival of Mabalacat City: Aeta Fiesta 2017.'www.youtube.com/watch?v=rNn2 KpIQs7o (accessed 12 November 2017).

'Caragan 2015 – Tribung Camachiles'. www.youtube.com/watch?v=X5Qpv2Qbo6k (accessed 12 November 2017).

Chan, Claire Suet Ching. 2015. 'Standardizing and Exoticising the Main Jo'oh: The Tourist Gaze and Identity Politics in the Music and Dance of the Indigenous Mah Meri of Malaysia,' *Asian Music*, 46(2): 89–127.

Chenoweth, Vida, Kathleen Van Arsdale and Artur Simon. 1998. 'Irian Jaya Province of Indonesia,' in Adrienne Kaeppler and J.W. Love (Eds.), *Australia and the Pacific Islands: The Garland Encyclopedia of World Music*, pp. 578–595. New York: Garland.

D'Cruz, Alan, dir. 2000. *Guardians of the Forest* [documentary on the Temuan released in 2000], www.magickriver.org/2014/06/guardians-of-forest-51-minute.html (accessed 20 November 2017).

Dibia, I. Wayan and Rucina Ballinger. 2004. *Balinese Dance, Drama and Music*. Singapore: Periplus.

Eliade, Mircea. 1972 [1964]. *Shamanism: Archaic Techniques of Ecstasy*. Princeton: Princeton University Press.

George, Kenneth. 1996. *Showing Signs of Violence: The Cultural Politics of a Twentieth Century Headhunting Ritual*. Berkeley: University of California Press.

Hobsbawm, Eric and Terence Ranger (Ed.). 1983. *The Invention of Tradition*. Cambridge University Press.

Jacobs, Karen. 'Kamoro Arts Festival 2003,' in Dirk Smidt (Ed.), *Kamoro Art: Tradition and Innovation in a New Guinea Culture*, pp. 66–71. Amsterdam: KIT Publishers (Rijksmuseum voor Volkenkunde-Leiden).

Kodi, I. Ketut, I. Nyoman Sedana and Kathy Foley. 2005. '*Topeng Sidha Karya*: A Balinese Mask Dance,' and 'Balinese Mask Dance from the Perspective of a Master Artist: I Ketut Kodi,' *Asian Theatre Journal*, 22(2): 171–213.

Lamb, Kate. 2015. 'Indonesia's Transgender Priests Face Uncertain Future,' *Al Jazeera*, 12 May, http://america.aljazeera.com/articles/2015/5/12/indonesias-transgender-priests-face-uncertain-future.html (accessed 15 November 2017).

Maceda, Jose. 1998. 'Upland Peoples of the Philippines,' in Terry E. Miller and Sean Williams (Eds.), *Southeast Asia: Garland Encyclopedia of World Music*, pp. 913–928. New York: Garland.

Manuel, Peter and Randal Baier. 1986. 'Jaipongan: Indigenous Popular Music of West Java,' *Asian Music*, 18(1): 91–111.

Matusky, Patricia. 1998. 'Borneo: Sabah, Sarawak, Brunei, and Indonesia,' in Terry E. Miller and Sean Williams (Eds.), *Southeast Asia: Garland Encyclopedia of World Music*, pp. 823–838. New York: Garland.

Mayberry, Kate. 2017. 'Port Project Threatens Indigenous Community in Malaysia,' *Aljazeera*, 3 March, www.aljazeera.com/news/2017/03/port-project-threatens-indigenous-community-malaysia-170303070150537.html (accessed 30 November 2017).

Miller, Terry. 1998. 'Lahu,' in Terry E. Miller and Sean Williams (Eds.), *Southeast Asia: Garland Encyclopedia of World Music*, pp. 538–540. New York: Garland.

Peterson, William. 2010. 'Performing Indigeneity in the Cordillera: Dance, Community, and Power in the Highlands of Luzon,' *Asian Theatre Journal*, 27(2): 246–268, www.jstor. org/stable/25782119 (accessed 17 April 2020).

Peterson, William. 2016. 'Time and Transcendence at Ati-Atihan,' in *Places for Happiness: Community, Self, and Performance in the Philippines*. Honolulu: University of Hawai'i Press. DOI:10.21313/hawaii/9780824851637.003.0006 (accessed 10 July 2020).

Pilo, Wilfred. 2016. 'Iban Legends and Fairytales Come Alive in Dance,' *Borneo Post*, 16 December, www.theborneopost.com/2016/12/16/iban-legends-and-fairytales-come-alive-in-dance/ (accessed 30 November 2017).

Pouwer, Jan. 2010. *Gender, Ritual, and Social Formation in West Papua*. Leiden: KITLV Press.

Roseman, Marina. 1991. *Healing Sounds from the Malaysian Rainforest: Temiar Music and Medicine*. Berkeley: University of California Press.

Roseman, Marina. 1998. 'The Indigenous Peoples (Orang Asli) of the Malay Peninsula,' in Terry E. Miller and Sean Williams (Eds.), *Southeast Asia: Garland Encyclopedia of World Music*, pp. 560–589. New York: Garland.

Ruriko Uchida and Amy Catlin in Terry E. Miller and Sean Williams (Eds.). *Southeast Asia: Garland Encyclopedia of World Music*, pp. 550–559. New York: Garland.

Rutherford, Danilyn. 2002. *Raiding the Land of the Foreigners: The Limits of the Nation on an Indonesian Frontier*. Princeton, NJ: Princeton University Press.

Smidt, Dirk. 1996. 'The Asmat Art: Expression of Life Transcending Death,' in Philippe Peltier and Floriane Morin (Eds.), *Shadows of New Guinea: Art from the Great Island of Oceania in the Barbier-Mueller Collections*, pp. 260–277. Paris: Musee Barbier Mueller.

Tan, Sooi Beng. 2005. ' "Akar Umbi" *Songs of the Dragon*: Indigenous Identity and Temuan Rights to the Forest,' *Aliran Monthly*, 25(5), https://aliran.com/archives/monthly/2005a/5g.html (accessed 17 November 2017).

van Zanten, Wim. 1995. 'Aspects of Baduy Music in its Sociocultural Context, with Special Reference to Singing and Angklung,' *KITLV* (Bidjragen tot de Taal-, Land- en Volkenkunde, Performing Arts in Southeast Asia), 151(4): 516–544, http://booksandjournals. brillonline.com/docserver/22134379/151/4/22134379_151_04_s03_text.pdf?expires= 1512081283&id=id&accname=guest&checksum=762FBA618AA73FB3A76662A9 C01A3357 (accessed 30 November 2017).

Vilarus, B.E.S. and R.A. Obusan. n.d. 'Ethnic tradition in Philippine Dance,' nlpdl.nlp.gov. ph:81/CC01/NLP00VM052mcd/v6/v2.pdf (accessed 12 November 2017).

Werner, Roland. 1973. *Mah Meri: Art and Culture*. Kuala Lumpur: Museum Department, University Malaya.

Glossary

aitu   spirit, Aeta, Philippines

aker   fishing dance, Biak, West Papua, Indonesia

anklung   shaken bamboo instruments, Baduy, Sunda, Indonesia

ayay   courtship poetry, Khmu, Cambodia

balyan   shaman-healer, Aeta, Igorot, Kalinga, Philippines

barong   body puppet of a wild animal, Java and Bali, Indonesia

bissu   transgender priest, Buginese, Sulawesi, Indonesia

bomoh   shaman-healer, Temiar, Mah Meri, Kelantan, Malaysia

dalang   puppet master, Indonesia and Malaysia

danyang   spirit, ancestor-protector, Java, Indonesia
dukun   shaman-healer, Indonesia
ensera   narratives, Iban, Borneo/Kalimantan, Malaysia/Indonesia
gangsa   gong, Igorot, Philippines
gawai   festival, Iban, Borneo/Kalimantan, Malaysia/Indonesia
gunungan   (cosmic) mountain image, Sunda, Java, Indonesia
huhud   epic song, Ifuago, Philippines
jaipongan   neo-traditional popular dance of West Java, Indonesia
kayon   tree of life image, Sunda, Java, Bali, Indonesia
kecapi   zither, Baduy, Sunda, Indonesia
khau xia   storytelling genre, Hmong, Vietnam, Thailand, Laos, Myanmar
kucapi   zither, Iban, Borneo/Kalimantan, Malaysia/Indonesia
kuda kepang   trance dance with woven bamboo horse figure, Java, Bali, Indonesia
kuntai   martial dance, Iban, Borneo/Kalimantan, Malaysia/Indonesia
kwv txhiaj   courting poetry, Hmong, Vietnam, Thailand, Laos, Myanmar
lemambang   storytellers, Iban, Borneo/Kalimantan, Malaysia/Indonesia
main jo'oh   mask dance, Mah Meri, Malaysia
main peteri   trance curing performance, Kelantan, Malaysia
manang   shaman-healer, Iban, Borneo/Kalimantan, Malaysia/Indonesia
naga   snake/dragon, Indonesia, Malaysia, Thailand
naw   mouth organ, Lahu, Thailand
ngajat   dance in place, Iban, Borneo/Kalimantan, Malaysia/Indonesia
pantun   Indo-Malay verse form of four lines of eight syllables, with the first two lines often a riddle and the second two the intended message, used in courting poetry, Indonesia (also storytelling form of Baduy, Sunda)
pa-nyah   courting poetry, Lao, Laos
penca, penca silat   martial arts dance, Indonesia and Malaysia
penglipur lara   storyteller, Kedah, Malaysia
pohon beringan   tree of life image, Kelantan, Malaysia
qeej   bamboo mouth organ, Hmong, Vietnam, Laos, Thailand, Myanmar
quan ho   courting poetry, Vietnam
ranyai   tree of life, Iban, Borneo/Kalimantan, Malaysia/Indonesia
sape   lute, Iban, Borneo/Kalimantan, Malaysia/Indonesia
serunai   oboe-like instrument, Indonesia and Malaysia
sewang   trance ritual dance, Temuan, Orang Asli, Malaysia
sisinderan   riddle poetry in pantun verse form, Baduy, Sunda, Indonesia
tarian jo'oh   mask dance, Mah Meri, Malaysia
tifa   drum, Biak, West Papua, Indonesia
timang   ritual chant, Iban, Borneo/Kalimantan, Malaysia/Indonesia
topeng banyet   courtesan dance, Sunda, West Java
tukang pantun   storyteller musician of Sundanese, traditionally a blind zither player, Baduy, West Java
ua neeb   honouring the spirit, Hmong, Thailand, Vietnam, Laos, Myanmar

wor   dance-music with trance roots, Biak, West Papua, Indonesia

wayang   traditional theatre with puppetry as model, Sunda, Java, Bali, Lombok, Kalimantan in Indonesia; Kelantan, Kedah, Malaysia

xam xoan,   string instrument music and storytelling, Vietnam

yospan   1960s music dance genre, Biak, West Papua, Indonesia

4

PERFORMANCE IN AUSTRALIA, AOTEAROA AND THE PACIFIC

*Tammy Haili'ōpua Baker, Maryrose Casey,
Diana Looser and David O'Donnell*

This chapter provides a sample of the breadth of performance traditions, practices and contemporary innovations from the peoples of numerous nations located on more than 25,000 islands across the Pacific, the island continent of Australia and the country of Aotearoa/New Zealand. These islands, large and small, spread out over more than 170 million square kilometres, have rich and varied histories of performance practices in cultures where choreographed performance has always been part of every aspect of life and social engagement. Traditionally, performance was a means through which peoples learned who they were and about their land and traditions. It was also an important part of communicating and representing identities and cultures to external communities. After European colonization of many of these lands, performance continued to play an important role in negotiating encounters and the aftermath of often violent settlement. Contemporary performance carries on intangible cultural heritages, filling a key role in reclaiming cultural practices and asserting cultural survival.

We examine the Pacific, including Australasia, as a complex space of crossings, where indigenous peoples negotiate tensions between the local/regional, grounded/networked and national/transnational. In each location, the relationship between performance and the land and the sea is a foundational aspect of knowledge and identity. These past and present performance practices also offer insight into traditions that continue to evolve and diversify, responding both to sociopolitical factors and to fresh artistic stimuli, both local and global.

Australia

In Australia there are two indigenous peoples: Aboriginal Australians and Torres Strait Islanders. Aboriginal Australian is a collective label that includes more than 500 separate nations or groupings with different languages, living in radically different physical environments: desert peoples, saltwater, freshwater and rainforest peoples, as well as groupings that hail from temperate parts of the country. These different groupings have different histories, modes of subsistence, cultural practices and technologies. Considered one of the oldest ongoing cultures in the world, Aboriginal Australians have occupied the continent and many of the islands off the coast for more than 70,000 years. The Torres Strait Islanders are indigenous to the islands in the Torres Strait to the northeast of mainland Australia. Torres Strait Islanders are regarded and identify as being distinct from mainland Aboriginal Australians. They are among the most southerly Melanesian communities. The main island groupings – Eastern Islands, Western and Central Islands – differ from each other and the Aboriginal peoples of the mainland linguistically and culturally. These groups speak different languages and draw on different performance and spiritual practices.

Both indigenous cultures have rich performance traditions, which continue to be an important part of everyday life. The cultural heritages differ, reflecting the different histories of the peoples. Though there are many commonalities, it would be impossible to present a meaningful account of the broad array of performance practices in this chapter. Therefore, as an example of practices, the focus is on Aboriginal performances, in particular those of the Yolngu peoples of Arnhem Land in the Northern Territory.[1] The Yolngu inhabit East Arnhem Land and their current homelands extend from the Gove Peninsula to Cape Stuart, and south to the Walker River. The Yolngu are an example of a people who have maintained strong connections with their land and culture throughout colonization and into the present.

As a generalization, a strong commonality across all traditional Aboriginal Australian cultures is that performance plays a central role. Every aspect of life from judicial to spiritual practices and from education to entertainment was performance-based in the sense of choreographed performances that the community learned and understood. Indigenous Australian performance is often described as "song" or "dance." In the context of Aboriginal performance practice, both of these terms (song and dance) do not refer to the singular art form as understood in a contemporary industrialized context. These performances combined multiple art forms, including visual arts through body painting, music, song, dance and narrative mime and dialogue. Performers were either all male or all female. When a scene calls for women in dances performed by men, their part is taken by men who decorate themselves accordingly. Performances were conducted in defined landscaped areas that provided a flat performance space with natural features to allow entrances or to act as a set, and a sloping area for audiences.

Mimetic performance is traditionally a strong feature of Aboriginal Australian performance practices. This choice relates to Aboriginal spiritual beliefs which hold that everything within the landscape – natural formations, animals, birds and humans – is connected to the creator beings and therefore has a spiritual life and connection to the sacred and sentient on a metaphysical level. This notion of the sacred is on a continuum, so sacredness is a question of degree rather than everything being the same. On this basis, a performance for entertainment does not share the sacrality of a spiritual ceremony, but at the same time respects the sacred.

As part of this engagement with the world as sacred, the physical movements of dance and mime express the connection between the people and events in the story with the effect of these on the Earth. So, the patterns of dancers, such as moving in lines or in circles, have specific meanings; on this basis, a dance from the desert will include sliding and shuffling movements reflecting the sand and wind. Sign languages are also common across Aboriginal groupings. These attribute specific meanings to particular parts of the body. For example, the Yolngu have a sign language based on the body in which different body parts represent relationships and actions, and this language is part of the dance. Performances are well choreographed and practised. Costume takes the form of body painting, masks and headdresses, and other types of physical adornment.

Traditionally, there were hundreds of genres of performance serving different social and political purposes. One example of a wide range of traditional choreographed performance is the judicial practices sometimes called war dances or war cries. In this form, conflict between Aboriginal people within a clan or between clans was mainly resolved through a choreographed dance. In the 1930s, William Lloyd Warner described a Yolngu version as an elaborate substitute war ritual that was part duel and part ordeal (1937: 174–76). After initial negotiations to meet to settle differences, the dancing ground is prepared. The men dance up to the challenged group then return to their side of the ground. The opponents similarly dance forward and retire. Then the "chief offender" moves into the ground and the offended parties throw spears at him. If he succeeds in avoiding them all, he dances what Warner styles "a descriptive dance" and then he presents himself for the judgement of elders who decide if he has fulfilled any requirements for justice. If they decide he has not, then he is speared in the leg. Then the two sides dance together as one group to indicate that the matter is resolved.

The most important types of performance relate to ceremonies that are either secret and sacred, or public and educational and topical performances for entertainment. Performances within the genre of sacred or public ceremony are based on what are generally known as Dreaming Stories. These can be narratives about the adventures of ancestral beings, magic and power, totemic songs, hunting, dramatic and epic stories, and fighting. The terms Dreaming or the associated Dreamtime are a mistranslation, effectively a homogenized European construction of traditional Aboriginal spiritual beliefs. Aboriginal performances associated with the creation and life of the world are put under the heading of Dreaming. The word in Yolngu is the word for law, Madayin. The stories and performances evoke laws about how Yolngu should live as people and care for the land, as well as the stories about the creation of people and the land. Performances related to Madayin can be part of secret ceremonies or public ceremonies to educate the community.

Given the orientation towards performance at all levels of life, it is not surprising that performances for entertainment were also prevalent. These performances range from gossip songs around the fire to complex narratives that critiqued contemporary life, including colonial violence. These topical performances are practically always comic, no matter how serious the subject matter. Comedies have played a central role across the millennia in Aboriginal cultures. They have been used by communities to manage the trauma of colonization in both the past and the present. The lightness of touch that maintains laughter continues as an important element in contemporary work.

An example of a performance for entertainment revealing an aspect of racialized violence is a Yolngu performance from Wave Hill. With biting humour, the performance satirizes the treatment of Aboriginal people by the British legal system as well as European attitudes towards Aboriginal women. The performers were all male; the female roles were played by young men. The narrative deals with a policeman leading a group of young women in chains while another white man attempts to steal them from him. Like many such Aboriginal satires, the performance focuses on revealing the foolishness of the white men in their greed and violence (Berndt and Berndt 1965: 324). There are many layers to such a performance narrative, including levels on which it is part of dealing with the overwhelming violence that was part of the colonial encounter.

Performances for fun based on topical issues were part of everyday life within small groups when they travelled through the country, when all the members of clans gathered together, and when there were large annual or biennial gatherings bringing everyone in a region together. These large-scale inter-community gatherings from across regions were historically part of social, economic and political life. They were organized for many reasons including sporting contests, trading, or political negotiations and marriage arrangements. At these gatherings, public songs, dances, stories and dramatized performances were bartered and exchanged between communities. These large regional gatherings continue in different parts of Australia. The Garma Festival brings together the 60 paterfilial groups that make up the 16 Yolngu clans. Though the practice had been officially discouraged and impeded, and had practically stopped by the 1930s, the gatherings at the ceremonial grounds of Gulkala have been revived. The Garma is organized by Yolngu people, primarily for Yolngu people to gather, perform and talk. As the organizers describe it:

> The ancient sound of the Yidaki (didjeridoo) is a call to all people to come together in unity; to gather for the sharing of knowledge and culture; to learn from and listen to one another. Annually the Yidaki (didjeridoo) announces the start of Garma, the largest and most vibrant annual celebration of Yolngu (Aboriginal people of north east Arnhem Land) culture.
>
> *(Yothu Yindi Foundation 2016)*

Garma, as a festival and coming together of Yolngu and others, aims to provide a contemporary environment "for the practice, preservation, maintenance and presentation of traditional knowledge systems and cultural traditions and practices, especially bunggul (traditional dance), Manikay (song), Miny' tji (art) and ceremony" (Yothu Yindi Foundation 2016).

The bunggul is a key traditional performance style that combines songs and dances to the accompaniment of clap sticks and the didjeridoo. The Yolngu songs and dances are performed with the permission of the owners of those stories and, as Franca Tamisari points out, the "Yolngu dance because they hold Law" (2000: 151–52). Ceremonial dances are performed, as are topical performances, such as the various Red Flag dances that have been in the repertoire for centuries.

There are numerous different Red Flag dances across Arnhem Land. The Nung-gubuyu people from Numbulwar, one of the Yolngu peoples, perform one that, like the others, is based in song, story and dance and tells of early encounters with Macassan traders, an Indonesian people from the island of Sulawesi. The Macas-sans had trading arrangements with the Yolngu peoples in Arnhem Land from at least 400 years before European settlement in 1788 until they were outlawed in the early 20th century. The performance called the Dhumbala (Red Flag dance) was created after some members of the Nunggubuyu people went travelling with the Macassans, possibly as early as the 18th century. On their return, they created per-formances based on their adventures. The song follows the journey and the return home. The accompanying dance uses extensive mime, intercut with stomping steps typical of the Yolngu to physically portray the story. The mime includes martial arts movements that were taught to the Nundhirribala by the Macassans, with the use of red flags on sticks as the sails of the boats, as telescopes looking out to see and as flags to wave. There is also mimed action of consulting maps, looking for and finding objects, raising the anchor, walking ashore, and investigating new lands and places.

Performance has continued as a crucial part of social and political life after colonization. Since the early 20th century, Aboriginal peoples have presented per-formances within the European theatre context. These have taken many forms: performances of traditional dance and song, shows that follow the European con-ventions of narrative theatre and shows that combine both in a variety of ways.

In the colonized context of Australia, Aboriginal performance is always a politi-cal act. Many shows have been created to actively engage with political issues. One from Elcho Island off the coast of Arnhem Land and home to 18 connected clan groups who are part of the Yolngu is *Ngurrumilmarrmiriyu: Wrong Skin* (2010). The show was created by a dance group of young Yolngu men known as Djuki Mala (formerly the Chooky Dancers). *Ngurrumilmarrmiriyu*, Djuki Mala's first full-length theatre show, not only presents and represents Yolngu law and traditions, it oper-ates within them. The show is spoken in language with surtitles in the introductory sequences, but without surtitles for the actual narrative. The show, created to com-municate with *Balanda,* or non-Yolngu audiences, focuses on their lives in relation to tradition and law, and their lives in relation to the impact of systemic racism and legislative action and representation. *Ngurrumilmarrmiriyu* offers multiple layers of life on Elcho including lives bound by law, late-night television and fried chicken. The Yolngu people of Elcho are part of a living tradition and the show is, on one level, a necessary step to maintain it as traditional and contemporary.

Ngurrumilmarrmiriyu is a series of moments of life on Elcho Island linked by a Yolngu version of *Romeo and Juliet.* The context of star-crossed lovers is based in cultural tradition rather than family strife. The English version of the title, *Wrong Skin*, refers to someone marrying the wrong skin or moiety. Aboriginal society is structured around complex family or kinship systems. Two main systems, kin groups and moieties, organize all aspects of life and help to locate an individual in society and in their country. All other people and all the features of the natural and spiritual world, land, animals and wind belong to one or the other of two moieties. In Yolngu traditional teachings, there are two moieties and the world is divided up between those two: Yirridja and Dhuwa. These systems – kin groups and moieties – jointly help to determine many aspects of social or religious behaviour, including who you can speak to and who you can marry. Moieties play a central part in the story since the "wrong skin" is about marrying someone of the wrong moiety or skin group. The cast includes two Yolngu senior songmen, Djakapurra Munyarrun and Djali Donald Ganambarr, each representing and performing songs from their respective moieties with didjeridoos and clap sticks.

In the 21st century, Aboriginal performance continues to be a living tradition whether created by urban people dislocated from their traditional lands or groups such as the Yolngu living in remote parts of Australia. Through performance they share their ontologies and epistemologies, making an offer to others of a different way to be and to know.

Aotearoa/New Zealand

The evolution of contemporary indigenous performance and theatre in Aotearoa/New Zealand is marked by the complex relationships between Māori and Pasifika (Pacific Island migrant) communities and artists. As indigenous performance in Aotearoa has become increasingly prolific and varied, it is impossible to make universal statements about style or themes. However, much of this work is connected to Pacific worldviews and connections with the cosmos, where cultural identity is related to and defined by the relationships between land and sea, genealogical connections to place and the journeys that have shaped contemporary Aotearoa. Māori are the indigenous people of Aotearoa – tangata whenua (people of the land). The word whenua, meaning land, also means placenta, making an association between birth, land and identity that is explored in a multitude of ways in Māori performance and playwriting. Māori arrived in Aotearoa approximately 1,000 years ago on sea-going waka (canoes) after epic migrations through the Pacific Islands, while Pasifika people migrated to Aotearoa from various Pacific Islands in large numbers since World War II in search of economic opportunity. The largest Pasifika populations in Aotearoa are Samoan, Cook Islander, Tongan and Niuean. Alice Te Punga Somerville re-contextualizes Aotearoa as a Pacific nation (rather than as a Westernized ex-British colony, as it is often perceived), defining Māori as "indigenous Pacific" and Pasifika as "migrant Pacific" (Te Punga Somerville 2012: 155). While the Pacific Island diaspora has spread to other countries such as the US and Australia, Auckland has the largest Polynesian population in the world. During the post-war period, Pasifika people were migrating to the cities at the same time that

Māori were moving in large numbers from their traditional rural bases to urban areas. Māori and Pasifika ended up in the same suburbs of the major cities, where they had to "scramble for the few resources available" in terms of employment, education, housing and health (Te Punga Somerville 2012: xxii). Although separate Māori and Pasifika theatre traditions have developed since the 1980s, they are linked by a focus on voyaging/journeying, reflecting the long histories of migration and trade routes around the Pacific, the relationship between land and sea, and the close connection between landscape and cultural identity.

Māori performance has become synonymous with the international profile of Aotearoa/New Zealand. The national rugby team the All Blacks have performed a haka prior to test matches since 1905. The English definition of haka as a "dance" is inadequate to describe a performance tradition which is "an aesthetically and culturally complex intertextual mode whereby meaning and function are contingent on the chanting that accompanies the physical movement" (Hyland 2015: 68) The modern tradition of kapa haka (Māori performing arts) developed in the 1930s, led by Māori leaders such as Princess Te Puea Herangi, who feared that the culture would die out if it was not practised in visible, public ways. Most Māori educational institutions have kapa haka groups that "enhance the ability of the institution to practice other tikanga [customs] such as traditional waiata, the haka, action songs and poi" (Mead 2003: 313). The biennial national kapa haka competition Te Matatini has become one of the largest cultural events in Aotearoa since it began in 1972, with up to 50,000 participants and spectators. Used for formal ceremonial functions as well as widespread performances in tourist performance, sports, schools, spontaneous celebration, and contemporary theatre and dance, haka is "an evolved and evolving cross-disciplinary form . . . a living practice" (Hyland 2015: 80). Haka such as "Toia Mai," commonly used at pōwhiri (formal welcoming ceremonies), re-enact the rowing and pulling in of waka, evoking "the twin acts of voyaging and coming to land" (Baker et al. 2016: 45). As scripted Māori drama evolved from the 1970s onwards, it became a syncretic form that blended international theatrical forms with aspects of tikanga and Māori performing arts (Balme 1999: 62–76). For example, Hone Kouka's *Nga Tangata Toa* (1994) opens with a karanga (ritual chant) and haka pōwhiri, as Māori soldiers returning from fighting in World War I are welcomed on the wharf. The scene powerfully evokes the voyages made by Māori in the post-colonial era to become combatants in global warfare and their return to the whenua, while also symbolically serving as a welcome to the audience from the actors in the company.

Prior to European colonization, Māori practised performing arts in a purpose-built house located on the pa (village) known as Te Whare Tapere (House of Entertainment). Whare Tapere practices were discontinued due to colonial pressures, but in the 1990s, Te Ahukaramū Charles Royal began to reconstruct knowledge of how the Whare Tapere operated through archival accounts and oral histories. Royal identified activities conducted in the Whare Tapere including kōrero (storytelling), karetao (puppetry), waiata (songs), haka (dance) and taonga pūoro (musical instruments) (Royal 2007: 201–3). In 2004, Royal formed Ōrotokare, an organization designed to explore and renew Whare Tapere art forms. From 2010 to 2014, Ōrotokare brought together indigenous artists with the aim of revitalizing Whare Tapere as a multidimensional performing arts form (Royal 2016). Royal's work connects with wider explorations in blending traditional and contemporary Māori arts. This work continues to reach wider and wider audiences. In 2016, for instance, Ōrotokare participants Horomono Horo and James Webster presented a dynamic display of karetao and taonga pūoro at the 12th Festival of Pacific Arts in Guam.

As European-style theatre developed throughout Aotearoa during the 19th century, Māori became performers in popular theatre works such as George Leitch's sensation melodrama *Land of the Moa* (1895), which featured a concert party performing haka. Māori performance became synonymous with the tourist experience, especially in tourist centres such as Rotorua (Werry 2011). In 1965, the New Zealand Opera Company produced *Porgy and Bess* featuring the Māori opera singer Inia Te Wiata, supported by a largely Māori cast. This production was the catalyst for the formation of the Māori Theatre Trust, and by the 1970s, Māori performers were achieving success as actors in theatre and television. This was paralleled by a growth in Māori literature, which led to established writers such as Harry Dansey, Rore Hapipi and Hone Tuwhare creating works for the stage.

Dansey's *Te Raukura* (1972) was the first professionally produced play by a Māori playwright, foregrounding Māori resistance to colonization in the Taranaki region during the New Zealand Wars from the 1860s to 1880s (Looser 2014: 115–26). Hapipi's *Death of the Land* (1976) focuses on land rights by dramatizing a hearing in the Māori Land Court. This play and Tuwhare's *In the Wilderness without a Hat* (1985) both feature ancestral spirit characters who "come to life" to advise the characters on contentious issues, a theatricalization of Māori views that ancestors are part of the present as well as the past – that "the universe is inhabited by wairua [spirits]" (Mead 2003: 55). Roma Potiki acknowledged the incorporation of traditional forms such as waiata, chant, haka and karanga (female welcome call) into Western dramaturgy, and defined Māori theatre as "tino rangatiratanga [self-determination] in action" (Potiki 1992: 153). For Potiki, Māori theatre must be "both written and controlled by Māori, and largely performed by Māori," and is "a visible claiming of the right to control and present our own material using self-determined processes which suit us and achieve our political, cultural and artistic aims" (Potiki 1992: 153). Thus, early Māori drama can be seen both as a continuity of pre-colonial Māori performing arts and as a potent expression of political activism and cultural identity.

As the energy of Māori theatre grew, there were close partnerships between Māori and Pasifika artists. One of the first companies was Taotahi, formed by a group of young Māori and Pasifika who met while students at high school. Co-founder Samson Samasoni articulated the connection between performance and politics:

> The co-operative nature of theatre, as opposed to the individual existence of writers, is becoming more and more attractive to Maori and Pacific Islanders.

Black politicos are fast coming to recognise that theatre, or play acting, has a role in the struggle.

(Samasoni 1986: 15)

In 1984, Taotahi created the first full-length Samoan play – *Le Matau* – written by Samson Samasoni and Stephen Sinclair. This portrays the journey of a young Samoan man to Aotearoa, and his assimilation into Palagi (white) society as he rejects his family and fa'asamoa (traditional Samoan values) to become "successful" in the Palagi world as a real estate agent. *Le Matau* provocatively depicts the migration process as leading to assimilation and the loss of cultural identity.

Le Matau was one of many Pasifika and Māori plays performed at The Depot, a theatre founded in Wellington in 1983 devoted exclusively to New Zealand drama and dance. By the early 1990s, The Depot had evolved into Taki Rua Theatre, and the focus had switched to Māori and Pasifika work. Taki Rua's name is derived from a customary weaving pattern, meaning "to go in twos," symbolizing the company's bicultural foundations in the spirit of the Treaty of Waitangi (1840) (Kouka 1999: 17). Thus, the production of theatre links to traditions of cultural preservation and the construction of taonga (treasured objects) made from natural materials derived from the land. In 2013 Taki Rua celebrated its 30th anniversary as the leading production company for Māori theatre.

In the 1990s, Māori theatre expanded from fringe venues into the mainstream, and writers Hone Kouka and Briar Grace-Smith moved beyond political activism to create plays that reflected Māori experience in more complex ways. Kouka's *Waiora* (1996) portrays the post-war Māori urban drift, focusing on one whānau (family) who move from their Ūkaipō (traditional homeland) in search of employment and better opportunities for their children. Thus, Māori are shown as migrants in their own land, and consequent pressures on the whānau lead to conflict and breakdown. Both *Waiora* and Grace-Smith's *Purapurawhetū* (1997) are set on a beach, these liminal spaces reflecting the symbolic associations of the sea with voyaging and migration, where characters can connect with tipuna (ancestors) who have made the journey to the spirit world Hawaiiki (Dale 1997: 26). In *Purapurawhetū*, the re-building of a wharenui (meeting house) ultimately enables a fragile healing process to take place in a whānau divided by traumatic past events. *Purapurawhetū* remains one of the most internationally critically acclaimed Māori plays: "[Grace-Smith] creates a strikingly powerful hybrid dramatic form, situated between Māori mythic storytelling and Western tragedy" (Maufort 2003: 231).

The development of Māori theatre connects to the revival of Te Reo (Māori language), which became an official second language of Aotearoa in 1987. During the 1980s, Kōhanga Reo (Māori language pre-school) and Kura Kaupapa (Māori language schools) were established. Apirana Taylor's play *Kōhanga* (1986) dramatizes conflicts within a mixed Māori/Pākehā whānau over whether a child should attend kōhanga reo. Recognizing the educational benefits of drama in Te Reo, Taki Rua have toured an original Māori language play to marae, schools and community centres since the 1990s. While most Māori theatre is performed in English, many plays include dialogue, speeches, songs and chants in Te Reo. Hone Kouka's *Mauri Tū* (1991) features a memorable scene where a kaumatua (elder) speaks in Te Reo as the lights are gradually dimmed to blackout, whereupon the character disparages the audience for "switching off" when Te Reo is spoken. In 1990, Don Selwyn directed a Te Reo production of Shakespeare's *The Merchant of Venice*, which he adapted into a feature film in 2002. In 2012, London's Globe to Globe Festival opened with a performance of *Tōroihi rāua ko Kāhira*, a Māori language production of Shakespeare's *Troilus and Cressida*.

Some companies and artists have used the "safe" frame of theatre as a method for community reflection on collective trauma such as crime and child abuse. John Broughton, a Māori health specialist, wrote several plays that used theatre as an expression of healing. For over 25 years, director Jim Moriarty has worked with his company Te Rākau Hua o Te Wao Tapu in prisons and with at-risk youth, often having perpetrators narrate or re-enact traumatic events within a tikanga Māori performance framework to create a collective catharsis for performers and audiences (Maunder 2013: 93–115). Such theatre has held a crucial function in Aotearoa in strengthening indigenous communities left fragmented by the forces of colonialism and globalization. In 2015, Moriarty collaborated with Fijian/New Zealand director Nina Nawalowalo to create *The White Guitar*, which tells the story of the journey of the Luafutu aiga (family) who migrated from Sāmoa in the 1950s. Although the story is framed through the ancestral figure of the great-grandmother who plays her white guitar in a dream-like memory of Sāmoa, the main theme is masculinity, as we see fathers and sons perpetuating cycles of criminal activity, domestic violence and addiction. The work suggests that there is no "happy ending" to this migrant story. The story is enacted by the real participants in the story, Fa'amoana (John) Luafutu and his sons Matthias and Malo (also known as the famous rapper Scribe). The dark themes are balanced by ironic, playful humour and the father's skilful playing of rock anthems on his guitar. Moriarty's confessional, therapeutic methodology combines with Nawalowalo's expertise in physical theatre and visual imagery to create a work that is highly original in form. Theatre's potential for healing is also the basis of *Shot Bro* (2016), written and performed by actor/playwright Rob Mokaraka, who in 2009 attempted suicide by provoking police to shoot him. Mokaraka created *Shot Bro* as a way of using his theatre skills to help others suffering from depression. *Shot Bro* references the introduction of European firearms, which was disastrous for Māori in the colonial era, as well as more recent police shootings of Māori men, yet its innovative mix of mime, haka, stand-up comedy and audience interaction has been uplifting and empowering for audiences.

In the 1990s, Pasifika theatre developed alongside Māori theatre as a potent force in New Zealand arts and culture. Christian churches function as social centres for many migrant Pasifika communities in Aotearoa; therefore, a significant number of Pasifika professional actors had their first experience of acting in church productions. In Auckland, Samoan director Justine Simei-Barton founded Pacific Theatre, a company which developed from staging plays by non-white writers from the US and UK to creating original Pasifika works. In Christchurch, Pacific Underground was established by a core group of Pasifika performers. Both companies toured Theatre in Education shows to schools as well as mainstage productions. Influenced by the traditional Samoan comic sketch form fale aitu (house of spirits), many Pasifika plays and performances use comedy as a way of opening up difficult social issues. For example, the all-male comedy troupe The Naked Samoans have explored contentious topics such as racism and child abuse through transgressive comedy.

The process of migration has been revisited over and over again in Pasifika plays, with differing emphases. Pacific Underground's first major work, *Fresh off the Boat* (1993) by Oscar Kightley and Simon Small, presented migration as a painful and inconclusive process as the central character alienates himself from his New Zealand-based relatives and ends up living a rough life on the streets. Makerita Urale focuses on female migrants struggling for economic survival and reconnection with Samoan culture in *Frangipani Perfume* (1997), while in *Falemalama* (2006), Dianna Fuemana depicts the life of her own mother as a challenging series of journeys between Sāmoa, Niue and Aotearoa. One consequence of migration has been the growing number of afakasi (mixed race) Pasifika people, characterized by poet Karlo Mila as "the caramello generation."[2] Samoan playwright Victor Rodger has produced a rich sequence of plays exploring different facets of afakasi identity, including the semi-autobiographical *Sons* (1995), *My Name is Gary Cooper* (2007) and *At the Wake* (2012). Influenced by his Fijian and English genealogy, Toa Fraser writes vivid mixed-race characters in *Bare* (1998) and *No. 2* (1999) that evoke the increasingly multicultural nature of Auckland as a centre of the Pacific diaspora. Fraser's *Paradise* (2001) reflects a legacy of family breakdown brought on by the mixed legacies of colonization and migration, as the central character travels to Fiji to find his father who abandoned his family when he was a child. *Paradise* is one of very few plays that reflect New Zealand's political role in the wider Pacific, as well as touching upon the consequences of the 1987 and 2000 *coup d'états* in Fiji.

Since 2000 many more playwrights have entered the indigenous theatre community, leading to an increased range of themes and genres from the perspective of a younger generation. This generation is exemplified by Miria George, a playwright/producer of Māori and Pasifika (Cook Island) descent. George described her play *and what remains* (2005), set in a near future in which Māori have been exiled en masse from New Zealand, as "indigenous science fiction." In the same vein, Whiti Hereaka's *Te Kaupoi* (2010) shows the future New Zealand as a police state where Māori activists have been driven underground, and Aroha White's *2080* (2015) depicts a dystopian future in which New Zealand has become segregated into three ethnic zones following an environmental catastrophe. This trend for young female playwrights to imagine pessimistic futures expresses anxieties about globalization and refugee crises that present new threats to indigenous identity and autonomy. George's *The Vultures* (2016) taps into ecological debates, showing a grotesque, wealthy Māori family profiting from intensive agricultural practices that are destroying the natural environment in New Zealand, satirically contesting the image of Māori as "guardians of the land."

The new millennium has seen a proliferation of initiatives in Māori theatre, including new companies, venues and festivals. Significantly, several of these events focus around celebrations for Matariki (Māori New Year) signalled by the mid-winter rising of the star formation known as the Pleiades. Since 2000, official celebrations of Matariki have grown in popularity throughout Aotearoa, with associated festivals such as that curated by Te Papa, the national museum in Wellington. Since 2010, Tawata Productions, a company co-founded by Hone Kouka and Miria George, has produced the Matariki Development Festival, an international script development workshop that has included work by indigenous Australian and Canadian writers, as well as local Māori and Pasifika work. In 2015, a Te Reo adaptation of *Romeo and Juliet* was staged as part of Auckland's Matariki Festival, while in Wellington, several Māori theatre companies combined to produce the Ahi Kaa Festival at Matariki. Ahi Kaa marked the first time every Wellington professional theatre venue has simultaneously staged Māori work. This festival illustrated Māori practitioners continuing experimentation with form. This included a show by The White Face Crew, an ensemble of Māori actors who have created a distinctive blend of hip-hop and contemporary dance with French-style mime and clowning. Ahi Kaa also featured Hone Kouka's *The Beautiful Ones* (2015), which combines a poetic love story with a fusion of hip-hop and dance culture in a nightclub setting mediated by a range of digital technologies. In the same year, Ruia Taitea Creative opened a new theatre space in Auckland, Te Pou, which they branded "The Auckland home for Māori theatre." Te Pou has made a strong investment in the future development of Māori theatre, including staging the first production of Briar Grace-Smith's *Purapurawhetū* in Te Reo Māori as part of Auckland's 2016 Matariki Festival. In Wellington, Tawata Productions has continued to produce annual festivals of new writing (re-named Breaking Ground), and the first Ahi Kaa event evolved into the Kia Mau Festival. Commenting on the diversity and innovation that characterized the 2016 Kia Mau productions, critic Adam Goodall described the festival as "a vital and exciting showcase for new work. . . . Perhaps, even, the country's best annual celebration of theatre" (Goodall 2016).

In 2014, the combined Edinburgh festivals invited a large contingent of New Zealand performing arts companies to perform in a celebration of New Zealand arts in a season called *NZ at Edinburgh*. The majority of these were indigenous companies presenting work by artists of Māori and Pasifika heritage, including a touring version of Te Matatini, as well as Lemi Ponifasio's MAU physical theatre; Black Grace dance company; *The Factory*, a musical from South Auckland's Pasifika company Kila Kokonut Krew; and plays *Strange Resting Places* by Paolo Rotondo and Rob Mokaraka, and *Black Faggot* by Victor Rodger. This programming provides a snapshot of the diversity of indigenous performance in Aotearoa, from the "living tradition" of kapa haka to drama to popular entertainment and avant-garde performance art. The increasingly frequent journeys made by indigenous companies to international performance venues mark continuity with Pacific voyaging traditions and indigenous engagement with globalization.

Contemporary indigenous theatre in Aotearoa combines diverse performance heritages from throughout the Pacific, enhances creative relationships between Māori and Pasifika peoples, and both critiques and celebrates traditions of voyaging and migration in the Pacific region. Indigenous performing arts in Aotearoa have become a multidimensional, intercultural and interdisciplinary force that is strongly connected with debates in society at large, with the re-generation of community and the creation of employment through tourist performance and commercial theatre. It reflects the literal and metaphorical journeys taken by Pacific peoples in the region in the past, present and future.

Pacific Islands

Any discussion of Pacific Islands performance must contend with the challenge of covering an area of such expanse and diversity. Encompassing more than 20,000 islands grouped into 26 countries and territories spread over more than a quarter of the Earth's surface, the Pacific Islands region contains a multitude of performance practices drawn from its hundreds of indigenous languages and cultures, its manifold social structures and its multiple colonial legacies. Consequently, any attempt in this chapter to address "indigenous Pacific performance" must be highly selective at best. Our approach here is to identify the Pacific as a complex space of crossings, centring the ocean – a defining geographical and cultural feature of the region – as a vehicle of connection and interrelation. This approach does not downplay the crucial importance of land, but foregrounds a dialectic between land and sea that resists perceptions of Pacific Islands and island cultures as remote, isolated, bounded and static. This angle also avoids a pedestrian country-by-country account of performance or a problematic discussion of Polynesia, Melanesia and Micronesia as discrete geo-cultural categories. While not every community in Oceania is, or has been, on the move in the same way, we understand Pacific indigeneity to be both grounded and mobile, and movement and networking have been integral and recurrent features of Pacific performance, past and present. As Pacific scholar Katerina Teaiwa argues, human identification and activity across the Pacific are marked by the rooted/stable and the travelling/dynamic working together in shaping identity and sustaining social life (2005: 173): "history and culture are only ever contingent and always happening between people and place, bodies and lands, and the vast oceanic spaces that hold, connect and transform them" (Teaiwa 2005: 176).

As in many other indigenous societies worldwide, performance played, and continues to play, central and multifaceted roles in the social, religious and ceremonial life of Pacific communities. Historically, key expressive arts included dance, song and chant, storytelling, puppetry and dramatic sketches (mainly comic or satiric), performed on their own or in combination. Comic performance, both secular and sacred, which ranged from short, spontaneous episodes of interpersonal clowning to prepared comic enactments driven by a plot, was probably very widespread throughout the pre-contact Pacific (Hereniko 1994: 1–28), and early written records by foreign visitors in the late 18th and early 19th centuries testify to its popularity in various sites. This genre provides good examples for considering both specific and shared traditions of Pacific dramatic representation; while displaying local diversity, common formal features speak to cultural and genealogical connections between different communities, especially across central and eastern Oceania. Plot-driven sketch comedies were prevalent in the Society Islands (now part of French Polynesia), particularly on the islands of Tahiti, Ra'iātea, Bora Bora and Huahine. Performed predominantly (but not exclusively) by members of the arioi, a religious sect that worshipped the war god "Oro," they typically took the form of broad, farcical interludes acted by men in between dramatic dances performed by women, within a larger entertainment known as a heiva (Oliver 1974: I.339–40; Looser 2011: 526). These interludes, while no longer extant, had commonalities with the Cook Islands nuku, comic dramas typically based on historical themes (Buck 1932: 198), as well as with the fale aitu comedy of Sāmoa (Sinavaiana 1992: 192–218), both of which are still performed today.

These comic performances served important local functions by recording historical and contemporary events, and by reinforcing social and moral norms for the immediate village community, but they are also significant for the ways in which their subject matter frequently registered the circulation of people and ideas. In recalling the exploits of visitors from different islands, wars with other communities, exploratory voyages and adventures and contact with Europeans, these works revealed a vivid connection and engagement with a wider world. The dynamic incorporation of new tropes, structures and materials is an ongoing characteristic of the dramatic sketch in Oceania. There is ample evidence of the comic sketch still being employed in Sāmoa, Tonga, Tokelau, Fiji, Cook Islands and Solomon Islands to comment on post-contact and contemporary concerns, including colonial institutions, biblical dramas and histories of conversion, stories of emigration and of corrupt politicians (Hereniko 1995: 146–49), augmenting the indigenous form with Western equipment and techniques.

Because Pacific cultural production, historically, was oral, full scripts from before the mid-20th century are very rare. On the island of Mangaia in the Cooks group, British missionary and folklorist William Wyatt Gill recorded a version of a *Pe'e Manuiri (Visitor's Song)* devised in c.1780 by a warrior named Tioi, which presented a satiric, indigenous view of Captain Cook's attempted landing on the island in 1777 (Gill 1880: 180–82). Another full scriptural record, *Te Reko no Tutepoganui, te Ariki ko te Moana (The Recitation/Drama of Tutepo[n]ganui, Lord of the Ocean)*, was documented in 1912 by French traveller and anthropologist A.C. Eugène Caillot on the island of Hikueru in the central Tuamotu archipelago, in what is now French Polynesia (Caillot 1912: 95–109). Dramatizing the story of the ocean lord Tutepoganui's journey ashore to search for two of his subjects, the whale and the turtle, who have been detained by the people of the land, the reko (talk, recitation) serves as an illuminating example of the meaningful interrelation between the sea and the land in Pacific performance, as well as varied intercultural exchanges and creative syntheses of pre- and post-European elements in theatrical composition. Beyond its formal commonalities with comic dramas produced in the Society Islands and the Cook Islands (Buck 1932: 203), the reko's conventions, subject matter and circulation highlight a range of indigenous mobilities. The ancestral presence of Tutepoganui, half-man and half-fish and legendary progenitor of the Tuamotuan people (Millaud 2012: np), reinforces the identity of the performers as people of the sea as well as of the land; while references to pan-Polynesian locations such as Ruahatu/Hawaiki,[3] and characters like the trickster-demigod Māui and the female voyager Hina, bind the play's local traditions to larger geographical and cosmological schemes. As a piece performed by pearl fishermen, the reko exemplifies how that networked marine industry provided the stimulus and sustenance for theatrical performance when hundreds of people from throughout the archipelago convened at pearl-diving islands (Luomala 1977: 133). Moreover, the spectacular mask worn by the actor playing Tutepoganui, created by craftspeople from Mangareva (625 miles from Hikueru), showcases trans-indigenous cultural traffic in the manufacture of theatrical properties.

Just as the early 20th-century Pacific saw the consolidation of many of the colonial projects established during the 18th and 19th centuries, the post-1960s period witnessed widespread decolonization initiatives throughout the region. These initiatives were accompanied by a new wave of scripted drama produced by Pacific playwrights who experimented with innovative syntheses of indigenous performance forms and Western theatrical frameworks and production contexts to produce works that spoke urgently to local concerns about belonging, social change and self-determination. Comprising plays in English, French, vernacular languages and local lingua francas, this corpus began to emerge across Oceania at approximately the same time. In the same year that Māori playwright Harry Dansey produced *Te Raukura* (1972) in Aotearoa/New Zealand, Maco Tevane inaugurated Tahitian popular theatre with his play *Te pe'ape'a hau 'ore o Papa Penu e o Mama Roro (The Incessant Disputes of Papa Penu and Mama Roro)* (1972). These works were coeval with the establishment of Kumu Kahua Theatre in Hawai'i (1971), the production of the first Fijian play, *Rachel* (1973), by Pio Manoa, and Georges Dobbelaere and Jean-Marie Tjibaou's *Kanaké* (1975) from New Caledonia. These came only a few years after the first scripted play from the Solomon Islands, Francis Bugotu's *This Man* (1969); the first published English-language plays from Papua New Guinea, Turuk Wabei's *Kulubob* and John Wills Kaniku's *Cry of the Cassowary* (both 1969); the first Guamanian play captured in a print medium, Linda Cruz's *White Lady on the Bridge of Maina* (1969); and the inaugural Tapati cultural festival on Rapa Nui/Easter Island (1969) (Looser 2014: 8; Saura 2012: 101).

Although these playwrights wrote within their own local traditions and directed their artistic work largely towards past and present social concerns in their own societies, their work was also enabled by broader regional endeavours. The establishment of the regional University of the South Pacific (1968), the South Pacific Creative Arts Society (1973) and the Festival of Pacific Arts (1972) were some of the literary and cultural enterprises that facilitated artistic connections between various

Pacific sites. The period since the 1970s has seen the flourishing of major Pacific playwrights and theatre-makers. In addition to the Māori and Pasifika playwrights based in Aotearoa/New Zealand and mentioned earlier in this chapter, this cohort includes Vilsoni Hereniko and Larry Thomas in Fiji; Henri Hiro, John Mairai, Jean-Marc Tera'ituatini Pambrun and Valérie Gobrait in Tahiti; Pierre Gope in New Caledonia; Peter Onedera in Guam; Wan Smolbag Theatre in Vanuatu; John Kolia, John Kasaipwalova and Nora Vagi Brash in Papua New Guinea; and Victoria Kneubuhl, Alani Apio and Tammy Haili'ōpua Baker in Hawai'i.

During the past generation, a key trend in Pacific theatrical performance has been a move beyond postcolonial plays focused on settler-indigenous concerns to encompass performances that explore transnational linkages and a positioning of indigeneity within a global milieu. This more recent output is also characterized by a diversification of form away from scripted dramas towards more integrated performance genres, greater collaboration between different island communities and increased international circulation of creative works, and an increasingly robust body of work in indigenous Pacific languages. In Hawai'i, for instance, the work of Hālau o Kekuhi, a hula hālau (school) that counts eight generations of kumu hula (hula masters) in their lineage (Edith Kanaka'ole Foundation), has pioneered the genre of Hawaiian dance theatre. Utilizing dance and chant drawn from hula genealogies, each performance is a recitation of the travels, challenges and triumphs of an ancestor or ancestral hula deity. The ensemble's first production, *Holo Mai Pele (Pele Travels)* (1995), exemplifies the relationship between land and sea through a dramatization of elemental forms. The epic narrative recounts the travels of the volcano deity Pele, her youngest sister Hi'iakaikapoliopele (Hi'iaka-in-the-bosom-of-Pele) and their clan from the Polynesian homeland of Kahiki. Crossing the South Pacific Ocean, the family brings religious practices and idols with them in search of a new home. After visiting and paying respect to their relatives on the Hawaiian islands of Kaua'i, O'ahu and Maui, they make their home at Halema'uma'u, a crater of Kīlauea volcano on the island of Hawai'i. The story also relates Hi'iaka's journey to fetch Pele's lover Lohi'au from the island of Kaua'i. The many dances and chants in the production honour Pele and Hi'iaka as patrons of the hula; the performances reveal Pele's supernatural abilities as a creator of land and a powerful matriarch, as well as Hi'iaka's role as a healer and source of inspiration (Kame'eleihiwa et al. 2001: 4–8).

In a similar vein, the works of Ka Hālau Hanakeaka (established in 1995) bring traditional Hawaiian stories to the stage via hana keaka, an amalgamation of customary performance forms and Western dramatic practice. Performed entirely in 'ōlelo Hawai'i (the Hawaiian language), Ka Hālau Hanakeaka's productions are based on oral tradition and 19th-century texts. The characters in the plays are ancestors and famous figures in Hawaiian history, some of whom were deified for their deeds. In addition to providing entertainment, the troupe's indigenous Hawaiian theatre aesthetic contributes to efforts to revitalize Kānaka Maoli (Native Hawaiian) language and culture. Several of Ka Hālau Hanakeaka's pieces have toured widely throughout the Hawaiian archipelago and Oceania, connecting with indigenous communities across the Pacific. The company's longest running show, *Kamapuaʻa* (*Hog-Child*, 2004–7), also adopts an epic structure, chronicling the journeys of Kamapuaʻa in 23 scenes as he searches for his mother, Hina, who abandoned him at birth. The play depicts the various transformative events in Kamapuaʻa's life – his travels across land and sea, battles with adversaries and his maturation from a puaʻa (hog) into a man – telling lesser-known stories of his compassion and leadership in the communities he served.

A significant phase in the evolution of hana keaka is the institutionalization of the practice at the University of Hawaiʻi at Mānoa. Established in 2014, the Hawaiian Theatre Program offers a Master in Fine Arts degree, advancing the study and analysis of indigenous Hawaiian theatre and training in both traditional and contemporary Hawaiian performance forms. The program has produced three full-length productions since its inception; the program's inaugural production *Lāʻieikawai* (2015), *Nā Kau a Hiʻiaka* (2017) and *ʻAuʻa ʻIa: Holding On* (2019). Both *Lāʻieikawai* and *Nā Kau a Hiʻiaka* were constructed from oral tradition and 19th-century Hawaiian literature. *ʻAuʻa ʻIa: Holding On* is revolutionary in the field of hana keaka because it tells a modern story set in 2019. The play follows four Kanaka Maoli university students who interact with their ancestors via archival research, leading them to engage and interrogate pivotal moments in Hawaiʻi's history. The students tackle issues of identity, religion and politics, finding resilience in the practice of aloha ʻāina (patriotism/love for the land), which decrypts what it means to be Kanaka Maoli in contemporary times. Through the support of Ka Hālau Hanakeaka and Haleleʻa Arts Foundation, these university productions have toured the Hawaiian archipelago, the continental United States and Aotearoa/New Zealand.

A very different performance style is expressed in the work of MAU dance theatre, led by Samoan artist and choreographer Lemi Ponifasio and based in Aotearoa. Founded in 1995, MAU (named after the 1908 Samoan independence movement and meaning "vision," "revelation," "truth" or "my point of view") consists of a shifting group of artists of various Pacific heritages, and is one of the region's most prolific and internationally recognized dance and theatre companies, featuring regularly at major theatres and festivals worldwide. Ponifasio's avant-garde approach merges Pacific ritual and performance traditions with contemporary dance practices, and favours a monochromatic visual scheme imbued with abstract symbolism and non-linear chronology, presenting images and ceremonies that aim to bring audiences to new states of awareness. MAU performances engage profound and serious subjects, such as the social and environmental impact of colonization in *Paradise* (2003); motifs of loss, mourning and renewal in *Requiem* (2006); state power, refugees and human rights in *Tempest: Without a Body* (2007); the mutable and transformative character of the city in *Le Savali* (2011); the threat of pollution and global warming in *Birds With Skymirrors* (2010); and panoptical surveillance in *The Crimson House* (2014). As a corpus, MAU's work recasts prevailing notions of "Pacific performance" both in terms of its aesthetic character and its role in engaging issues of global concern.

Theatre-maker Nina Nawalowalo, who is of Fijian and British descent, also takes a coalitional approach to creating Pacific performance. Nawalowalo's company The Conch has developed an international reputation for its striking visual imagery that merges dance, puppetry and stage illusionism into a lush and layered mise-en-scène. Of especial note are Nawalowalo's cross-cultural collaborations with women from various parts of Oceania, with a particular emphasis on employing theatre for social change. In projects like *Vula* (2002), which celebrates the rapport between Pacific women and the sea; *Stages of Change* (2013–14), which uses theatre as a vehicle to help reduce domestic abuse of women in the Solomon Islands; and *Marama* (2016), in which female performers from Aotearoa, Fiji, Solomon Islands, Sāmoa and Kiribati choreograph a haunting protest against deforestation, Nawalowalo poses pressing questions about the relationships between female embodiment, landscape and violence in the Pacific region.

The Oceania Centre for Arts, Culture and Pacific Studies at the University of the South Pacific in Fiji is an important artistic initiative presently engaged in re-sculpting the profile of contemporary indigenous performance in the Pacific Islands. Founded in 1997 by Tongan scholar Epeli Hau'ofa, the centre was conceived as a creative extension of Hau'ofa's compelling vision of Oceania as an interconnected "sea of islands" – a concept devised as a counter to belittling Western views of the Pacific as "islands in a far sea" (2008a: 31). Implicit in Hau'ofa's ideal of unity-in-diversity is an acknowledgement of, and response to, the multiple legacies of conflict and disjuncture that have also shaped and refracted the Pacific region. Taking the sea's motion and relationality as an artistic compass, the centre has sought to create works that cut across the Pacific's imposed geopolitical boundaries, that emphasize co-operation, that blend customary and contemporary Oceanic performance forms with a range of international influences, and that travel to connect with maritime peoples in other parts of the world (Hau'ofa 2008b: 86–7, 92–3).

Since Hau'ofa's death in 2009, the centre has flourished under the artistic directorship of Rotuman playwright and filmmaker Vilsoni Hereniko, who, together with Hawaiian choreographer Peter Rockford Espiritu and Samoan composer Igelese Ete, has pioneered a series of "music-dance-dramas" with an experimental Oceanian fusion aesthetic. *Vaka: The Birth of a Seer* (2012) and *Drua: The Wave of Fire* (2012) are two related works that explore the historical assemblage and inter-island journeys of the drua, the Fijian long-distance voyaging canoe, underscoring through the form and content of the performances the social networks that have connected Fiji to multiple communities throughout central Oceania. Their subsequent show, *Moana: The Rising of the Sea* (2013/15), approaches the ocean from a different angle by dramatizing the urgent threat to island communities posed by climate-induced sea level rise, and in its Oceanic and European tours, the performance has served as an exigent medium of advocacy and appeal. In combining modes of theatricality that are locally specific and regionally coherent, rooted and routed, the Oceania Centre expresses an artistic and political solidarity that seeks to transcend histories of division and dissension and to perform a strategic "Oceanian" identity.

Conclusion

Performance has occupied, and continues to occupy, a central place in the social and political lives of the peoples indigenous to the Pacific, Australia and Aotearoa. These histories of practice have been forged within heterogeneous geographies, epistemologies and cultural exchanges, yet there are commonalities that bind these activities across Oceania's vast, networked domain. Performers across the region have drawn on performance's multivalent vocabularies to respond strategically to the precariousness wrought by colonial intervention; to seek communion with a spiritual realm that deeply infuses the mundane world; to consolidate, communicate and question cultural norms and customs; and to contribute actively to the construction of existing and emerging communities, both local and international. As indigenous performers from Australia, Aotearoa and the Pacific Islands take an increasingly prominent place on the world stage, actively charting their own itineraries and negotiating their own transactions, their work testifies to the ongoing dynamism of indigenous cultures in the 21st century.

Notes

1 The examples of Yolngu performances are drawn from and discussed in more detail in Maryrose Casey. 2014. 'Making Fun of Trauma: Laughing at Racialised Violence,' *Performing Ethos: International Journal of Ethics in Theatre and Performance*, 4(1): 9–23; Maryrose Casey. 2012. *Telling Stories: Aboriginal & Torres Strait Islander Performance*. Melbourne: Australian Scholarly Publishing; Maryrose Casey. 2011. 'Performing for Aboriginal Life and Culture: Aboriginal Theatre and *Ngurrumilmarrmiriyu*,' *ADS*, 59: 53–68.
2 "Caramello" is a milk chocolate bar with a caramel centre.
3 A sacred place of origin and return for many societies across Oceania. Ruahatu is the Tuamotuan name for Hawaiki.

References

Baker, Tammy Haili'ōpua. 2019. 'The Development and Function of Hana Keaka (Hawaiian-Medium Theatre): A Tool for the Empowering Kanaka Maoli Consciousness,' PhD thesis, Hamilton, New Zealand: The University of Waikato.

Baker, Tammy Haili'ōpua, Sharon Mazer and Diana Looser. 2016. '"The Vessel Will Embrace Us": Contemporary Pacific Voyaging in Oceanic Theatre,' *Performance Research*, 21(2): 40–49.

Balme, Christopher B. 1999. *Decolonizing the Stage: Theatrical Syncretism and Post-Colonial Drama*. Oxford: Oxford University Press.

Berndt, Ronald M. and Catherine H. Berndt. 1965. *The World of the First Australians; An Introduction to the Traditional Life of the Australian Aborigines*. Sydney: Ure Smith, (First impression 1964) Second Impression.

Buck, Peter (Te Rangi Hīroa). 1932. *Ethnology of Manihiki and Rakahanga*. Honolulu: Bishop Museum.

Caillot, A.-C. Eugène. 1912. *Mythes, Légendes et Traditions des Polynésiens*. Paris: Ernest Leroux.

Dale, Judith. 1997. '"On the Beach": Questions of Identity in Recent Maori Drama,' *Illusions*, 26: 39–42.

Edith Kanaka'ole Foundation. www.edithkanakaolefoundation.org/ (accessed 25 July 2016).

Foley, Kathy. 1993. 'Oceania,' in James Brandon (Ed.), *The Cambridge Guide to Asian Theatre*, pp. 203–210. Cambridge: Cambridge University Press.

Gill, William Wyatt. 1880. *Historical Sketches of Savage Life in Polynesia: With Illustrative Clan Songs*. Wellington: George Didsbury.

Goodall, Adam. 2016. '"I am more important than Shakespeare": Ten Moments in Wellington Theatre,' *The Pantograph Punch*. https://www.pantograph-punch.com/post/ten_moments_wellington_theatre_2016 (accessed 24 April 2020).

Hau'ofa, Epeli. 2008a. 'Our Sea of Islands,' in *We Are the Ocean: Selected Works*, pp. 27–40. Honolulu: University of Hawai'i Press.

Hau'ofa, Epeli. 2008b. 'Our Place Within: Foundations for a Creative Oceania,' in *We Are the Ocean: Selected Works*, pp. 80–93. Honolulu: University of Hawai'i Press.

Hereniko, Vilsoni. 1994. 'Clowning as Political Commentary: Polynesia, Then and Now,' *The Contemporary Pacific*, 6(1): 1–28.

Hereniko, Vilsoni. 1995. *Woven Gods: Female Clowns and Power in Rotuma*. Honolulu: University of Hawai'i Press.

Hyland, Nicola. 2015. 'Beyoncé's Response (Eh?): Feeling the Ihi of Spontaneous Haka Performance in Aotearoa/New Zealand,' *TDR: The Drama Review*, 59(1): 67–82.

Kame'eleihiwa, L., P.K. Kanahele-Kanaka'ole and N. Kanaka'ole. 2001. *Holo Mai Pele Educator's Guide*. International Cultural Programing and Pacific Islanders in Communication.

Kouka, Hone. 1999. 'Introduction,' in Hone Kouka (Ed.), *Ta Matou Mangai: Three Plays of the 1990s*. Wellington: Victoria University Press.

Looser, Diana. 2011. 'A Piece "More Curious Than All the Rest": Re-Encountering Pre-Colonial Pacific Island Theatre, 1769–1855,' *Theatre Journal*, 63(4): 521–540.

Looser, Diana. 2014. *Remaking Pacific Pasts: History, Memory, and Identity in Contemporary Theater from Oceania*. Honolulu: University of Hawai'i Press.

Luomala, Katharine. 1977. 'Post-European Central Polynesian Head Masks and Puppet-Marionette Heads,' *Asian Perspectives*, 20(1): 130–171.

Maufort, Marc. 2003. *Transgressive Itineraries: Postcolonial Hybridizations of Dramatic Realism*. Brussels: Peter Lang.

Maunder, Paul. 2013. *Rebellious Mirrors: Community-Based Theatre in Aotearoa/New Zealand*. Christchurch: Canterbury University Press.

Mead, Hirini Moko. 2003. *Tikanga Māori: Living by Māori Values*. Wellington: Huia.

Millaud, Hiriata. 2012. 'Tūtepoganui,' Flyer produced for the Assembly of French Polynesia, Papeete, Tahiti. Not paginated.

Oliver, Douglas. 1974. *Ancient Tahitian Society*, 3 Vols. Honolulu: University of Hawai'i Press.

Potiki, Roma. 1992. 'Confirming Identity and Telling the Stories: A Woman's Perspective on Māori Theatre,' in Rosemary Du Plessis (Ed.), *Feminist Voices: Women's Studies Texts for Aotearoa/New Zealand*, pp. 153–162. Auckland: Oxford University Press.

Royal, Te Ahukaramū Charles. 2007. 'Ōrotokare: Towards a New Model for Indigenous Theatre and Performing Arts,' in Marc Maufort and David O'Donnell (Eds.), *Performing Aotearoa: New Zealand Theatre and Drama in an Age of Transition*, pp. 193–208. Brussels: Peter Lang.

Royal, Te Ahukaramū Charles. www.orotokare.org.nz/ (accessed 11 July 2016).

Samasoni, Samson. 1986. 'Maori and Pacific Island Theatre in New Zealand – Past and Future,' *Act*, 11(2): 15–16.

Saura, Bruno. 2012. *Tahiti Mā'ohi: Culture, Identité, Religion et Nationalisme en Polynésie Française*. Tahiti: Au Vent des Îles.

Sinavaiana, Caroline. 1992. 'Where the Spirits Laugh Last: Comic Theatre in Samoa,' in William E. Mitchell (Ed.), *Clowning as Critical Practice: Performance Humor in the South Pacific*, pp. 192–218. Pittsburgh: University of Pittsburgh Press.

Tamisari, Franca. 2000. 'Knowing the Country, Holding the Law': Yolngu Dance Performance in North-eastern Arnhem Land,' in Culture, Neale, Margo, Sylvia Kleinert and Robyne Bancroft (Eds.), *The Oxford Companion to Aboriginal Art and Melbourne*, pp. 146–152. New York: Oxford University Press.

Teaiwa, Katerina M. 2005. 'Our Sea of Phosphate: The Diaspora of Ocean Island,' in Graham Harvey and Charles D. Thompson Jr. (Eds.), *Indigenous Diasporas and Dislocations*, pp. 169–191. Aldershot: Ashgate.

Te Punga Somerville, Alice. 2012. *Once Were Pacific: Māori Connections to Oceania*. Minneapolis: University of Minnesota Press.

Warner, William Lloyd. 1937. *A Black Civilization: A Social Study of an Australian Tribe*. New York: Harper and Bros.

Werry, Margaret. 2011. *The Tourist State: Performing Leisure, Liberalism and Race in New Zealand*. Minneapolis: University of Minnesota Press.

Yothu Yindi Foundation. 2016. 'About Garma,' www.yyf.com.au/pages/?ParentPageID=116&PageID=117 (accessed 1 July 2016).

5

"THEORY COMING THROUGH STORY"

Indigenous knowledges and Western academia

Hartmut Lutz

A few years ago, the German newspaper *Süddeutsche Zeitung* carried a small article by Swiss-Canadian author Bernadette Calonego entitled "Sanfte Wölfe" (gentle wolves). She reports that biology professor Chris Darimont of Simon Fraser University found out that certain wolves inhabiting islands along the coast of British Columbia were thriving on seafood and had developed a gentler social behaviour than their more aggressive relatives on the mainland. In its last paragraph, the article mentions that Heiltsuk (Bella Bella) hunter Chester Starr had alerted professor Darimont to this difference between "coastal wolves" and "timber wolves" as a phenomenon which Aboriginal peoples in BC had known for a long time. The article concludes: "So now the attentive observations by Indigenous people have found a scientific confirmation by Darimont's studies."[1] This is just one example of how Western scientists are beginning to use Aboriginal Traditional Ecological Knowledge (TEK). But why is it that they seem to think that indigenous knowledge needs to be accredited by Western science? Why do they feel that expert knowledge, which has been gained empirically over extended periods of observation and interaction with nature, have to be corroborated by a Western scientist's field studies? These are the questions I shall try to find answers for in this chapter.

But first of all, following a widespread indigenous protocol, I have to begin this by locating – not positioning – myself in relation to the topic that I am trying to address.

Locating myself

I was born in April 1945 in a small town in Northern Germany that had then doubled its inhabitants due to the influx of displaced persons, expellees and refugees from Eastern Central Europe, like my own family. I was born exactly three months after the liberation of Auschwitz concentration camp by Russian troops, and 12 days before World War II ended the German Nazi terror in Europe. My family roots stretch along the Baltic rim from Schleswig-Holstein, Hamburg and Pomerania to what was formerly East Prussia. I grew up in a mainly matriarchal family, since my uncles had not returned from the war and my father died before I was five, so that my grandfather, a retired East-Prussian schoolteacher, became my mentor and role model. He introduced me to "Indianer" or Indians, so that in my childhood and youth I was exposed to the widespread German romantic infatuation with "Indianer" and developed a lasting interest in indigenous North America. After a PhD in English literature (Lutz 1975), I took up the old interest again with my habilitation (Lutz 1985), and I have been involved in Native American studies and later Canadian First Nations, Métis and Inuit studies for over four decades. My research was first culturally self-reflective, investigating which historical influences shaped our epistemological framing of "Indianer" (Lutz 1985) and trying to understand the phenomenon I came to call "Deutsche Indianertümelei" or "German Indianthusiasm" (Lutz 2003; Lutz et al. 2020). I was intrigued by the fact that a nation steeped so deeply in racism like Germany should romanticize peoples so far away from us. After that, besides teaching and researching American and Canadian literatures in general, I began to read, teach and publish about indigenous literatures and cultures. And I was fortunate, because in the process I learned from Aboriginal teachers, won guest professorships at indigenous universities and departments, and I also enjoyed repeated research visits to other native studies centres, including the En'Owkin Center at Penticton on unceded Syilx Okanagan territory in present day British Columbia.

Looking back at my experiences of four decades in indigenous studies, I feel truly blessed, and I am deeply grateful, because my journey gave me the incredible privilege and joy to learn from indigenous researchers, authors, editors, teachers, students and elders. In the process, I often encountered "connecting moments," in which things fell into place in such remarkable ways that my Western rationalist self gradually began to accept the notion that, indeed, things are all connected. This was a hard process for a Leftist like me, who fancied himself embarked on the "Long March through the institutions" and looked at the world with a Marxist frame of perception. But a few years ago in Margaret Kovach's wonderful study *Indigenous Methodologies* (2009: 182), I stumbled across a passage on "connecting moments" that I can fully empathize with, and I quote:

> I still do not understand these experiences fully. I have tried to analyze, theorize, and rationalize, but there are some things that you cannot deconstruct. As an Elder said, some knowledges you cannot know. What I am left with is an acceptance that these knowings matter to me inwardly, and because I allowed them they impacted my research path in a good way.

Following such thoughts and in writing this chapter, I consulted the works by a number of indigenous researchers like Jeanette Armstrong, Richard Atleo, Marie Battiste, Vine Deloria, the late Jo-Anne Episkenew, the late Jack Forbes, Margaret

Kovach, Rauna Kuokkanen, Neil McLeod, Mary Simon, Karla Jessen Williamson and Shawn Wilson, as well as non-indigenous scholars in native studies, like Keith Basso and Colin Calloway, and European scientists and philosophers.

Based on this background, I shall address the following four questions:

1   Why have we as Europeans or Westerners apparently been unable to listen to and learn from indigenous knowledges?
2   What is it that we seem to have failed to learn from indigenous knowledges?
3   Why are indigenous knowledges of paramount interest to us today?
4   Are there bridges to build relationships?

1 "Why have we as Europeans or Westerners apparently been unable to listen to and learn from indigenous knowledges?"

The European inability to learn from Aboriginal American epistemologies is puzzling, because, after all, Europeans have taken so much material wealth and technological know-how in what Alfred W. Crosby in 1972 called the *"Columbian Exchange."* This exchange profoundly altered both the Americas and Europe, and the Atlantic became a *"Red Atlantic,"* as Cherokee scholar Jace Weaver so aptly called it more recently (2014), thereby echoing Paul Gilroy's foundational 1993 study of the *Black Atlantic*. Non-indigenous scholars like Warren Lowes (1986), Jack Weatherford (1988, 1991) and Ronald Wright (1992) have described the fundamental transfer of material wealth and agricultural practices from the Americas to Europe which facilitated the astounding demographic and economic growth of the post-Columbian West (Lutz 2013: 137–40) and formed the nutritional base for the Industrial Revolution in detail. The Powhatan and Lenape ethnohistorian Jack D. Forbes even investigated *The American Discovery of Europe* (2007).

Here, I am looking at the Columbian exchange again, not at material wealth and technologies, but to find out why indigenous epistemologies were not included in the transfer. Clearly, this is not the fault of indigenous teachers, because for centuries there have been many deliberate attempts by Aboriginal knowledge keepers to instruct settlers and newcomers in their ways, but the Europeans would never listen. It is not within the scope of this chapter to go into such teaching attempts in detail, but believe me, there are many, and the European inability to listen to First Nations is notorious. In 1970, Lakota lawyer and philosopher Vine Deloria published his book *We Talk, You Listen*, in which he demanded that after centuries of one-way communication between Europeans talking to, or about, and instead of Native Americans, the process be reversed. In 1976, the Bavarian journalist Claus Biegert published (together with Carl-Ludwig Reichert) a translation of Vine Deloria's *We Talk, You Listen*, but chose the German title *"Nur Stämme werden überleben"* (Only Tribes Will Survive), thus arguing for re-indigenization as a sustainable way of life. I shall return to Biegert's statement later.

Colonialism/racism

One possible answer to the question "Why have Europeans or Westerners been so un-enabled to listen and learn from indigenous knowledges?" seems for me to reside in the fact that our European relationship to indigenous cultures is profoundly colonial – even in those countries which never had any colonies in North America. A colonialist mind-set is racist. It denigrates and dehumanizes the colonial objects, making it easier for the colonizer to abuse, exploit or even kill the subalterns. The colonial relationship is a form of structural violence as defined by the Norwegian peace researcher Johan Galtung.[2] It victimizes the colonized, and at the same time stunts the colonizer's intellect and totally blocks his capacity to accept indigenous epistemologies. An "Indianthusiast" who has learned to expect First Nations people to be feathered, dancing, fighting and buffalo hunting *Indianer* is *un*-enabled today to meet indigenous persons as complex human beings and academic researchers. Inuit scholar Karla Jessen Williamson says much the same about our take on "Eskimos":

> A substantial amount of the writing about the Eskimos omitted real Inuit perspectives and was uncritically predicated upon assumptions directly stemming from Eurocentric, paternalistic, patronizing and belittling paradigms; it was, at the very least, colonialist. Furthermore, the Christian doctrine played a great role in discounting other ways of being.
>
> *(2000: 127)*

Christianity

Obviously, monotheism, and in the European case, Christianity, has a lot to answer for when it comes to our inability to learn from indigenous knowledges. A monotheist axiom claims that there is only one true god and only one truth about the world. Most churches seem to insist that there is only one correct way of worshipping and that there is only one religious Truth, which they hold. Such epistemological hubris and narrow-mindedness foreclose listening to and learning from indigenous knowledges with an open heart and mind – otherwise, I am certain, we would have learned about more conversions going in the other direction.

Enlightenment

The Enlightenment comes to mind as another mental obstacle to learning from indigenous knowledges. Now, I have a very hard time in admitting that to myself, because it makes me feel a bit like a traitor to the epistemological place I come from, and to the emancipatory impact the Cartesian shift entailed for Europeans. I remember when, as a high school student, I first heard the Cartesian notion *"cogito, ergo sum"* (I think, therefore I am). I then thought, "Wow! How true!" and I was fascinated by the existentialist radicalism of this axiom. But after four decades of learning in indigenous studies, I am not so certain any more. Taken literally (and deliberately out of its semantic context), *"cogito, ergo sum"* is a statement that is entirely isolationist and shockingly solipsistic. It constructs the thinking subject as removed from any relations with the surrounding world, from time or place, from social relations and the ecosystem, and even from his or her own physical being. The *"ego"* in *cogito ergo sum* needs no body (nobody!), no land, no emotions, no others, regardless of whether they are finned, winged, scaled, mineral, rooted, four legged or human. Wouldn't statements like "I have a mother, therefore I am"; or "I eat and defecate, and therefore I am"; or "I live on this place on Earth, therefore I am" be equally pertinent, less egocentric and certainly more life sustaining? The exquisite Cartesian logic and rationality of the enlightenment estranges us from indigenous knowledges.

For Aboriginal scholars, the Enlightenment's complicity is all too clear, as Jo-Ann Episkenew put it poignantly and tongue-in-cheek in her illuminating study *Taking Back our Spirits* (2006: 1):

> In my second year as an undergraduate student, I had an epiphany. I realized that all knowledge worth knowing – or more specifically, knowledge that my university considered worth teaching – was created by Greeks, appropriated by the Romans, disseminated throughout western Europe, and through colonialism made its way to the rest of the people of the world, who apparently were sitting on their thumbs waiting for enlightenment.

The Sami scholar Rauna Kuokkanen, in her immensely well-researched and theorized doctoral dissertation *Reshaping the University: Responsibility, Indigenous Epistemes, and the Logic of the Gift* (2007: 6), aims her critique at the heart of Western epistemology, when she contends:

> The empiricism of the Enlightenment marked a radical break from participatory, respectful relations with the world. The Cartesian view of the world became characterized by hyperseparation as well as by the fantasy that the world can be measured.

I shall return to this "hyperseparation" as scientific method later.

Literacy vs. orality

A fourth obstacle in our reception of indigenous knowledges is both epistemological and methodological, contingent on modes of knowledge acquisition and dissemination.

A paramount essential in Western science is literacy. Western academia – and my focus here is in philology and cultural studies – privileges printed texts presenting heuristic conclusions in impersonal language, substantiated by massive readings of secondary sources – and that is fine, and particularly important in Europe.

Indigenous epistemologies vary from nation to nation, but all the indigenous researchers which I have consulted so far – Inuit, Sami, First Nations, Métis and Maori – seem to share the methodologies and axiology of the oral traditions which lie at the heart of indigenous cultures. As early as 1991, Lee Maracle explained that indigenous knowledge is "Theory Coming Through Story" (172). Indigenous researchers tend to privilege emploted story over abstract formula, experiences over theoretical learning and orality over literacy. Besides, and this seems increasingly important, indigenous sciences in oral traditions are fluid, malleable and relational, not frozen into letters. These are characteristics which our Western academia has a hard time to recognize, accommodate or validate, let alone accept.[3]

2 "What is it that we seem to have failed to learn from indigenous knowledges?"

Relationality, accountability and what, for the lack of any adequate or more established term, I here call "land embeddedness" are complexly interconnected, but again, I'll try to present them consecutively.

Relationality

One of the first phrases anybody approaching indigenous North American cultural practices will hear is "All My Relations" – a spiritual formula that translates the Lakota phrase "Mitakuye Oyasin,"[4] which expresses "a tribal sense of relation to all being" (Lincoln 1983: 2), and is central to indigenous epistemology and axiology. In his 1973 study *God Is Red*, Lakota scholar Vine Deloria says that even the "possibility of conceiving of an individual alone in a tribal religious sense is ridiculous" and being isolated would constitute a "terrifying loss of identity" (Deloria 1973: 201). More recently, Bonita Lawrence explained that:

> For Native people, individual identity is always being negotiated *in relation to* collective identity, and *in the face of* an external, colonizing society. Bodies of law defining and controlling Indianness have for years distorted and disrupted older Indigenous ways of identifying the self in relation not only to collective identity but also to the land.
>
> *(2003: 4; emphasis in original)*

And a year later, Nu-cha-nulth scholar Umeek or Richard Atleo explained: "In the Nuu-cha-nulth worldview it is unnatural, and equivalent to death and destruction, for any person to be isolated from family or community" (Atleo 2004: 27).[5]

Individualism and egocentrism run counter to the relational worldview and ethics by which Aboriginal people traditionally position themselves in relation to, and as part of, all of creation, not as masters of nature but as members of it, on equal terms with other forms of life, all of whom must and do network together to sustain life on Earth. Goodness invests in sustaining life, evil in its destruction.

This transcultural Aboriginal episteme informs indigenous scholarship. Based on sharing and collectivity, it respects the individual not as self-defining *ego*, but as constituted by an infinite web of spatial, physical, social, psychological, spiritual and mental relations, without whom the individual could not and indeed, does not, exist. Cree scholar Shawn Wilson contends:

> Indigenous research . . . is the knowing and respectful reinforcement that all things are related and connected
>
> *(2008: 60)*

and he explains later:

> An Indigenous paradigm comes from the foundational belief that knowledge is relational. Knowledge is shared with all of creation. It is not just interpersonal relationships, not just with the research subjects I may be working with, but it is a relationship with all of creation. It is with the cosmos, it is with the animals, with the plants, with the earth that we share this knowledge. Who cares about those ontologies? It's not the realities in and of themselves that are important; it is the relationship that I share with reality.
>
> *(2008: 91–2)*

In the material realm, relationality is manifest in what Sami scholar Rauna Kuok-kanen in the subtitle of her study referred to as the *Logic of the Gift* and described in detail as "the gift economy" (2007: 23f.). Richard Atleo identifies "[g]iving as a general community practice" and an "economically feasible principle" (2011: 39). A gift economy cherishes giving as much as receiving, not in the sense of bartering or exchange, because a gift expecting a return is not a present given but a trade, but giving as an essential mode of interaction. It seems modelled on the boundless generosity of Mother Earth herself, who has nourished and supported us all (and our relations) since life began.

Wilson also states that in his understanding "An Indigenous research paradigm is relational and maintains relational accountability" (2008: 71).

Accountability in orality

More so than in literate cultures where lies, plagiarisms, misquotations or other fraud can be exposed and corrected by objective and impersonal research, the recipients of knowledge in oral cultures have to depend on the wisdom and integrity of the one who provides the information, the more precariously so, because oral stories and knowledges live and die with their keepers, and are therefore always only "one generation from extinction" (Johnston 1990: 10). Each speaker is responsible for the truthfulness and the lasting effects of her own words, which, once she has spoken them, she cannot call back, burn, delete or send through the shredder. The speaker is accountable in what the Cree storyteller and knowledge keeper Alexander Wolf called "a copyright system based on trust" (1988: xiv). Thus, orality needs and does have an inbuilt ethics that I would like to call "*Wahrhaftigkeit*" in German, because "*Der Sprecher haftet für die Wahrheit seiner Worte*" – the speaker is liable for the truth of his words – and that truth clings to (*haftet*) and is attached to the speaker's life and honour, even at the risk of penalization (*Haftung*). Cree scholar Margaret Kovach puts it like this: "It is about standing behind one's words and recognizing collective protocol, that one is accountable for one's words" (2009: 148).

In Western academia, we traditionally shirk personal exposure and try to hide idiosyncrasies and experiential subjectivity by striving for "objectivity" and using "neutral" language. Fortunately, this denial of individual experience has gradually somewhat changed since feminist scholars claimed exposing the political in the personal, and the personal in the political, thus validating reflected subjectivity, experiential learning and the emotional. In the many speeches by Aboriginal orators I have listened to, and in the indigenous research studies I have read, the speakers or writers usually begin by locating themselves – as I did in the beginning of this chapter – in relation to her or his origins, and with regard to the research and the informants, elders and colleagues who have helped them along, not to self-indulge or draw attention to their own persons, but to give credit to the participants in the web of their learning processes. This protocol may be compared to our bibliographies at the end of scholarly studies, which also represent a kind of scholarly lineage and make the author accountable to the community of scholars trained in his or her language.

Land embeddedness

Inuit scholar Karla Jessen Williamson writes about the Inuit relationship to *nuna*, the land:

> on our land we found peace, contentment, and a good life. Obviously, this can only be gained by a deep understanding of the reciprocal relationship with the land and its riches. For us the land is a soul enriching totality, which by its own integrity has allowed human existence. The allowing of life on *nuna* is premised by a strong sense of affinity with all other beings. A relationship with the land, the animals, and their souls has assured the Inuit a sustainable way of life over the last four or five millennia. This relationship has given us a strong sense of identity, one solidly bonded with the land. The sense of belonging to the land of our birth remains remarkably significant and very few Inuit have contested this by moving away from their place of birth.
>
> *(2000: 127–28)*

Aboriginal scholars seem to agree that belonging to specific places in the land constitutes the most important paradigm of indigenous ethnic identity. I think that it is by their millennial trans-generational collective relationship with the land – something we don't have in Europe, due to wars and ethnic cleansings – and by their observance of the obligations which that relationship entails, that indigenous scholars and elders tend to explain an indigenous episteme. First Nations creation stories, for example, tend to establish geographic relationality by stressing life's embeddedness in the land and its ecosystem, thus fostering human ecological accountability.

Okanagan scholar Jeannette Armstrong focused her doctoral thesis on the Syilx-Okanagan story of "How Food Was Given,"[6] a traditional *captik* that teaches us that those processes which facilitated the beginnings of human life on Earth are not singular acts by an omnipotent creator, but rather the outcomes of a collective process of interdependent actions by a network of players whose wisdom is based on, and conveys to others, their learning from their experiences of living with the land. The "message" of stories like this one, to put it in a more abstract Western format, is that humans cannot exist vis-à-vis but only as part of and in relation to an ecosystem, and it is therefore their inescapable obligation to keep it intact.

And this realization brings us to the third question.

3 "Why are indigenous knowledges of paramount importance to us today?"

Jeannette Armstrong once said that her father told her the land is a teacher, and she explained in individual essays, as well as in her doctoral dissertation, how during millennia of living and flourishing in the same region her Syilx Okanagan people developed a vast and comprehensive, and yet nuanced and detailed, understanding of their regional history and ecosystem. This empirical knowledge came to constitute their very being as an indigenous people. Their land-gained knowledge and cultural and physical land-embeddedness is given voice in stories, and they must be considered at least on par with any scientific ecological knowledge gained by hard-core Western empiricism expressed in scientific formula.

But land is not only a teacher to understand its own ecosystem. Land is also an episteme for learning, structuring and understanding history. Specific mountains, lakes or rocks provide mnemonic formations, inscribed by experiences and events as chronotopes (Basso 1996: 62) and palimpsests (Lutz 2004: 176) which constitute indigenous historiography not in a linear sequence but within a place-related structure. Rather than emploting historical events chronologically as a retrospective teleology, the indigenous cultures I learned about tend to see history as structured within a network of relations tied to places, as non-indigenous researchers like Basso, Nabokov (2002) and Calloway (2003) show in their respective studies.

I have written about this elsewhere, but let me just share with you one example, where I came to perceive history in a totally different way while learning from an indigenous scholar. We tend to say "we see the future before us" and "leave the past behind." My then colleague at the Native American Studies Department of Dartmouth College in Hanover, New Hampshire, the Nez Percé linguist and historian Dennis Runnels, saw this as a heuristic fallacy. He explained in a personal conversation in the fall of 2001:

> Europeans believe in progress. You say you leave the past behind, you see the future, and you move on into the future. In our understanding that's a fallacy. The past is not behind! The past is right before us, right under us. We stand on the bones of our ancestors, on the bodies of plants and animals that went before. Even the buildings we see right in front of us are from the past. Everything we see is history. It is from the past. It's right there in front of us. But: the future? The future is behind our backs, unseen. So, we don't believe the past is behind us, and the future before us. Quite to the contrary, the past is right before us. Everything, all the history, is in the land. We walk into the future going backwards, while looking at the past receding from us.
>
> *(Runnels 2001)*

Often, our daily language contains knowledge which we may not even be aware of when using it. Such seems the case when in English we say "history takes place" (and not time), or likewise in German, when we say *"ein Ereignis findet statt"* (an event takes place) – in both cases, the languages on the lexicological level seem to insist on a semantic that events are located (sic) at a geographical space, not at an abstract point in time. That perception literally puts history "in its place."

If Western science ever matures to learn from indigenous epistemes, academia/ we will have to respect and utilize Aboriginal stories and rituals on a par with the periodic system, because both *captik* and the periodic table address the same complexity called nature, as Jeannette Armstrong explains in her thesis:

> Science is the human ability to observe, understand and explain nature. Whether through the use of microscope, quantum or abstract theory, the fact remains that *science is nature's intelligence being translated into the human mind*. Organizing what appears as chaos into cognizant patterns is no less critical to human intelligence whether through scientific formulae or through words. The fundamental difference between the two as method is that *words constructed into story provide open access to societal members through intellectual and emotional intelligence* while access to science is limited to those schooled in its language.
>
> *(2009: 330f., my italics)*

Armstrong concludes her doctoral dissertation by stating that to halt and heal the further destruction of all our lives, we need to "re-indigenize" – and her definition of indigeneity is based on learning and place, not race. She says about the role of indigenous scholars:

> Clearly, necessary towards re-indigenization is the need for Indigenous scholars to contribute the level of quality research and dialogue required to

reconstruct into contemporary context the underlying precepts of Indigeneity which foster strong environmental ethics common to Indigenous peoples and now largely absent in non-Indigenous society.

(2009: 323)

But re-indigenization does not mean that Europeans must return to the Stone Age, but rather to develop an ethics and an axiology of survival.

Nowhere in the world does the need to heed indigenous knowledges seem more obvious and more pressing than in the Arctic (Battarbee and Fossum 2014; Knopf forthcoming). Mary Simon, director of Tapriirisat Kanatami, called Arctic Inuit people "the 'canary in the mineshaft' with respect to the regionalized impact of global climate change" (2011: 884), and she explains:

> We have the vocation to be the frontline environmental watchdogs and police. This does not make us hostile to new forms of development or locked into a kind of paralyzing nostalgia for the days of old. It does, however, make us a critical force in ensuring that the development of Arctic resources is done in ways that are measured, informed, transparent, and accountable, and that make the wellbeing and cultural continuity of Inuit necessary and central considerations.
>
> *(2011: 889–90)*

Indigenous knowledges provide a guiding paradigm to halt the ongoing ecocide, and indigenous scholars have known this fact for a long time. Indigenous and non-indigenous scholars in native literary studies have tried again and again to convey this realization to Western academia. In her pioneering book on Aboriginal literatures as seen from a German immigrant Canadian perspective, *Travelling Knowledges*, the late Renate Eigenbrod (2005) clearly remarked that we need a new epistemology and ethics when approaching indigenous literatures and cultures, and by extension, I would conclude that a radically altered ethics is needed if we are to survive on this planet together. But, given the fact that Christian axiology has failed so abysmally in its 2,000-year effort to make way for goodness, I am not too optimistic. Yet I know that the ethics and epistemology of re-indigenization are direly needed to unsettle the globalized rampage of unleashed capitalist greed. In my conclusion to Jack D. Forbes' *Columbus und andere Kannibalen*, I wrote the following more than 20 years ago – and there is nothing new I can add today:

> The cannibalism of Western-Christian culture is expressed merely in symbolic terms in wine and bread turning into the flesh and blood of Christ. But whoever has witnessed the gaping wounds and cancerous growths on our Mother Earth, does see in concrete terms how right Jack Forbes is in his challenge, that we are greedily consuming life itself in a cannibalistic manner. The fact that Forbes decided to rewrite and republish his book once again for us Europeans in 1992, eleven years after its original publication in Germany,

and 500 years after the Columbian Exchange began, is evidence of the fact of his and other Indigenous people's hope, to find allies in Europe, because it depends on all of us whether racism, fascism, sexism and ecological insanity will continue to spread, or whether we will succeed in leaving the straight road of our linear progress towards death and re-enter the circle to which we all belong, and which is called "life."

(1981: 179, my translation)

Today, contemporary Aboriginal scholars like Atleo, Armstrong, Cornplanter, Episkenew, Kovach, Kuokkanen, Lawrence, McLeod, Williamson and Wilson are explaining in great theoretical detail the indigenous epistemology, axiology and methodology which the Western world is in dire need of in order to survive.

4 "Are there bridges to build relationships?"

I mentioned earlier that offers by indigenous people to teach newcomers their ways have existed for centuries. Within the last 100 years, their efforts have grown ever more pressing. In 1922, Hiamovi, High Chief of the Tsistsistas and Dakota peoples, wrote in his foreword to Natalie Curtis' monumental *The Indian's Book*: "I want all Indians and white men to read and learn how the Indians lived and thought in the olden time" (1968: ix), and 11 years later, the Lakota actor, author and educator Luther Standing Bear wrote in an often quoted passage:

> Our annals, all happenings of human import, were stored in our song and dance rituals, our history differing in that it was not stored in books, but in the living memory. So, while the white people had much to teach us, we had much to teach them, and what a school could have been established upon that idea!

(1978: 236)

In the 1920s, Deskaheh, the highest official of the Haudenosaunee, tried in vain to address the League of Nations in Geneva about his confederacy's grievances with the British Crown and Canada (Weaver 2014: 182–88), and since then there have been a series of interventions by Haudenosaunee, Hopi and other knowledge keepers to warn the Western world against its self-destructive abuses of Mother Earth. In the 1970s, pan-indigenous delegations repeatedly visited Europe to talk to the United Nations in Geneva and local NGOs to protest resource extractions on indigenous lands and the increasing destruction of our entire planet. As exemplary, I would like to refer readers to *A Basic Call to Consciousness*, a booklet first published in Geneva, Switzerland in 1977 with illustrations by Kahonhes, then copyrighted in 1978 and often reprinted by *Akwesasne Notes* in North America. The third (revised) printing of *A Basic Call to Consciousness* shows a photograph of Philip Deere (Muskogee Creek, AIM spiritual leader), Hopi elder David Mon
onghye and the Haudenosaunee Tadodaho walking in front of the indigenous

delegation, holding the Hopi elder by the hands. There was regular reporting on such delegations and issues by Gesellschaft für bedrohte Völker/Survival International in their journal *Pogrom*, and among German journalists it was, again, Claus Biegert who reported most persistently on these issues.

As already mentioned, Biegert entitled his translation of Deloria's *We Talk, You Listen* in German *Nur Stämme werden überleben* (Only Tribes Will Survive). Now, that was almost half a century ago, long before Jeannette Armstrong's appeal for re-indigenization. Biegert's book was published by a small but committed publisher and had a very limited distribution. So the appeal or prophecy in the title of Biegert's translation, that re-indigenization would ensure survival, remained largely unheeded, but today there are more and more signs indicating that Western academia seems to be opening up to Aboriginal knowledges. Encouragingly, such epistemological openings occur not only within the soft-science disciplines related to indigenous studies, but even in the hardest core of natural sciences, namely physics, as well as in new forms of philosophizing.

Soft sciences and indigenous studies

Syilx scholar Jeannette Armstrong went right into the lion's mouth of Western academia and did her PhD at a German university, and so did the late Métis scholar Jo-Ann Episkenew a few years earlier. Besides, there have been many visits by Aboriginal authors and artists to European universities over the last 30 or 40 years, and there have been lecture tours and even guest professorships by Aboriginal scholars teaching native studies to European students. I recall a speech by the then director of the En'Owkin Center, Métis scholar Don Fiddler, who on 12 October 1992, exactly 500 years after the colonization of the Americas had begun, spoke to a German audience from the rostrum in the castle hall of the University of Osnabrück. But it was really with Jeannette Armstrong's dissertation that indigenous knowledges as such were first presented and defended by a First Nations scholar within the rigorous scholarly framework of a traditional pre-Columbian university (Greifswald University was founded 1456) and in front of an interdisciplinary PhD-committee that combined scholars in linguistics, philosophy (environmental ethics), Slavic philology and North American literatures and cultures. One of her two supervisors was professor of philosophy Konrad Ott, a former PhD candidate of none less than Jürgen Habermas. Prof. Ott then held the only chair in environmental ethics in Germany. He had a particularly hard time at first accepting indigenous epistemologies and methodologies, but Armstrong convinced him by discussing indigenous environmental epistemes in comparison with a set number of staunch Western theories of environmental ethics, and she also convinced the linguist and the literature scholars by unearthing the foundational importance of Aboriginal languages and stories from the oral traditions for defining a locally embedded indigeneity that carries global implications. After her graduation, we even managed to have a Four Foods fest, combining local North German harvest festivities with the Syilx Okanagan *captik* "How Food Was Given."

While this may be just one isolated and individualized example of the transfer of indigenous knowledges to Western academia, there are other encouraging signs by researchers like Groß (2011), Knopf (2011) or Mackenthun and Hock (2012), showing that Western academia in Europe has begun to listen. The 2014 Canadian Studies conference at Grainau, Bavaria, which brings together about 200 scholars each year from the German-speaking countries, Poland, Scandinavia, Britain and Canada, focused on "Indigenous Knowledges and Academic Discourses" – a special issue of their journal, *Zeitschrift für Kanadastudien*, on "Indigenous Knowledges" came out in February 2018. In March 2016, the University of Bremen hosted an international conference on "Postcolonial Knowledges" (in their series "Language and Literature in Colonial and Postcolonial Contexts"), which was convened by indigenous studies specialist Kerstin Knopf – the recent president of the German Association for Canadian Studies and now president-elect of the International Council for Canadian Studies, who also edited the special issue of *Zeitschrift für Kanada-Studien* mentioned previously. The Bremen conference brought together speakers from Asia, Africa, Europe and Turtle Island, including Jeannette Armstrong. This book in the Key Concepts series is further proof in hand.

Hardcore natural sciences

While there is this growing readiness in the arts to listen, the doors to certain areas of hardcore science seem to be opening, too. As Nu-cha-nulth scholar Richard Atleo pointed out in his study on *Principles of Tsawalk* (2011: 37), there are phenomena in quantum physics which traditional physics cannot explain, but which seem to overlap and be explicable within indigenous epistemes.

I am not able to go into detail in this – for reasons of lack of space, but much more so because of a lack of expertise in physics on my side – but I would like to share with you what appears to me as a striking congruence on the phenomenological and even iconographic level between two metaphors, one used by an indigenous educator, the other by a Western physicist, to visualize the relational interconnectedness of all of life's material phenomena.

Cree scholar Shawn Wilson in his study on "Indigenous Research Methods" (subtitle), *Research is Ceremony* (2008), relates how through a dream-vision he came to conceptualize his own connectedness to all of creation. In his vision he knew himself to be a single knot of light in dark space, and then very slowly and gradually he observed the formation of another dot of light out there, and then slowly but steadily an increasing number of individual knots of lights appeared consecutively. These knots of light then began a process of weaving shining threads of light between all of them, thus creating a filament – an expanding and ever accelerating and growing web of relationality and all-connectedness. And, he continues:

> Now as you open your eyes, you can see all of the things that are around you. What you see is their physical form, but you realize that their physical form is really just a web of relationships that have taken on a familiar shape. Every

individual thing that you see around you is really just a huge knot – a point where thousands and millions of relationships come together. These relationships come to you from the past, from the present and from the future. This is what surrounds us, and what forms us, our world, our cosmos, our reality. We could not be without being in relationship with everything that surrounds us and is within us. Our reality, our ontology is the relationships.

(2008: 76)

The late German physicist Hans Peter Dürr re-published a collection of essays under the title *Physik und Transparenz: Die großen Physiker unserer Zeit über Begegnungen mit dem Wunderbaren* (Physics and Transparency: The Great Physicists of Our Time About Their Encounters With the Miraculous) in 2012, with contributions by some leading 20th-century physicists including Niels Bohr, Max Planck, Werner Heisenberg and Albert Einstein. In his preface, Dürr recounts the development of quantum physics after Niels Bohr, and he marks a departure from traditional physics after Werner Heisenberg, which opened the discipline to epistemologies far beyond the material. Dürr explains:

Instead of an initial base that is primarily materialist and mechanist, and which is followed by everything else like form and movement only as a secondary step, there is now a non-material and non-separable web of relations in the primary position, entailing the familiar characteristics matter and energy as secondary phenomena.[7]

(Dürr 1986: 9)

Such an approach to physics, I think, could be corroborated by indigenous epistemologies, methods and axiology. This seems the more obvious when we look at Dürr's metaphor to visualize his model for this "Beziehungsgefüge" (web of relations), which closely resembles what Wilson saw in his dream. Dürr wrote:

If we visualize mind as a web of relations constituted by threads, then their knots would result in a kind of spatial clusters like those in a fishing net or a sweater. But these are only parables, which help us to let our imagination get closer to the incomprehensible. We must not misuse them as explanations for that which can be understood by (scientific) proof.[8]

(Dürr 1986: 10)

Whether perceived as shiny knots in a filament of light or more profanely as the knots in a fisher's net or a sweater, both Wilson and Dürr insist that things are far more intricately connected than meets the quotidian Western eye.

Systemics vs. hyperseparation

Just recently, while working on and thinking about this topic, I came across a book that was given to me by a colleague in linguistics when I retired from university service nine years ago, entitled *Die andere Intelligenz: Wie wir morgen denken werden*

(The Other Intelligence: How We Will be Thinking Tomorrow). The book contains essays and conversations by a number of mostly German-speaking scholars who have been meeting for a number of years to discuss questions of mutual interest. While the general tone of the book is philosophical, the scholars themselves come from various disciplines, mostly from the natural sciences. Parts of what I read there seem to echo or run parallel with what I had learned from Aboriginal thinkers. While the contributors seemed unaware of the latter, I learned from the introductory chapter by Bernhard von Mutius that the discussants were addressing issues like "relational thinking" (Foerster & Floyd 2004: 25)[9] and "that connections are more important than the parts" (2004: 27)[10] or that

> by tuning in on the emotionally determined worlds of the imaginations and relations of the other, and by the inclusion of that which had been hitherto excluded by logic, we could develop new kinds of solutions and ways of action.[11]
>
> *(2004: 29)*

To me, that sounded like an epistemological interface between Western knowledge and those indigenous knowledges that I had learned about over the years. In conclusion, I would like to share with you just one final example from that recently rediscovered gift.

In a dialogue on "Systemics, or Seeing Connections" (*Systemik oder: Zusammenhänge sehen*), two German-speaking scholars – the trained mathematician Christina Floyd and the trained physicist Heinz von Foerster – discuss the difference between what they call "science vs. systemics," or analytical vs. synthetic/synthesizing thinking. Science, Foerster contends, is based on separation and differentiation:

> That is the strategy of reductionism. If it is too difficult to understand the whole, you cut it up into small pieces. If they are still too complicated, you keep on cutting up until you arrive at something, which you believe you understand. What is so attractive about this method is, that it is always successful. But the price you have to pay for this success, are the lost connections, which make the parts into a whole.[12]
>
> *(Foerster and Floyd 2004: 58)*

This echoes the "hyperseparation" Rauna Kuokkanen talks about. Foerster then argues for an understanding of the complementary character of science and systemics:

> It is important to understand the interplay, the complementarity of science and systemics. Science is concerned with causality. Systemics are needed whenever relations are important.[13]
>
> *(Foerster and Floyd 2004: 59)*

Please don't get me wrong. I am not quoting these German scholars to endorse indigenous knowledges. Far from it! Indigenous knowledges don't need such corroborations – remember the coastal wolves mentioned in the beginning of this

chapter. Rather, I quote them to show that indigenous knowledges may corrobo-
rate Western science, and that by studying nature's intelligence as translated into
the human mind, we may encounter phenomena which open windows towards
relationality, accountability and, lastly, re-indigenization in Western academia.

Notes

1 The original reads: "So haben nun aufmerksame Beobachtungen von Eingeborenen
durch Darimonts Studie eine wissenschaftliche Bestätigung gefunden" (Bernadette Calonego, "Sanfte Wölfe," *Süddeutsche Zeitung*, 21. 08. 2014, 16).
2 The colonial relationship is paradigmatic of what the Norwegian peace researcher Johan
Galtung (1969) described as structural and personal violence. Galtung defines violence
as any situation in which a person is not allowed to develop to her fullest intellectual,
psychological and physical potential, and he clearly differentiates between personal and
structural violence. The German scholar Jörg Becker (1977) has taken Galtung's theories a step further by defining racism as a form of violence in the Galtungian sense, and
showing how racism not only violates the victims most fundamentally, but at the same
time stunts and violates the racist himself in his perceptions. The most important implications of Galtung's definition remains for me to be the ethics to overcome any economic, social and political systems which are based on and impose structural violence.
3 I do not want to bash Western academia here. I think that our system of documenting
evidence is pertinent and well-grounded. Detailed bibliographies not only document
the acumen of the researchers' learnedness based on reading, but they also acknowledge
and honour, name by name, the acumen and reading of those who went before her or
him. A good bibliography gives the lineage of the scholar's learning. While indigenous
research protocol generally puts the self-location of the speaker in relation to his sources
(dreams, elders, talking circles, visions) at the beginning, Western academic conventions
put the "genealogy" of research (readings) at the end. Both explain and demarcate where
the scholar and the study come from and they acknowledge relationships, each contextualizing their referential universe. Some indigenous studies I have read lack the Western
form of bibliographic contextualization – their bibliographies are sometimes meagre
and thus allow for copious subjective solipsism and neologism – and nearly all Western
studies I know lack the former indigenous form of personal contextualization, almost
obliterating the researcher's ideological whereabouts and ethics, and lacking axiological
accountability.
4 There are various spellings of this well-known Lakota phrase. I take this spelling from
Kenneth Lincoln in his *Native American Renaissance* (1983: 2), and from a chapter heading in Kenneth Lincoln and Al Logan Slagle's *The Good Red Road* (1987: 247).
5 To demonstrate the interrelatedness and mutual dependency of all creatures on Earth,
Jack D. Forbes once explained the human dependence on the ecosystem by compar-
ing humans and trees and how they are related. Trees have roots that go into the soil,
which is composed of the dead bodies of all our relations that went before us. Humans,
like trees, have roots, but ours don't go into the earth through our feet, but into the air
through our noses and mouths. The air holds the oxygen produced by trees and other
plants. The earth holds the bones, composted flesh and feces, which nourish the trees.
No matter how powerful we may consider ourselves, if our nose and mouth roots are cut
or sealed shut, we die like a tree dies when its roots are severed from the soil (personal
recollection).
6 An official bilingual English and Okanagan version of this foundational tale was published by the Okanagan Tribal Council (2004). Two years later, Jeannette Armstrong
told it in English at a conference in Greifswald, and it is now available in the conference
proceedings (2007: 31–2). More recently I have reprinted and discussed this *captik* myself
in Lutz (2013).

7 My translation of the following German original: *"Anstelle einer primär unverbundenen materiell-mechanistischen Ausgangsbasis, der alles Übrige wie Form und Bewegung an zweiter Stelle folgt, tritt nun ein immaterielles, unauftrennbares Beziehungsgefüge an die vorderste Position, mit den uns geläufigen Eigenschaften wie Materie und Energie als sekundäre Erscheinungen."*

8 My translation of the following German original: *"Wenn wir uns den Geist als Beziehungsgeflecht von Fäden vorstellen, so ergeben dessen Knotenpunkte eine Art räumliche Bündelungen wie bei einem Fischernetz oder Pullover. Doch das sind alles nur Gleichnisse, die uns helfen, in unseren Vorstellungen näher an das Unbegreifliche heranzukommen. Wir dürfen sie nicht als Erklärungen für ein beweisbares Verständnis missbrauchen."*

9 *"das relationale Denken"*

10 *"dass die Verknüpfungen wichtiger als die Teile sind"*

11 *"wie wir durch Einstimmung in die emotional geprägten Vorstellungs- und Beziehungswelten des anderen und durch die Einbeziehung des bislang logisch Ausgeschlossenen neue Lösungs- und Handlungsperspektiven entwickeln können."*

12 *"Das ist die Strategie des Reduktionismus. Ist es zu schwierig, ein Ganzes zu verstehen, zerstückelt man es in kleinere Teile. Sind auch die zu kompliziert, teilt man weiter, bis man bei etwas ankommt, das man zu verstehen glaubt. Das Attraktive an dieser Methode ist, daß sie immer erfolgreich ist. Aber der Preis, den man für diesen Erfolg zahlen muß, sind die verlorengegangenen Verbindungen, welche die Teile zum Ganzen machen."*

13 *"Es ist wichtig, das Zusammenspiel, die Komplementarität von Wissenschaft und System, zu verstehen. Bei Wissenschaft geht es um Kausalität. Systemik ist dort gefordert, wo Relationen im Vordergrund stehen."*

References

Armstrong, Jeannette Christine. 2007. 'Kwtlakin? What is Your Place?,' in Hartmut Lutz and Rafico Ruiz (Eds.), *What is Your Place? Indigeneity and Immigration in Canada*, pp. 29–33, Beiträge zur Kanadistik Bd. 14, Augsburg: Wissner.

Armstrong, Jeannette Christine. 2009. 'Constructing Indigeneity: Syilx Okanagan Oraliture and tmixʷcentrism,' Dissertation phil. U Greifswald, http://ub-ed.ub.uni-greifswald.de/opus/volltexte/2012/1322

Atleo, Richard (Umeek). 2004. *Tsawalk: A Nuu-chah-nulth Worldview*. Vancouver: UBC.

Atleo, Richard (Umeek). 2011. *Principles of Tsawalk: An Indigenous Approach to Global Crisis*. Vancouver: UBC.

Basso, Keith H. 1996. *Wisdom Sits in Places: Landscape and Language Among the Western Apache*. Albuquerque: University of New Mexico.

Battarbee, Keith and John Erik Fossum. 2014. 'Introduction: Indigenous Perspectives in the Arctic,' in Keith Battarbee and John Erik Fossum (Eds.), *The Arctic Contested*. Brussels: P.I.E.: Peter Lang S.A. Canadian Studies No. 24.

Becker, Jörg. 1977. *Alltäglicher Rassismus: Die afro-amerikanischen Rassenkonflikte im Kinder- und Jugendbuch der Bundesrepublik*. Frankfurt and New York: Campus.

Biegert, Claus. 1976. *Seit 200 Jahren ohne Verfassung – 1976: Indianer im Widerstand*. Reinbek: Rowohlt.

Calloway, Colin G. 2003. *One Vast Winter Count: The Native American West before Lewis and Clark*. Lincoln and London: University of Nebraska.

Cornplanter, Jesse J. 1938. *Legends of the Longhouse*. Reprint Ohsweken. Ontario: Iroqrafts, 1992.

Crosby, Alfred W. 1972. *The Columbian Exchange: Biological and Cultural Consequences of 1492*. Westport, CT: Greenwood.

Curtis, Natalie (Recorder and Ed.). 1968. *The Indians' Book: Songs and Legends of the American Indians*. New York: Dover, 1923.

Deloria, Vine. 1973. *We Talk – You Listen: New Tribes, New Turf.* New York: Delta Books.

Deloria, Vine. 1973. *God Is Red.* New York: Dell.

Deloria, Vine. 1976. *Nur Stämme werden überleben: Indianische Vorschläge für eine Radikalkur des wildgewordenen Westens,* Translated and Edited by Claus Biegert and Carl-Ludwig Reichert. AG Nordamerikanische Indianer München, München: Trikont.

Dürr, Hans-Peter (Ed.). 1986. *Physik und Transzendenz: Die großen Pysiker unserer Zeit über ihre Begnungen mit dem Wunderbaren.* Cesky Tesin, Czeck Republic: Driediger Verlag, 2012.

Eigenbrod, Renate. 2005. *Travelling Knowledges: Positioning the Im/Migrant Reader of Aboriginal Literatures in Canada.* Winnipeg: University of Manitoba.

Episkenew, Jo-Ann. 2006. 'Beyond Catharsis: Truth, Conciliation, and Healing In and Through Indigenous Literature,' Dissertation phil. U Greifswald.

Episkenew, Jo-Ann. 2009. *Taking Back our Spirits: Indigenous Literature, Public Policy, and Healing.* Winnipeg: University of Manitoba.

Foerster, Heinz von and Christiane Floyd. 2004. 'Systemik oder: Zusammenhänge sehen,' in Bernhard von Mutius (Ed.), *Die andere Intelligenz: Wie wir morgen denken werden,* pp. 57–74. Stuttgart: Klett-Cotta.

Forbes, Jack D. 1979. *A World Ruled by Cannibals: The Wétiko Disease of Aggression, Violence, and Imperialism,* DQU Pre-Print Series, Davis: DQ-U. [Later published as a trade book under the title: *Columbus and Other Cannibals: The Wétiko Disease of Exploitation, Imperialism and Terrorism,* 1992]. Brooklyn, NY: Autonomedia.

Forbes, Jack D. 1981. *Die Wétiko-Seuche: Eine indianische Philosophie von Aggression und Gewalt,* Translated and Edited by Indianerprojektgruppe Osnabrück. Wuppertal: Peter Hammer, repr. 1984. [1992, new rev. edition *Columbus und andere Kannibalen: Die indianische Sicht der Dinge,* Uwe Zagratzki (Ed.), Hartmut Lutz, Nachwort (afterword), Wuppertal: Peter Hammer.].

Forbes, Jack D. 2007. *The American Discovery of Europe.* Urbana and Chicago: University of Illinois Press.

Galtung, Johan. 1969. 'Violence, Peace, and Peace Research,' *Journal of Peace Research,* 6(1): 167–191.

Galtung, Johan. 1977. *Strukturelle Gewalt: Beiträge zur Friedens- und Konfliktforschung.* Reinbek: Rowohlt, 1975.

Gesellschaft für bedrohte Völker. 1977. 'Indianer Sprechen: Forderungen – Programme – Erklärungen,' *Sonderausgabe Pogrom,* 8: 50–51.

Gilroy, Paul. 1993. *The Black Atlantic: Modernity and Double Consciousness.* Cambridge, MA: Harvard University Press.

Groß, Konrad. 2011. 'Traditional Ecological Knowledge and the Image of the Green Aboriginal,' in Kerstin Knopf (Ed.), *North America in the 21st Century: Tribal, Local, Global,* pp. 131–144. Festschrift für Hartmut Lutz, Trier: Wissenschaftlicher Verlag Trier.

Johnston, Basil. 1990. 'One Generation from Extinction,' in W.H. New (Ed.), *Native Writers and Canadian Writing,* pp. 10–15. Vancouver: UBC.

Knopf, Kerstin (Ed.). 2011. *North America in the 21st Century: Tribal, Local, and Global. Festschrift für Hartmut Lutz.* Trier: Wissenschaftlicher Verlag Trier.

Knopf, Kerstin. 2015. 'The Turn Towards the Indigenous Knowledge Systems and Practices in the Academy,' *Amerikastudien/American Studies* 60. 2/3, 179–200.

Knopf, Kerstin. forthcoming. 'Indigenizing Science?! Global Warming, Inuit Knowledge, and Western Scientific Discourses,' in Stephan Alexander Ditze and Jana Nittel (Eds.), *Reflections on the Far North of Canada in the Twenty-First Century.* Bochum: N. Brockmeyer.

Kovach, Margaret. 2009. *Indigenous Methodologies: Characteristics, Conversations, and Contexts.* Toronto, Buffalo, London: University of Toronto.

Kuokkanen, Rauna. 2007. *Reshaping the University: Responsibility, Indigenous Epistemes, and the Logic of the Gift*. Vancouver: UBC.

Lawrence, Bonita. 2003. 'Gender, Race, and the Regulation of Native Identity in Canada and the United States: An Overview,' *Indigenous Women in the Americas*, 18(2): 3–31.

Lincoln, Kenneth. 1983. *Native American Renaissance*. Berkeley: University of California.

Lincoln, Kenneth and Al Logan Slagle. 1987. *The Good Red Road: Passages into Native America*. San Francisco: Harper and Row.

Lowes, Warren. 1986. *Indian Giver: A Legacy of North American Native Peoples*. Penticton, BC: Theytus Books.

Lutz, Hartmut. 1975. *William Goldings Prosawerk im Lichte der Analytischen Psychologie Carl Gustav Jungs und der Psychoanalyse Sigmund Freuds*. Frankfurt am Main: Akademische Verlagsgesellschaft.

Lutz, Hartmut. 1985. *"Indianer" und "Native Americans": Zur sozial- und literhistorischen Vermittlung eines Stereotyps*. Hildesheim: Georg Olms.

Lutz, Hartmut (Ed.). 1991. *Contemporary Challenges: Conversations with Canadian Native Authors*. Saskatoon: Fifth House.

Lutz, Hartmut. 2002. *Approaches: Essays in Native North American Studies and Literatures*. Beiträge zu Kanadistik 11. Augsburg: Wissner Verlag.

Lutz, Hartmut. 2003. 'German Indianthusiasm: A Socially Constructed German National(ist) Myth,' in Colin G. Calloway, Gerd Gemünden and Susanne Zantop (Eds.), *Germans and Indians. Fantasies, Encounters, Projections*, pp. 167–184. Lincoln and London: University of Nebraska Press.

Lutz, Hartmut. 2004. 'Race or Place? The Palimpsest of Space in Canadian Prairie Fiction, from Salverson to Cariou,' *Textual Studies in Canada*, 17: 171–185.

Lutz, Hartmut. 2005. 'A History of Native American Studies/Canadian First Nations Studies in the Germanys/Germany,' in Hans Bak (Ed.), *First Nations of North America: Politics and Presentation*, pp. 72–85. Amsterdam: VU University Press.

Lutz, Hartmut. 2007. '"To Know Where Home Is": An Introduction to Indigeneity and Immigration,' in Hartmut Lutz and Rafico Ruiz (Eds.), *What is Your Place? Indigeneity and Immigration*, pp. 9–28. Beiträge zur Kanadistik Bd. 14, Augsburg: Wissner.

Lutz, Hartmut. 2011. '"The Land is Deep in Time": Natives and Newcomers in Multicultural Canada,' in Ewelina Bujnowska, Marcin Gabryś and Thomaz Sikora (Eds.), *Towards Critical Multiculturalism: Dialogues Between/Among Canadian Diasporas/Vers un multiculturalisme critique: dialogues entre les diasporas canadiennes*, pp. 47–64. Katowice: Agencja Artystyczna PARA.

Lutz, Hartmut. 2013. 'Whom Do We Eat? – Thoughts on the Columbian Exchange and "How Food Was Given",' in Annekatrin Metz, Markus M. Müller and Lutz Showalter (Eds.), *F(e)asting Fitness? Cultural Images, Social Practices, and Histories of Food and Health*, 137–148. Festschrift für Wolfgang Klooß, Trier: Wissenschaftlicher Verlag Trier.

Lutz, Hartmut. 2014a. '"Writing Back", "Writing Home", and "Writing Beyond?": Native Literature in Canada Today,' in Weronika Suchacka, Uwe Zagratzki and Hartmut Lutz (Eds.), *Despite Harper: International Perspectives of Canadian Literature and Culture*, pp. 153–162. Hamburg: Kovač.

Lutz, Hartmut. 2014b. *Contemporary Achievements: Contextualizing Canadian Aboriginal Literatures*. Studies in Anglophone Literatures and Cultures 6. Augsburg: Wissner.

Lutz, Hartmut, Florentine Strzelczyk and Renae Watchman (Eds.). 2020. *Indianthusiasm: Indigenous Responses*. Waterloo, ON: Wildfrid Laurier University Press.

Mackenthun, Gesa and Klaus Hock. 2012. 'Introduction: Entangled Knowledge, Scientific Discourse and Cultural Difference,' in Klaus Hock and Gesa Machenthun (Eds.),

Entangled Knowledge: Scientific Discourses and Cultural Difference, pp. 7–27. Münster: Waxmann.

Maracle, Lee. 1991. 'Lee Maracle (Interview),' in Hartmut Lutz (Ed.), *Contemporary Challenges: Conversations with Canadian Native Authors*, pp. 169–179. Saskatoon: Fifth House.

McLeod, Neal. 2007. *Cree Narrative Memory: From Treaties to Contemporary Times*. Saskatoon: Purich.

Nabokov, Peter. 2002. *A Forest of Time: American Indian Ways of History*. Cambridge: Cambridge University Press.

Okanagan Tribal Council (Eds.). 2004. *Kou-Skelowh/We Are The people: A Trology of Okanagan Legends*. Illustrated by Barbara Marchand. Penticton, BC: Theytus Books.

Ott, Konrad. 2011. 'Beyond Beauty,' in Kerstin Knopf (Ed.), *North America in the 21st Century: Tribal, Local, Global*, pp. 119–129. Festschrift für Hartmut Lutz, Trier: Wissenschaftlicher Verlag Trier.

Runnels, Dennis. 2001. 'The Past is Right Before Us', personal information given to Hartmut Lutz, September, Dartmouth College, Hanover, NH.

Schlesier, Karl H. 1985. *Die Wölfe des Himmels: Welterfahrung der Cheyenne*, Translated by Stephan Dömpke. Köln: Eugen Diederichs.

Simon, Mary. 2011. 'Canadian Inuit: Where We Have Been and Where We are Going,' *International Journal*, Autumn: 879–899.

Smola, Klavdia. 2013. 'Slawisch-Jüdische Literaturen der Gegenwart: Wiedererfindung der Tradition,' in Klavdia Smola (Ed.), *Osteuropäisch-jüdische Literaturen im 20. Und 21. Jahrhundert: Identität und Poetik/Eastern European Jewish Literature of the 20th and 21st Centuries: Identity and Poetics*, pp. 103–130. München, Berlin and Washington: Otto Sagner.

Standing Bear, Luther. 1978. *Land of the Spotted Eagle*. Lincoln and London: University of Nebraska, 1933.

Weatherford, Jack. 1988. *Indian Givers: How the Indians of the Americas Transformed the World*. New York: Fawcett Columbine.

Weatherford, Jack. 1991. *Native Roots: How the Indians Enriched America*. New York: Fawcett Columbine.

Weaver, Jace. 2014. *The Red Atlantic: American Indigenes and the Making of the Modern World, 1000–1927*. Chapel Hill: University of North Carolina.

Williamson, Karla Jessen. 2000. 'Celestial and Social Families of the Inuit,' in Ron F. Laliberte et al. (Eds.), *Expressions in Canadian Native Studies*, pp. 125–144. Saskatoon, Saskatchewan: University of Saskatchewan Extension Press.

Wilson, Shawn. 2008. *Research is Ceremony: Indigenous Research Methods*. Halifax and Winnipeg: Fernwood.

Wolf, Alexander. 1988. 'Introduction,' in Alexander Wolf (Ed.), *Earth Elder Stories*, pp. xi–xxiii. Saskatoon, SK: Fifth House.

Womack, Craig S. 1999. *Red on Red: Native American Literary Separatism*. Minneapolis and London: University of Minnesota.

Wright, Ronald. 1992. *Stolen Continents: The "New World" Through Indian Eyes Since 1492*. Toronto: Penguin Books of Canada.

6

PERFORMANCE AMONG ADIVASIS AND NOMADS IN INDIA

G. N. Devy

The grammar of performance in India

The continuous history of the human population in India goes back to nearly 40,000 years (Reich 2018). However, the known history extends back only to the period of the Sindhu river culture, known to the world as the Harappan civilization, which is a period of about 45 centuries to 40 centuries before our time. What is known, though, is based on archaeological evidence; and not enough is known about the language and literature of the Harappan people (Robinson 2002). Their script has still remained undeciphered. When it gets deciphered in the future, it may become necessary to make a radical restatement of Indian history. The earliest Indian history about which scholars are able to speak with a reasonable degree of confidence belongs to the era known as the Vedic period, an era during which oral poetry was beginning to be composed. These poems, known as the Veda, continue to exist and are carried forward through oral memory by a small class of people specially trained in the art of memory (Sri Aurobindo 1956). The Vedic Age is identified with the period some 35 centuries to 30 centuries before our time. There is a considerable debate about its precise date, particularly among the neo-nationalist political scholars. In India, cultural history with any degree of certainty begins with Gautama Buddha's time, which is approximately 25 centuries before our time. Major texts written since this period are available in our time. Some of these were texts on performance (Devy 2003). The most remarkable of these is the *Natyashastra*, which in English translation would mean "Dramaturgy." Its authorship is ascribed to Bharata or Bharata Muni.

The *Natyashastra* holds as much importance in the tradition of Indian literature and theatre as does Aristotle's *Poetics* in the tradition of Western literature and theatre. It analyses dramatic production in terms of the audience experience, categorized in eight distinct types of emotional states. The *Natyashastra* terms these states as *rasa* (singular) and *rasas* (as the English plural goes). This classification and the description of the *rasas* exerted a great influence on the production of literature and drama in India through the ages until during the 19th century, Indian theatre practices started imbibing elements of Western drama due to the colonial cultural impact. Apart from the dramaturgy of Bharata, other texts related to dance were produced in ancient India. Some of these relate to movements and gestures used in dance. The science of the gestures was known in the Sanskrit tradition – the language in which such texts were written in ancient India – as *mudra-shastra*, the science of gestures, or the *chinha-shastra*, the science of signs (Devy 2014). When the meanings associated with certain gestures and movements are accepted by a given culture, and are then noticed and catalogued, they get canonized as meaningful signs.

In ancient India, two types of signs were chosen for formulating a system or grammar of signs: one, the signs that the body can generate; and two, the signs inscribed on/in the body. The latter category was covered by the *chinha shastra*, the former by the *natya shastra*. It would not be inappropriate to translate *chinha shastra* as "metaphysical semiology." This branch, a highly popular branch of Indian hermeneutics, is further sub-divided in the field into the *samudrik* and the *jyotisha*. The *samudrik* dealt with the interpretation of lines and marks on the body of a person, such as *shankha* (crouch), *padma* (lotus), *chakra* (circle), etc., claimed to be imbued with spiritual significance. It was expected of a person deemed fit to be a ruler to have certain kinds of marks on the forehead, neck and other parts of the body, as well as a certain configuration of lines on the palms. These were known as *"lakshana"* (which was also the term that Indian linguistics used to describe one layer of meaning of words; the term literally means the stated or visible meaning). However, it was accepted that the *"lakshanas"* were all the handiwork of destiny or supernatural powers. The other development in the field of interpretation of signs was related to those signs which are socially created, conveyed and accepted as meaningful signs.

The branch of science that dealt with these came to be known as *natya shastra*. Though the term immediately evokes the name of Bharata Muni, it is necessary to bear in mind that dramaturgy was a well-developed branch of interpretative sciences in ancient India and that Bharata Muni was only one of the theorists to have commented on *hasta-mudras* (signs used in dance and drama to convey meaning). Several centuries before Bharata Muni, Nagnajita and a Buddhist scholar had described the correspondence between *mudras* and meaning. His work, unfortunately lost to Sanskrit scholarship in subsequent periods but miraculously available to us now thanks to its translation into Chinese (and from Chinese to German and then from German to English), focused on the Buddhist practice of sculpture in his times (Nardi 2006). Nagnajita discusses the importance of proportion and balance in sculptural *mudras* (the expression on the face of Buddha figures) for communication of *bhava*, the feeling conveyed, in his treatise on the correspondence between form and meaning. Thus, one of the sources of Bharata's dramaturgy was the Buddhist sculptural tradition, and it had a profound impact on Bharata's understanding of how meanings work in relation to signs generated by body move-ment. Not surprisingly, the *mudras* as conceptualized in the *natya shastra* were seen as essentially symbolic and not as a mime for objects or experiences (for concrete or abstract signification).

The twin principles along which Bharata presented his ideal of *mudras* were opposition and balance. If one were to think of signs created through body move-ments for height or ascending high, or the divine or royal stature of a person – as in a person at a high position – a normal mime would tend to use the rising of hands or fingers high in the air. In Bharata's conceptualization, this is to be done by bending the head and the body backward as much as possible and bringing them closer to the ground. On the stage, this movement of the dancer/actor makes the audience look "down" rather than "up," and yet, as the convention is now well established, the audience understands this as a reference to something high. Similarly, for indicating the wild flapping of the wings of a wounded bird (such as Jatayu – a mythical flying being – or a royal swan), a straight mime would require the actor to spread her or his arms and flip-flap them violently. In the *Natyashastra* tradition of *mudras*, this is accomplished by bringing both arms together in front of one's face and moving them in the manner of gentle waves. By using these principles of balance and opposition, Bharata turned the *mudras* into a science of symbolic gestures rather than a mechanical translation of meaning or feelings. His interpretation of the artist's body movements later became the foundation for the entire *Bharat Natyam* tradition of dance (and probably that is why it was called the *Bharat-Natyam*, though *natya* would mean drama while *nritya* would mean dance).

New languages and forms of expression

While the *Bharat-Natyam* received royal patronage all through India over the cen-turies enabling it to become canonical, a different kind of *mudra* tradition or *chinha shastra* continued to flourish in India, mainly in the area of iconography. The con-ventions of iconography originate in the nature of the material medium used for making figures of godheads. Though in most cases the material used was rock, it was a widespread practice to make terracotta figures of godheads, *gram-devatas*, ancestors, specific cult-related pantheons and natural elements, and cosmic bodies. These originated from the craft traditions of India. Within these craft traditions, exuberance dominated the making of figures. Thus, large eyes, long noses, thick lips, very broad chins, multiple arms, tails, etc. became elements of these *murtis* (torsos or body-sculpture). This kind of iconography then became the source of characterization in popular theatre as well as in various painting traditions (Devy 2010). The *Ramayana* and the *Mahabharata* scenes, as depicted in various wall paintings or scroll-paintings, exemplify this. The figures in the work of Raja Ravi Verma, an early 20th-century artist, had such figures in his work that stand out by their exuberance of colour and line rather than by their suggestive power. In modern times, the *murti* iconography came to impact the depiction of characters in theatre and cinema. Quite naturally, the *murti* tradition, too, has had a deep impact on the meanings associated with various body movements and signs. For instance, the combined movement of head and hands by a young woman suggesting a denial but indicating acceptance, widely in circulation in Indian visual culture, is drawn more upon the *murti* tradition rather than the *natya-nritya* tradition. An easier example would be the way Indians point a finger to the skies, fold all other fingers and move the hand (somewhat semi-folding the arm) to ask "Wh" questions: what, when, where, why, etc. This sign can communicate, with no assistance from any additional verbal signal, the meaning. The origin of this particular sign is in theatre arts dominated by the use of masks (rather than dance), and such mythological plays in particular need to depict *rakshasas*, the supernatural diabolic characters. This particular gesture is not to be used by heroic characters.

The history of gestures, signs, eye movements and body movements for communication in India, brought to every member of the society through a myriad of performance, visual representation, narration of myth, social relations and norms of behaviour in public places, all jointly and imperceptibly influence the unconscious association between gestures or signs and the meaning they convey. Therefore, when a person is left to convey meaning with no other means but gestures, signs and body movements invariably draw upon the wealth of such gestures and signs canonized in Indian history and society.

The Sanskrit language had its sway in literature till the end of the first millennium, about ten centuries before our time. By then, new languages had started emerging in all parts of India (Devy 1992). They emerged from a combination of Sanskrit on one hand and Pali and several varieties of Prakrit on the other hand. Pali and the Prakrit had been in existence in northern parts of India. Similarly, Tamil had been in existence in the south. From it, too, new languages emerged around the turn of the millennium. Thus, new languages, with a new kind of imaginative and social vitality, had emerged. They included Kannada, Malayalam and Telugu in the south and Kashmiri, Punjabi, Hindi, Gujarati, Marathi, Sindhi, Oriya, Assamiya and Bangla in the north. The languages named here were among the major ones. And all of these inherited the grammar of gestures and the manner and method of performance in dance and drama signs from the earlier times. However, the genres of performance had changed, and their diversity was quite eye-catching at the beginning of the second millennium, and also through subsequent centuries up to the 19th century. New forms were being constantly added to previously existing forms.

The colonial construction of the indigenous

When India confronted European traditions of performance, the Indian civilization had already developed an amazing variety of the forms of composition, singing, narrative, storytelling, dramatic presentation, rendering of episodic narratives, serialized presentations, mime and shadow play, puppetry, athletic dances, group dances, chorus, symbolic and sacred arts, ritual performances, social forms of reciting traditional songs, oral traditions associated with agriculture, food making, food processing, fishing, rowing, walking long distance, pilgrimages, prayers, sooth say-ing, lullabies and burial or crematory songs. If not all of these, certainly many of these had been inherited by the communities that came to be designated as "tribal" or the "indigenous communities" during the last quarter of the 19th cen-tury as a combined result of the stringent forest regulations, political expediency and the confused response of the colonial rulers to India's vast society with its ethnic diversity (Damodaran 2006). This elaborate introduction is necessary for anyone approaching the performance tradition of the indigenous peoples and the knowledge embedded in the indigenous performances.

The nine decades of colonial rule in India from 1857, when the East India Company passed on India to the British Sovereign, to 1947 when India gained independence, witnessed two crucial phenomena in the history of the indigenous communities. One was the increasing control of the state; the other was the rise of an anthropological view of the adivasis (as the indigenous communities like to identify themselves). By the beginning of the 20th century, the adivasis had been fully anthropologized, with their imagery making the rounds at European muse-ums along with similar imagery of the indigenous peoples drawn from other con-tinents (Damodaran 2006). They had been completely subsumed within the state authority. At the beginning of the 20th century, the general population in India had already started viewing the adivasis through the gaze of European anthropol-ogy, and had turned them into "strangers."

The colonial impact on the demographic self-recognition of India was so pro-found that, by this time, Indians had started thinking of the indigenous peoples as some odd remnants of primitive communities. It took the life-work of Verrier Elwin to bring back at least a degree of respect and recognition on the part of the Indian people towards the indigenous communities (Elwin 2008). It was Elwin's historic burden to re-examine the category, turn it upside down and gain sympathy – if not respectability – for the tribes. He carried out this seemingly impossible task with an unparalleled dedication (Oxford India Elwin 2008). Given the timing of Elwin's arrival in India, it is not surprising that the young Elwin felt attracted towards Mahatma Gandhi. However, it was not Gandhi but Jamanalal Bajaj, Thakkar Bapa and Sardar Patel who drew Elwin's attention to tribals. Thakkar Bapa provided Elwin the initial exposure to tribals by taking him to Dahod and Jhalod. Elwin arrived in India in November 1927; he finally decided to move to Karanjia in Man-dla District in January 1931. He came in close contact with Gandhi during 1930, and started spending time at the Sabarmati Ashram and travelling with associates of Gandhi to various parts of India. Gandhi was not just the most popular leader that India has known, he was also, and perhaps more essentially, a moral universe. Though Elwin came under the spell of this moral universe, he decided to trespass it in favour of his quest for understanding the tribals.

Elwin spent over three decades living among the tribals, serving them, learning their languages and culture, documenting oral traditions, preparing policy docu-ments, advising the government on tribal issues and writing about them. It was the sequential unfolding of his many-sided love for the tribals during the three decades of an intimate engagement with them that led to Elwin's production of such mighty works as *The Baiga, The Agariya, Maria Murder and Suicide, Folk-Tales of Mahakoshal, Folk-Songs of Chattisgarh, The Muria and the Ghotul, The Tribal Art of Middle India, The Myths of Middle India, Songs of the Forest, Folk-Songs of the Maikal Hills* and *Leaves from the Jungle*. Elwin's love for the tribal communities of India has almost no parallel, with the later-day exception perhaps of Shankar Guha-Niyogi, Ram Dayal Munda and Mahasweta Devi. His involvement with them went far beyond an anthropological dedication, aesthetic fascination or altruistic community work. Through the decades of his work, Elwin became increasingly aware that defending tribal well-being was his responsibility.

Thanks to Elwin's work, since Independence several institutions in India started taking an interest in adivasi culture and performance traditions. The most important among these was the Bhopal-based Bharat Bhavan. Bhopal, being the capital city of Madhya Pradesh with the highest percentage of adivasis in any single state, found it necessary to offer space for adivasi performances. The Bharat Bhavan was headed by an enlightened civil servant, Ashok Vajpeyi, who was himself a poet of high merit. He brought in a man of an exceptional empathy for the indigenous and a great understanding of the principles of their arts and performance traditions. It was J. Swaminathan's (1928–94) genius that created high visibility for the adivasi music, dance and theatre of the adivasis of Madhya Pradesh and attracted the attention of many high-profile Indian painters and singers of the day. The remarkable music genius Tejanbai shot into international fame after she was given a platform at the Bharat Bhavan. The other institution that decided to focus on the indigenous population was the Museum of Man, the *Manava-sangrahalaya*, an extremely innovative cultural centre, again based in Bhopal. Under the leadership of Dr. K. K. Chakravarty, who was also a civil servant like Ashok Vajpeyi, the Manava-sangrahalaya changed the philosophy of museums altogether. He advocated for the new Museum Movement, which treated the entire society as the cultural arena and the museum institution as the co-curator of it. Thus, the museum started going out to the habitats of the indigenous and worked with them *in situ* in order to empower their creative expression. One more institution that contributed to gaining dignity for the adivasi performance traditions was the Delhi-based Indira Gandhi National Centre for the Arts (IGNCA). It was driven by the passion and learning of an exceptionally gifted scholar-artist, Dr. Kapila Vatsyayan. It took on the work of documenting all the forms of arts and performances of the adivasis in India. The IGNCA provided space for the long-overdue initiative of collecting manuscripts from all over India. This led to the discovery of many texts that had been circulating in oral traditions.

Such, then, was the situation of the adivasis and their arts and performances at the turn of the century. I entered the scene about a decade before India entered the 21st century. For me, the turning point was an informal discussion held at the hilly indigenous village Saputara, in the state of Gujarat, western India. Before I come to the discussion of several types of performances and the knowledge embedded in them, it may be necessary to present an overview of the indigenous communities in India during the first two decades of the 21st century.

Indian adivasis and nomads

The Indian federation has 28 states and eight Union Territories. The area and the population of the Union Territories are generally small. Among the 28 states, the adivasis are spread over Kerala, Tamil Nadu, Karnataka, Goa, Telangana, Andhra Pradesh, Maharashtra, Gujarat, Madhya Pradesh, Chhattisgarh, Jharkhand, Odisha, West Bengal, Rajasthan, Himachal Pradesh, Uttarakhand and Assam. The states of Punjab and Haryana have no or very minuscule adivasi populations. The north-eastern states such as Sikkim, Arunachal Pradesh, Tripura, Meghalaya, Nagaland, Mizoram and Manipur also have "indigenous" populations, but they have been offered a slightly different legal status than the communities in other states. In all of the states, except the north-eastern states, the population of the adivasis is a minority in them, mostly in a single-digit percentage, except in Orissa, Jharkhand, Chhattisgarh and Madhya Pradesh. Over the last 50 years, the population of the adivasis has fluctuated between 8% and 9% of the total population of the country. In 2019, the population of the indigenous was at 135 million (Census of India website). The major adivasi groups in the country are the Munda, the Gond, the Santal and the Bhil. Numerous sub-groups of these four major types, besides many other ethnic isolates such as Sidis who migrated to India centuries ago from East Africa, inhabit India. In addition to the adivasis, there are other tribe-like communities in large numbers which include pastoral and nomadic communities. They are mostly spread over the Himalayan states and the western states.

There are also other migratory communities whom the British had branded as "criminal tribes" and had placed them under area restriction or in reformatory settlements (Devy 2007). The branding was, in the first place, based on several faulty social principles and random identification; and since Independence, that has been withdrawn. These communities are, therefore, known as the Denotified tribes. The total estimated population of the Denotified and Nomadic tribes (or communities) is approximately 110 million. Only some of these are included in the official list of the adivasis (the scheduled tribes, in official terminology). Thus, the population one is talking about in this chapter, discounting the marginal overlap between the scheduled tribes and the Denotified tribes, may be approximately 200 million. The number of communities covered under all these official categories may be close to 600. With so many communities and such a large population, though each community may be a tiny minority in its own states, the "indigenous" in India form quite a "continent of culture."

When I entered their world in 1994, this continent of culture was close to being submerged under the tsunami of globalization, urbanization and caste-dominated politics in India. During the 1980s, stringent forest land regulations were brought in by the Indian government. The first affected by these regulations were the ones who dwelt in forests or close to the forests. One started noticing that by the end of the 1980s, the number of pauperized and displaced adivasis going to the nearby cities looking for daily wage work had increased. The nation used to see them colourfully dressed to dance during the Republic Day parade, held on every 26th of

January in the national capital. But, the sheer artificiality of the official assemblage of "culture" was clear in the sad eyes of the adivasis. The anger towards the other classes living in their insomniac cities could also be perceived in their indifferent glances.

Whenever the adivasis arrived in the cities looking for work, usually walking long distances of a hundred kilometres or more, they normally chose not to speak to the city dwellers. They remained aloof, camping at the worksite and spending their evenings in their own groups at the worksite or playing flutes to themselves. During those years, the militant left-wing "ultras," known in India's political history as the "Naxalites," were multiplying in number, and the violent acts of these fringe-groups often caused killings or plain plunder. Therefore, the government had started setting up greater policing in the adivasi areas, and the police forces specially trained for the task of curbing the Naxalites had been given greater authority to "liquidate" the Naxalites. As a result, sadly, the trust level between the adivasis and the non-adivasis had hit a low (Devi 1997). Similarly, the Denotified communities, the ones that had been wrongly stigmatized as "criminal tribes," were being hounded out of urban neighbourhoods by people who had no clue who they were and of their age-old contribution to the arts and society. This was the context. During the 1980s and the early part of the 1990s, I used to teach at a university in Gujarat. The state has a large population of adivasis and Denotified tribes (approximately 13 million in 1995). I had been watching the adivasis and the nomads. I was keenly interested in their languages – in documenting them and in learning them. My interests led me to spend long periods of time with these communities. This required frequent trips to their villages and settlements. Fortunately, since I had been given a professorship fairly early in life, it was relatively easy for me to adjust all my academic work within the first three days of every week and then set out for long trips to the adivasi villages.

The adivasi epics

In 1994, I decided that I would leave my university position altogether and settle in one of the adivasi villages before they became entirely submerged in the continent of culture. With this in mind, I convened a meeting of some similarly interested individuals, from a variety of disciplines and backgrounds, in March 1996 at the hilly village Saputara. Among those who participated were adivasi artists, painters and photographers from non-adivasi society, writers, journalists, linguists and activists. We all decided that an institution should be created for providing space for the adivasi arts and languages. I accepted the responsibility for locating land, building a campus, creating funds, identifying people to join the institution and to run it, all in an honorary way. Now, 25 years later, as I look back on the entire experiment, I feel amazed at how much and how well my adivasi colleagues associated with the institution have achieved. It is known as the Adivasi Academy, situated at the Tejgadh village in adivasi area and is recognized as a Centre of Excellence by the Indian government's Ministry of Tribal Affairs and accepted by UNESCO as an inter-governmental member for its programme on Intangible Heritage. It has a museum of voice created by adivasis themselves, a multilingual school, a reasonably good library on adivasi culture, history and society, a studio for crafts and textiles, an open-air museum of languages called "the Forest of Languages," and a great amount of data on adivasi health, economy, education, sports and culture. Indigenous peoples from all continents visit the Academy, performances take place all through the year, art workshops are held week upon week and a tremendous amount of learning on these subjects is offered by the Academy. It is there that I saw plays, dances and performances of the indigenous of India innumerable times. Among them, the most striking was the experience of witnessing an oral epic.

We all hear of the *Iliad* and *Odyssey*, whose authorship is ascribed to Homer, as examples of oral epics in ancient Greece, and of the *Mahabharata*, whose authorship is ascribed to Vyasa, in ancient India. However, they come to us today as printed books. It is rare that one gets to experience the oral epic in its entirely oral form. Several such purely oral epics are in practice among the adivasis of India. They are found in Karnataka, among the nomadic Banjara community, in Chhattisgarh and Orissa. On the border of Rajasthan and Gujarat, there is a sub-group of Bhils known as the Garasiya Bhils. They sing/perform several oral epics. The most fascinating among them is recognized by them as *Bharath* (Patel 2004), and is fairly close to the mainstream *Mahabharata*. There can be, though, significant differences in the plot lines of the two epic traditions. The story runs as follows. There is a frog. It decides to go to the Ganga River. On the way, it gets maimed by wandering cattle. Its soul enters the body of a baby about to be born in the family of a small-time trader. On becoming an adult, the baby – a boy – starts disliking the family profession. So he decides to go to Indra, the king of gods. Indra looks at this boy and feels very amused that such a boy – who knows next to nothing – has such an ambition. So Indra sarcastically tells him that he would employ him as his advisor. The offer is promptly accepted. But Indra fails to pay to the boy the big salary he had agreed to pay. On a morning when the boy is sitting outside his house doing *datun*, brushing his teeth with twig of a tree, he spots a woman who is cleaning the streets, and he is smitten by her. He approaches her, but he only says "You are my sister. What can I give to you?" She says, "Normally I don't get good clothes. If you give me some clothes, I'll be happy." So he decides to give her clothes stolen from Indrani's robes made of gold. A few days later this woman goes to Indra's city, the Indraprasth. Indra sees her and gets very wild. "Only the Indrani can use such clothes, how can this woman use such clothes? Who is the idiot who has given her such clothes?" So the boy is accused. The *Indra-sabha* is convened. "You must immediately be sacked because only Indrani can wear such clothes," commands Indra. "Wait, you're sacking me but you never paid my wages, so give all those wages to me." It was, indeed, a huge amount. Indra ends up giving him several mounds of coins. The boy says, "Of course, I have to go back home but before that why don't I go and visit Ganga once." So he fares forth to Ganga and, on the way, one of the bullocks of the cart in which he is travelling collapses. It is already dark and there is forest on all sides. So this boy prays to Surya (the sun god). Surya appears and demands,

"I can rescue you provided you give me some bribe." The young man promises to give half of the coins to Surya. Immediately, the bullock comes back to life and the young boy, rather the young man, reaches the Ganga River. Struck by her beauty, he says, "What will I do with all the wealth that I have, I'm going to give half of my wealth to Ganga." So he sinks half of the money into the river. Then on his way back, Surya stops him and says, "Where is my half?" He says, "but I gave your half to Ganga, my half is with me." Suryadeva says, "this is unfair, this is not how a self-respecting tribal ever behaves. You are behaving like a wolf, you'll become a wolf." So the young man instantly turned into a wolf. He is angry, and he starts chasing Ganga, as he had suffered because of Ganga. Ganga starts running, and goes to her *guru*; her *guru* protects her for a while but not for a very long time. And finally – after many strange things happen to both of them – Ganga decides to marry the man turned into a wolf. It is at the moment of their wedding that the wolf returns to a human form, and it is revealed in the story for the first time that his name is Shantanu.

The names of the characters are from Vyasa's *Mahabharata* (Sukhathankar et al. 1971), but the plot details in the adivasi *Bharath* are entirely rooted in tribal context. The artists who perform this to present the story to their rural audiences spread over several days. On every day, the performance begins with propitiation of the musical instruments and prayers to adivasi deities. What is remarkable is that a fresh painting using natural colour powders is made at the "apron" of the make-shift stage made for the recital. These paintings depict the "scene" to be performed on that particular day. The group of three or four narrators open the recital and then slowly transform themselves into dancers and singers, "doing" various characters all by themselves. They sing, dance and respond to the audience as they are dancing, but rarely do they change any word or line from what they have learnt as *Bharatha*. They do not improvise, add, alter, modify or tamper with the "poem" that they have inherited from the preceding generation of singers. When one experiences this performance, it becomes clear as to how oral epics would have survived through centuries when writing and printing were not known to humans.

Painted words and possessed speech

The adivasi community near Tejgadh, the village where I had decided to commence the work planned in 1995, is Rathwa. These are highly dignified, self-respecting and reticent people, full of courtesy. In the initial weeks of my work at Tejgadh village, I made it a point to visit as many adivasi houses as possible. I had expected them to be hovels in a pathetic condition. What I found, however, was quite contrary to my expectations. The houses were built of mud and brick, and the windows were relatively small. However, the size of the rooms inside was much larger than rooms in urban houses. On average, they were 40 to 50 feet long and about 15 feet or more in width. What was even more surprising for me was that in most houses, one of the walls in the front room was adorned with a painting that was stunning in its conception and colours. At that time, I did not know that this painting is, in fact, a kind of a performance. All that I had learnt in my life till then about arts, literature, culture and history had not equipped me to imagine painting as a performance – not metaphorically but literally. In order to give an idea of what it is, let me first draw a word picture of Tejgadh for the reader to visualize the phenomenon that I am going to describe.

Tejgadh is situated on the border of Gujarat and Madhya Pradesh, 90 kilometres east of Baroda. The name of the village seems to have been drawn from the Koraj Hill nearby. The relics of an 11th-century settlement seen at the foot of the hill show a fortified area which was possibly the Tejgadh fort at one time. There is, however, no memory of this fort in the local folklore. The population of Tejgadh and the surrounding villages is predominantly adivasi. These villages were ruled in the past by petty chieftains, and each one of them built a fortification in the Rajput style for themselves. Tejgadh may have been one of those kingdoms. However, the present village is situated 3 kilometres away from the Koraj Hill. The oldest settler family there can recall a history not older than 100 years. The family that claims to be the earliest family to settle in the present location of Tejgadh is of the merchant class. However, the largest segment of population is adivasi, and their lifestyle is in continuity with the ancient and medieval tribal lifestyle in the region. In terms of the village architecture, Tejgadh shows five layers of settlement. The earliest of these appears to have been the area of the village pond, near which a 16th-century step-well is still in existence, though it is now out of use. The pond is approximately 400 metres away from the northern bank of the river Orsang. The next historical layer seems to be what is now known as Haridaspur, which is a cluster of about a 170 tribal families. Most of these families carry on the traditional animistic practice of worship and have preserved their sacred groves. The third layer of habitation is at the foot of the Koraj Hill. However, the families settled there show no traces of lineage-relation with the historical Tejgadh fortification. They are all tribal families, and are clan relations of the families settled in Haridaspur. It is quite likely that they moved out of Haridaspur subsequent to the decline of Tejgadh's political power and claimed the land there for agricultural use. The fourth layer of settlement is the Limdi Falia, or the straw-market, around which the houses of the Hindu and Muslim shop-keepers are built, which may not be even a century old. The last layer of settlement is the Rohit Falia, the colony of low-caste Hindus, with houses built on the fringe of farms owned by the merchant class.

There are traces of three village ponds in Tejgadh. The oldest pond is closest to the river Orsang, and holds water even today. The second pond is close to the Rohitvas, about half a kilometre from the old pond, but it is now no more than a dry depression. A new road has been built to span it and it has been partially filled for that purpose. The third pond is near the Koraj Hill; it has completely dried up, but a view of the dry pond from the top of the hill shows how majestic it must have been at one time.

The river Orsang is a dry river with a sandy basin almost half a kilometre wide. It only has water during the monsoon months, but it turns to a trickle during the late-winter months, when the river bed is used for watermelon cultivation. There is no temple in the river bed or along the banks of the river. On the whole, the Orsang does not enjoy much centrality in the emotional life of the villagers in Tejgadh, nor does it enjoy a place of privilege in their festivals and rituals. It is rather seen as the line of natural defence. There are no wells in Tejgadh which enjoy the status of community wells.

The Tejgadh village can be seen as a chain of rings, each larger than the previous one. Thus, the innermost ring forms the habitation of the Hindu merchants. The next, slightly larger, is the habitation of Muslims and the Harijans. The next is the habitation of adivasis who consider themselves "developed" tribals. The next ring, which is very large in expanse, is the habitation of the adivasis. And the last ring, which covers an area of nearly 12 kilometres in length, has isolated habitation of the poorest of the adivasis, who still survive on forest-gathering and farm labour. Three different places are used for cremation. One of those is for Hindu merchants and the Harijans, the second for Muslims and the third for the adivasis. All of them are at least a kilometre away from the village centre that is the Limdi Bazaar. For the disposal of dead animals, there is only one place reserved, which is next to the railway track. Since there are families that do the scavenging and the skinning of the dead animals, the disposal system is fairly efficient.

There are three public places of worship in Tejgadh. The most organized is the mosque, where prayers are offered punctually according to the customs of the Muslim families. There are two other temples, one of which has a Hindu deity of Mata or Laxmi and the tribal hero Bhathuji. There is one temple in Haridaspur which is devoted exclusively to Bhathuji. However, there is a public meeting hall for the Vaishnavas, within which idols of Krishna are displayed and worshipped on special occasions. Near the Koraj Hill, there is a beautiful temple precinct, but it is not in use now since the idols there have cracked. It shows relics of a Shiva temple and a broken Linga.

The painting, or what I initially called "painting," is described by the Rathwa adivasis as "Babo Pithoro" (Figure 6.1). If one were to press for an etymology and the exact meaning of this label, it would translate to "the revered ancestor." Rathwas treat Pithoro as a divinity, a god-like presence. They do not "offer" worship to Pithoro. Rather, having Pithoro inscribed on the walls of their houses is, for them, the highest kind of worship. From their perspective, "Pithoro" is both a verb and a noun. "Doing Pithoro," as an outsider may say, is quite appropriate to the entire ritual. The Rathwa adivasis use the expression "Writing Pithoro" or "Performing Pithoro" – writing being, for them, the same as performance. This performance is a collective affair and the entire adivasi community in a given village and the villages nearby is expected to participate in it. One of them is the person who holds a special status for the purpose of this "performance." He is the master painter and is called "lakhara," which in translation will be "the writer or the author." When I say he is the Master Painter, it is not because he draws outlines and others merely fill colours in them. He sets the orientation of the painting and also "audits" each and every element in it when the work is done. The audit process is carried out after the Lakhara gets under a spell of being possessed by the spirit of the God

FIGURE 6.1   Babo Pithoro in a house at Tejgadh

Source: Adivasi Academy Archives, Tejgadh, Gujarat, India

Pithora. This requires a liberal amount of collective drinking. The ritual extends over several days, normally beginning on a Wednesday. On that day, the wall is white-washed and people start arriving to the house where the ritual is being done. The next day, they fast, while several volunteer painters create many figures on the wall marked for the purpose. On the third day, after the spiritual audit by the Lakhara is complete, and after he announces that Babo Pithoro has arrived to inhabit the "painting," the people assembled enjoy a big feast. The painting is a mix of a narrative and a symbolic realm. Within the symbolic realm, the symbols for the cosmos, natural energy, the process of generation and major events as remembered in history are painted. The space where these symbols are painted is interpreted by the painters in a surreal manner. The narrative part of the painting offers history as remembered and some contemporary events or concerns related to the life of the Rathwas. Women and men keep endlessly singing songs from a large repertoire throughout the three days of the ritual. There is also a long narrative of "Babo Pithoro," which is now documented by Narayan Rathwa and Vikesh Rathwa of the Adivasi Academy (Rathwa et al. 2016). They studied 111 Pithoras available during 2008 and 2014, and published a book in Gujarati about the Pithora performance. I was told by Narayan Rathwa, as I was writing this chapter, that there still are about 700 or more adivasi houses in the Rathwa cluster of villages where Pithora has been "performed." The dimensions of the painting vary, but they can be 8 to12 feet tall and 20 to 30 feet long. Rathwas, whose average annual income is roughly 80,000 Indian rupees, spend close to 1.50,000 rupees for having the

Pithora performed in their houses at least once in their lifetime. The painting is "repaired" every eight to ten years, depending on the financial provisions available to the owner of the house. Pithora is a mode of writing, and therefore a script of a kind; a mode of remembering, and therefore history of a kind; a mode of worship, and therefore religion of a kind; and also a social gesture, and therefore sociology of a kind – all rolled together in a single act of "performance."

The Lakhara has one more important function to perform, which is related to exorcising girl children and interpreting what the ancestors want to convey to the community. This ritual does not have a prior composed text, as is in the case of the Babo Pithoro "performance." The ritual begins with parents identifying children who can be initiated into the capability of "getting possessed." Often, the ritual is used as a cure for a short illness, but that is not an absolute precondition. This ritual takes place outdoors in the dark hour of midnight. The child selected is made to stand at a spot that has been made sacred through a full propitiation, and the Lakhara stands at some distance. For the purpose of this ritual, he is called "bava," the shaman. He speaks to the child in an inspired way, purportedly on behalf of a variety of deities. The child responds to each of his rhetorical moves using a symbolic movement of their head and hands. When the child indicates a degree of comprehension of his utterances, the bava starts moving ahead, step by step, moving closer to the child. The mutual recognition increases, literally step by step. Finally, the two of them are able to communicate in the "non-language rant-like symbolic communication." At this stage, the child also gets possessed, the communication is complete and the performance ends. I have seen this with interest, and have seen the audience that stands around the two in a pin-drop silence, enveloped in the darkness of the night. When the "possessed words" ritual comes to its conclusion, the villagers start lighting little oil lamps, and, when it comes to a complete end, they start conversing in excitement. This performance is believed to "purify" the "inspired speech tradition" of the Rathwas. In their normal life, they are extremely reticent. In a normal conversation with outsiders, they normally respond in monosyllabic words and go about their business in silence. Most of the time, when they meet socially, they are more silent than talkative.

The performative use of painting or colour diagrams is peculiar not just to the Rathwa adivasis. It is found in the Midanapur district of Bengal among the makers of what is known as the Patta-Painting. The "Patta," or a long cotton strip, is used for painting scenes from the heroic narrative from the oral tradition of the community. The audiences are required to listen to the oral narrative as the rolled cotton strip is unfolded scene by scene. The experience of the performance is kinaesthetic, of seeing and listening simultaneously. In Rajasthan, an intriguing box is made out of thin wood. It is painted inside and outside, and it opens and folds in multiple ways. Depending on which way one opens the box, the narrative takes a certain form. But, if the box is opened in another way, it becomes another, though not entirely unrelated, narrative. The box is called "*kavad*," which means "a basket of narratives carrying ancient memory forward." Similarly, there is a tradition of painting among the Gond adivasis, who know several narratives associated with the figures and their sequences. The most fascinating among them is the narrative related to the figure known as "The Tree of Life" – a complex image painted in stunning bright colours which reminds one of the Kabala tree image, one half dying and the other half taking on a new, lush life.

The Theatre for Forgetting

I now turn to the theatre practice of the indigenous peoples in India. The traditions of dramatic performances among them are so numerous that it would not be possible to comment on all of them in a chapter of this nature. Notable among them is the dance drama of the Sidi adivasis, originally from Africa. It is called Dhamal and has a breath-taking speed of movement and a hypnotizing drum-beat in accompaniment. There is also the complex, symbolic and myth-based Manipuri theatre, which became a major influence on the modern Indian theatre. Then, there are the dances from Chhattisgarh and the Dangs district of Gujarat which depend on the gymnastic skills of the performers. There is the solo performance of the Nayak community in which music is the soul. Here, I would like to briefly discuss the "Theatre for Forgetting" developed by the Chhara Denotified community (Figure 6.2). As mentioned earlier, the "Denotified" tribes are the communities that were wrongly branded during the colonial rule. The Chhara community was one of them.

In 1871, the colonial government brought in the first "Criminal Tribes Act" (CTA). The CTA was revised and modified several times between 1871 and 1924.

FIGURE 6.2   Denotified tribe artists in their conventional performance

Source: Photograph by Sandesh Bhandare

The list of communities specified as "criminal" were included in the Schedules of these Acts. The CTA enabled the colonial government to restrict the movements of these communities that had essentially been nomadic in habit. Special areas were created for them, and in many cases, reformatory settlements were established. One such settlement was located outside Ahmadabad, not too far from the Sabarmati ashram of Mahatma Gandhi. India became independent in 1947. Five years later, the government of free India decided to annul the CTA. In 1952, the Habitual Offenders Act replaced the colonial CTA. The settlements were opened and the communities imprisoned for three generations were made free. However, they did not have any land and any other habitat. Besides, the stereotype had been by then ingrained in the minds of Indians; and the society continued to look at these "Denotified" communities as essentially "criminal" in habit. Their nomadic habits, too, had been curtailed after being kept in settlements for several generations. Thus, these Denotified and Nomadic tribes, the DNTs, chose to form slums close to the former settlements and began a new life from there.

The Kuber Nagar Settlement in Ahmadabad is where the Chhara DNT settled in the 1950s. Since the people in Ahmadabad continued to look at them with suspicion, and since the police attitude inherited from the colonial times did not change in tune with the new law, Chharas had to live a life of utter poverty, civic neglect and petty crime. It was 1998, 45 years after their "denotification" that I happened to make my first visit to Chhara Nagar. No one from among my literate friends in Ahmadabad was willing to accompany me. I was accompanied by the well-known renegade Bangla writer Mahasweta Devi. When we met the Chhara people, we realized how suffocated they had been feeling. Many of them were in jail on charges of petty theft, others imprisoned on suspicion of brewing illicit liquor and yet others who found it difficult to seek jobs if they disclosed their identity. At the time we made the first visit to Chhara Nagar, Mahasweta Devi had filed a case in the High Court of West Bengal on behalf of a young DNT girl from Purulia, West Bengal, whose husband had died in police custody. The fact of the case was that he, a 22-year-old Budhan, was brutally beaten up by the police on mere suspicion of a minor theft. The beating proved fatal, and he died. The police declared that he had committed suicide. The police department was forcing his widow, Shyamali, to quickly cremate his body. Mahasweta Devi advised her to hide the dead body and wait for cremation till a proper post-mortem report was secured. The court intervened; the post-mortem report proved that it was not a suicide and that Budhan was, indeed, killed by the brutality of the police.

In those days, I used to publish a little magazine for promoting my campaign for the human rights of the DNTs. I decided to name the untitled journal *Budhan*. A copy of the issue in which I printed the West Bengal High Court's judgement in the Budhan murder case reached Chhara Nagar. When Mahasweta Devi and I made subsequent visits to Chharas, they quite surprised us by showing us a dramatized performance of the entire event, with Mahasweta Devi as one of the characters. This was done in the style of street theatre. It was powerful. We spoke about it to our friends in Ahmadabad, and requested them to invite the Chhara "actors" to perform the play. It proved so moving that the Chhara group received a series of invitations to perform the "play" – which was for them an everyday life experience – in Ahmadabad, in other cities of Gujarat and even outside Gujarat. Soon, the group acquired the name "Budhan Theatre." By now, we had succeeded in creating a small public library in that locality. The young people gathered there in the evenings and started playing other stories, composing songs, forming a band, writing plays for performance and inviting people to watch them perform. The story is long. During the last 20 years, the Budhan Theatre has acquired fame as an experimental theatre, have performed in more than 2,000 shows, have taken their ever-increasing group to other cities and other countries such as the US and UK, trained several hundred actors from various colleges and universities and has changed the image of the Chharas from being known as "thieves" to being known as artists. The moving spirit behind this entire glorious journey has been the direc-tor of Budhan Theatre, Dakxin Bajrange. After a decade of work with his theatre, he won a Ford Fellowship and trained himself at the Leeds University in England. Some of the other actors like Alok Gagdekar and Vivek later joined the prestigious National School of Drama in Delhi, some like Kalpana joined mainstream TV and cinema, and some others like Atish Indrekar became trainers in various theatre groups. They have performed plays by many modern dramatists, including the French nomad Jean Genet and the Italian Leftist Dario Fo. They have also entered the field of cinema and made successful films and documentaries, as well as feature films. I have sat through their performances on innumerable occasions. I have seen the lasting impact they make on their audiences. Their theatre, in my opinion, is for making the society overcome the colonial history of turning hapless tribal com-munities into criminals. I call it the Theatre for Forgetting.

Performing freedom

It is indeed impossible to pack everything related to the performance practices of the indigenous peoples of India. The diversity is too vast to allow that. In order to showcase the diversity as a means of regaining their self-respect, Kanaji Patel – my colleague at the Adivasi Academy and a well-known poet writing in Gujrati – thought of creating an annual performance festival of the indigenous. I thought it was a great idea. We made a modest beginning in 2000. The initial response was so overwhelming that we continued year after year. The festival is held in the Pan-chamahal district of Gujarat. The site chosen for this is close to an archaeological site with thousand-year-old relics called Kaleshwari – literally, the Goddess of Arts (Figure 6.3). Artists from Gujarat, Rajasthan, Maharashtra and Madhya Pradesh have been gathering year after year, one day a year. Thousands of others also go to Kaleshwari to experience the performances. All of the performances happen simultaneously, side by side, since the site is large enough to permit such a mix. The groups learn from each other, offer critical comments of performances, bring in innovations in their traditional skills and provide a fascinating window to the world on the performance traditions of the indigenous in India. They do not look for newspaper notices for their performances, do not charge fees and do not worry about the numbers present in the audience. They perform because the indigenous

FIGURE 6.3   Nomadic artists performing at Kaleshwari Arts Festival

Source: Photograph by Sandesh Bhandare

perform for joy, for transcending the rough and tumble of their daily life, and in praise of the creator of the world and as an offering to Mother Earth.

Conclusion

In this chapter, I have discussed three types of performance traditions still in practice among the adivasis and the Denotified communities of India: oral epic, ritual painting and theatre. This discussion is by no means exhaustive. There are other types of performances which combine dance and drama, such as *Akhyana*; visuals and narratives, such as the Kunkna heroic poems; group dances, such as the *Lehngi* of the Banjara community; and large-scale community festivals, such as the *Holi* in the Western and Central belt adivasis and the *Bihu* in Assam. The few examples that I have discussed should indicate that the performance traditions are still in active practice. However, there is a severe drop in the level of community patronage of these performances, and one does not know if, and for how long, these traditions can manage to survive.

References

Damodaran, Vinita. 2006. 'Colonial Construction of Tribe in India: The Case of Chhota Nagpur.' *Indian Historical Review*, January, 44–75.

Devi, Mahasweta. 1997. *Mother of 1084*, Translated by Samik Bandyopadhyay. Calcutta: Seagull Books,

Devy, G. N. 1992. *After Amnesia: Tradition and Transformation in Indian Literary Criticism.* Bombay: Orient Longman.

Devy, G. N. 2003. *Indian Literary Criticism: Theory & Practice.* Hyderabad: Orient Blackswan.

Devy, G. N. 2007. *A Nomad Called Thief.* New Delhi: Orient Blackswan.

Devy, G. N. 2010. *Consortium of Indian Tribal Museums.* Baroda: Purvaprakash.

Devy, G. N. 2014. 'The Chinha-shastra Indian Sgn Language(s),' in Tanmoy Bhattacharya, et al. (Eds.), *People's Linguistic Survey of India,* Vol. 38. New Delhi: Orient Blacksw.

Elwin, Verrier. 1936. *Leaves from the Jungle.* London: John Murray Publishers Ltd.

Elwin, Verrier. 1942. *The Agaria.* Calcutta: The Bapstist Mission Press.

Elwin, Verrier. 1944. *Folk-Songs of the Maikal Hills.* Oxford: Oxford University Press.

Elwin, Verrier. 1946. *Folk-Songs of Chattisgarh.* Oxford: Oxford University Press.

Elwin, Verrier. 1947. *The Muria and the Ghotul.* Oxford: Oxford University Press.

Elwin, Verrier. 1949. *The Myths of Middle India.* New Delhi: Oxford University Press.

Elwin, Verrier. 1950. *Bondo Highlanders.* New Delhi: Oxford University Press.

Elwin, Verrier. 1950. *Maria Murder and Suicide.* New Delhi: Oxford University Press.

Elwin, Verrier. 1964. *The Tribal World of Verrier Elwin.* New Delhi: Oxford University Press.

Elwin, Verrier. 1980. *Folk-Tales of Mahakoshal.* London: Arno Press.

Elwin, Verrier. 1986. *The Baiga.* New Delhi: Gian Publishing House.

Elwin, Verrier. 2008. *The Oxford India Verrier Elwin Selected Writings.* New Delhi: Oxford University Press.

Nardi, Isabella. 2006. *The Theory of Chitrasutras in Indian Painting.* London: Royal Asiatic Society Books and Taylor and Francis.

Patel, Bhagwandas. 2004. *The Mahabharath of the Bhils,* Translated by Nila Shah. Baroda: Purvaprakash.

Rathwa, Narayan and Vikesh Rathwa. 2016. *Bharatiya Adim Chitrakala: Rathwa Samajama Babo Pithoro* (in Gujarati). Baroda: Bhasha Research Centre.

Reich, David. 2018. *Who We Are and Who We Got Here: Ancient DNA and the New Science of the Human Past.* New York: Pantheon.

Robinson, Andrew. 2002. *Lost Languages: The Enigma of the World's Undeciphered Scripts.* New York: Thames and Hudson.

Sri Aurobindo. 1956. *The Secret of the Veda.* Pondicherry: Sri Aurobindo Ashram.

Sukhathankar, V.S., et al. 1971. *Mahabharata: The Critical Edition.* Pune: Bhandarkar Institute.

Website of the Census of India. http://censusindia.gov.in/2011Census/Language_MTs.html (accessed 20 April 2020).

INDEX

Note: Page numbers in *italics* indicate a figure on the corresponding page.